W9-AQR-430

IMPERIAL GERMANY
and the Industrial Revolution

Imperial Germany

and the Industrial Revolution

by
THORSTEIN VEBLEN

Introduction by Joseph Dorfman

Ann Arbor Paperbacks

THE UNIVERSITY OF MICHIGAN PRESS

PREFACE

Some apology may seem due on offering at this season so unwarlike a study as what here follows on the case of Imperial Germany and its place in modern civilisation. The essay was projected before the current war came on, though the complexion of subsequent events has also doubtless had its effect on the particular direction taken by the argument at more than one point in the inquiry. The inquiry in hand, therefore, is concerned neither with the controverted merits of the international quarrel nor with the comparative force and probable success of either belligerent. Its aim is the less polemical one of a comparison and correlation between the German case on the one hand and the English-speaking peoples on the other hand, considered as two distinct and somewhat divergent lines of the cultural development in modern times; and the ground on which the inquiry runs is that afforded by the economic, chiefly the industrial, circumstances that have shaped the outcome in either case.

It aims to account for Germany's industrial advance and high efficiency by natural causes, without drawing on the logic of manifest destiny, Providential nepotism, national genius, and the like. It is believed to be the first attempt yet made at an explanation, as distinct from description or eulogy, of this episode in modern economic history; unless Professor Sombart's *Deutsche Volkswirtschaft im XIX.*

Jahrhundert may be so regarded. Apart from Professor Sombart's study of this period, it is believed, nothing of consequence has appeared in the way of a theoretical inquiry into this Imperial era and the run of its industrial affairs, although many scholarly and workmanlike studies have presented the run of the facts from one point of view and another.

There is of course no intention here to impart information on the history of this period, whether political or economic; and the historical information made use of as material for argument is of the commonplace kind familiar by common notoriety or from the standard manuals accessible to all readers. Anything like a comprehensive citation of sources and authorities has accordingly been dispensed with, though citations and references covering given points have been brought in where special occasion appeared to call for it. The argument runs between the lines of the histories, as conventionally written, and does not lean on recondite material or niceties of detail.

To English readers, it is true, the chapter on the Old Order may appear in part to rest on recondite information. The argument bearing on this topic presumes a degree of familiarity with the archæology of the Baltic region, together with a fairly exhaustive first-hand acquaintance with what there is extant of literary remains in the Old Icelandic. It is not a matter in which the reader would be much helped out by a citation of sources; nor would a detailed enumeration of documents and textual passages appear to serve any useful end even in the hands of a specialist in this province of erudition, since the purpose for which this material is here used is such as would be served by nothing short of a somewhat protracted and inclusive familiarity with the entire range of literature in question. The early culture of the Germanic peoples, and of their pre-German forebears, that so comes in sight in these archæological and literary antiquities, is made use of as a term of contrast against which to exhibit the characteristic traits of the modern era, and as showing the cultural point of departure of these peoples, toward which any drift of reversion in their case will necessarily set.

It may also appear that a larger attention has been given to the case of the English-speaking community than would seem warranted by the caption of the title-page. Here, again, the need of a term of comparison has been allowed to decide, as well as the fact that, in the industrial respect, the current German situation is a derivative of the English and an outcome of the past development of the industrial arts as worked out in Great Britain. Some attention has therefore necessarily been given to this past development of industry and its consequences in the British community.

March 1915

CONTENTS

SUPPLEMENTARY NOTES

INTRODUCTION

If the men who count in the social sciences in the United States were asked today who was America's most creative thinker in this field, few would dissent from the choice of Thorstein Veblen. They might not approve his views in general, let alone the details, but they would acknowledge that he showed a far more penetrating insight into the nature and future course of development of the modern business civilization than any of his contemporaries or successors.

With the exception of the much misunderstood *The Theory of the Leisure Class*, Veblen's books have hardly been popular. Yet slowly his books rise from the obscurity of being out of print to take their place as significant interpretations of the current drift of events dating from the great crisis of 1929. Veblen died an embittered man, only a few months before the beginning of that memorable event, but since then the majority of his books have again emerged and new editions have been required.

From students perplexed anew by the inadequacy of traditional economics came a demand for *The Place of Science in Modern Civilisation and Other Essays*. Those who despaired of the ability of the prevailing higher education to cast light on pressing social problems called for *The Higher Learning in America: A Memorandum on the Conduct of Universities by Business Men*. The "technocracy" craze made *The Engineers and the Price System* a best seller for a period, although the connection of Veblen's book with the movement was at most accidental. The advent of the "New Deal" sent readers to *The Theory of Business Enterprise* and *The Vested Interests and the Common Man*. Today the course of international events calls forth *Imperial Germany and the Industrial Revolution*.

In one respect in particular, this book is the finest drama that Veblen ever wrote. So well had Veblen caught the spirit of the Third Reich twenty years before its birth that its accredited spokesmen sound as if they are merely obeying Veblen's logic not only in broad outline but in specific detail. Yet this book suffered a fate even more severe than did most of his other works. Published shortly after the outbreak of the World War, it was soon on its way to the heap of forgotten and unsold books. Even men of high reputation in liberal ranks who believed Veblen to be a genius were perplexed concerning the meaning of this book. Graham Wallas and Walter Weyl complained of its irony, reticence, and concealment. That was not all. They felt it was too detached. Wallas, professor at the London School of Economics, thought that Veblen was too hard on the English; Weyl, an American liberal with a German university education, felt that Veblen should have found some good in German culture.

America's entrance into the conflict in 1917 seemed to offer another opportunity for the book to make its contribution to current thinking, but again its objective character decreed otherwise. The official propaganda bureau of the American government urged newspapers to republish parts of the book as damaging evidence against Germany, but the

Postmaster General's office barred the book from the mails under the Espionage Act.

The equally penetrating *An Inquiry into the Nature of Peace and the Terms of Its Perpetuation* underwent a similar fate. Spokesmen of patriotic organizations denounced Veblen as a pacifist; agents of the Department of Justice held that the book called for more severe penalties upon Germany than were publicly advocated by the Entente powers.

In this book Veblen forecast the future history of the yet to be born peace treaty and the League of Nations, and presented at great length the plan and terms of what he conceived might be a permanent "pacific league." But the government overlooked Veblen as it scoured the country for economic advisers on these paramount questions; it preferred so it seems the usual run of the profession who were accustomed to ignoring Veblen's numerous constructive proposals by calling him, at best, a mere critic.

With the cessation of hostilities there was only a negligible demand for either of these works. Germany was now ostensibly a republic and those whom Veblen called the "subsidized pacifists" were in the saddle, proclaiming obsolete, innocuous solutions.

But today with the world trembling on the brink of war, and Germany going through those evolutions sketched by Veblen, his cosmic spirit again impresses a world that cannot escape from his persistent influence, because he understood its drives.

The scope of *Imperial Germany and the Industrial Revolution* extends far beyond the case of Germany. It requires no reading of his equally prophetic and neglected "Oppor-

tunity of Japan" written at the same time [1] to realize that
Japan is included. The western democracies also come in for
attention. The longest chapter in the book is entitled "The
Case of England," and the nine-page supplementary note,
tucked away in the back of the work, dealing with American
captains of finance should lead to a rereading of the main
text as "The Case of America."

In *Imperial Germany and the Industrial Revolution*, as
in all his books, Veblen employs techniques that permit him
to use a segment or aspect of culture as a spotlight to illu-
minate the underlying forces of the development of western
civilization. Thus something must be said of Veblen's character and the position of the book in his comprehensive
scheme, or readers may again be misled by its superficial
trappings, particularly by the illusion that he was writing
merely of the Germany of William II rather than of the
current posture of events, both national and international.

Nature endowed Veblen with an orderly brain, a high
sense of intellectual integrity, and an insatiable curiosity.
There was little that did not interest him, and he early
acquired and constantly augmented vast knowledge that
ranged from epic literature, theological dogma, and philosophical systems to the latest mechanical inventions and the
most recent anthropological and archaeological researches.
Circumstances beyond his control determined that his mind,
curiosity, and knowledge should be turned to the uses not
of an antiquary but to those of a dissector of the modern
order.

---

[1] Republished in Veblen's posthumous collection, *Essays in Our Changing Order*, edited by Leon Ardzrooni, New York, 1934.

As Professor Wesley C. Mitchell has so well shown,[1] Veblen's detached outlook developed from his having spent his early youth in a "little Norway" in the Middle West with its relatively self-sufficient agrarian scheme of things of a day fast disappearing, and then being thrown into the dominant Yankee business culture of the towns. Stripped thereby of a predilection for either scheme, he was able to see less obscurely than his contemporaries the development of those institutions that were transforming America into the most advanced product of capitalism; namely, the machine process and its concomitants under the regime of property—corporation finance and imperialism.

The story of the development of modern business enterprise was to be Veblen's main concern after his re-entrance into academic halls in 1891. Although he had received a Ph.D. from Yale in 1884, he entered Cornell as a graduate student. In the intervening seven idle years of waiting for a post he had ample opportunity to think deeply of the problem. During the decade that followed, he worked out the main threads of his argument. It was a decade known to historians as the "stormy nineties," and respectable sentiment expected academicians to refrain from seriously questioning the fundamental arrangements. Although Veblen's first article, which appeared at the beginning of the period, was called "Some Neglected Points in the Theory of Socialism" [2] it is not difficult to understand why his first book,

---

[1] "Introduction" to *What Veblen Taught,* selected writings of Thorstein Veblen, edited by Wesley C. Mitchell, New York, 1936.

[2] Republished in *The Place of Science in Modern Civilisation and Other Essays,* selected by Leon Ardzrooni, Wesley C. Mitchell, and Walter W. Stewart, New York, 1919; new edition 1930.

published in 1899, should have the title *The Theory of the Leisure Class*.

Veblen labored long and arduously over this book. For subtlety it has hardly an equal. The nature of the control of the predatory captains of finance over the material welfare of the community is worked out in terms of the canons and activities of the leisure class gentleman, and of his apparent prototype, the barbarian chieftain. Veblen brought into play much of that curious information he had accumulated, to characterize and analyze the meaning of the jarring effect on modern industry of the never-ceasing strategic maneuvers of the financial leaders in their contests for financial hegemony.

Veblen paid a heavy penalty for using such a technique. William Dean Howells lavishly praised it as a masterly ironic presentation of the wealthy aspiring to be English aristocrats, and of the contamination of all phases of life by the vulgar canons of the marketplace. Since Howells was the dean of American letters, praise from him meant fame to the recipient. Thus Veblen became known as a satirist possessed of an original style. He was not to be taken seriously as a student of economic affairs. That reputation Veblen never lived down. His subsequent works were always viewed in the shadow of this interpretation of *The Theory of the Leisure Class*, which became traditional.

As if seeking to correct that view, Veblen published *The Theory of Business Enterprise*. Here the argument was unfolded more bluntly, in terms of a conflict between modern business enterprise and the requirements of the modern state of the industrial arts, between the never-ending pursuit

for funded wealth and increased capitalization, by the pecuniary magnates in their competitive, wasteful struggles,
and the inordinate productivity of the comprehensive, deli-
cate machine process.

The results are, on the one hand, depression as the normal state, and, on the other, the need for business enterprise to assume more and more the character of contending imperialisms at home and abroad. Enduring peace, that
is, the uninterrupted, smooth functioning of the industrial
processes for the material welfare of the community, requires emancipation from unmitigated pecuniary management, but modern business enterprise, like the leisure class,
is animated by the institution of ownership.

Veblen's analysis moves to its end with a discussion of
the close resemblance of the present "princes by the grace
of ownership" and their canons of "pecuniary mastery and
commercial solvency" to the older barbarian "princes by
the grace of God" and their canons of "warlike mastery and
ceremonial precedence." Thus the outwardly peaceful but
actually contentious scheme of modern business enterprise is
essentially an unstable, transitory stage of culture and is
bound eventually either to return to unmitigated feudalism
and petty industry or to move forward to the industrial republic and the unhindered machine process.

The outbreak of the war in 1914 caused Veblen to hurry
his book *Imperial Germany and the Industrial Revolution*.
In one respect this was fortunate. He had less time for carefully planned literary stratagems, though there were still
enough of them to confuse the reviewers and the government agencies. The main argument of *The Theory of the*

Leisure Class and of *The Theory of Business Enterprise* stands out more sharply. Here and there in the text, and even more in the supplementary notes, Veblen openly calls attention to the potential nature of unrestrained business enterprise with its dynastic politics.

The argument runs in terms of a comparison of Imperial Germany with the ostensibly democratic English-speaking peoples as dominant types of social organization. In the former type Veblen includes Japan; in the latter he places the United States, which is an outlying province of the English cultural scheme.

Veblen finds little difference between these types so far as the welfare of the mass is concerned. The German Junker, the British gentleman, and the ideal American business man are brothers under the skin.

Veblen's immediate, explicit objective, as the title indicates, is to explain why and how Germany with its dynastic political organization made such rapid strides in the machine technology as to outstrip the democratic English-speaking peoples from whom emanated the modern industrial process. The explanation lies in the logic of business enterprise. The machine technology began in England, but the institution of ownership was and continues to be the paramount institution in the English scheme of things. Thus the growth and functioning of the technology were increasingly obstructed by the necessity of protecting the ever-augmenting nominal capitalized values of the "gentlemanly investors." As Veblen had already elaborately explained in *The Theory of Business Enterprise,* advancing technology lowers prices and profits in nominal values, but business solvency and success depend on the maintenance and advance of these nominal values even though the material values may actually be decreasing. This paramount necessity of protecting the funded wealth of the great owners may lead to an ever-increasing waste of the product and prospects of industry by a leisure class of business men, and an ever-increasing amount of distress for the masses.

Germany avoided this "penalty of taking the lead" in modern industry under private property by virtue of its more recent entrance among the great powers. Relatively free from the dead hand of funded capital, her technology could develop at a faster pace than in the lands of its birth. However, the surplus is devoted not to the material welfare of the community but to the intangible glory of the reigning house. The objective of a dynastic State is insatiable dominion, and economic life is organized to enhance fighting capacity. Since a dynastic State must in the modern scheme of private property work through business and the price system, and since the principle of the price system closely resembles that of the leisure class it is only a matter of time before the mature English and American situation will be reached and the competitive advantage of warlike force will be dissipated.

Indeed, Germany missed her opportunity, said Veblen, and struck too late. But Japan, he maintained, still has a chance. If she were wise, she would strike now, before the principles of business enterprise waste away her surplus of fighting strength.

Yet the dynastic State, like modern business enterprise,

derives its strength from the machine technology and so is increasingly threatened by what was termed, in *The Theory of Business Enterprise,* the alternative to feudalism for business enterprise—the industrial republic.

Thus *Imperial Germany and the Industrial Revolution,* seen in the light of Veblen's previous books, is revealed as not only a discussion of the nature and destiny of the dynastic States and the western democracies, but also as a most elaborate discussion of modern business enterprise. Even the so-called contrast between business enterprise and the dynastic State in the discussion of Germany's prospects of success for world dominion seems to be a double analysis of modern business enterprise; on the one hand as the institution of the leisure class, and on the other as the institution of the dynastic State.

The principle of the "penalty of taking the lead," as Veblen used it, has far-reaching implications. Not only may it help to explain the sudden tremendous increase in the military and industrial efficiency of the Third Reich after a good part of its funded wealth had been canceled, but it might also serve to guide inquiry into the Russian experiment and its fate. Russia, instead of going through what Marxians call bourgeois democracy, jumped from autocracy into communism, where theoretically the dead hand of ownership is not present. In its basic elements, however, the principle is Veblen's fundamental contrast between business and industry, between corporation finance and the machine technology, between ownership and the requirements of the community. A great industrial nation if freed from the restraint of pecuniary considerations avoids "the penalty of taking the lead," the penalty of business convulsions and increasing distress.

So this new edition is presented with no change in Veblen's original text, except for corrections of typographical errors, and a few minor verbal emendations which Veblen himself left behind, doubtless with a firm faith that time would vindicate him and create the present event.

JOSEPH DORFMAN

Columbia University
February 1939

IMPERIAL GERMANY

AND THE

INDUSTRIAL REVOLUTION

CHAPTER I

INTRODUCTORY — RACES AND PEOPLES

AMONG men who have no articulate acquaintance with matters of ethnology it is usual to speak of the several nations of Europe as distinct races. Even official documents and painstaking historians are not free from this confusion of ideas. In this colloquial use "race" is not conceived to be precisely synonymous with "nation," nor with "people"; although it would often be a difficult matter to make out from the context just what distinctive meaning is attached to one or another of these terms. They are used loosely and suggestively, and for many purposes they may doubtless be so used without compromise or confusion to the argument; so that it might seem the part of reason to take them as they come, with allowance for such margin of error as necessarily attaches to their colloquial use, and without taking thought of a closer definition or a more discriminate use than what contents those who so find these terms convenient for use in all their colloquial ambiguity.

But through all the current ambiguity in the use of these terms, and of others that serve as their virtual equivalents, there runs a certain consistent difference of connotation, such as to work confusion in much of the argument in which they are employed. Whatever else it may be taken to convey, "race" always implies a solidarity of inheritance within the group so designated; it always implies that the complement of hereditary traits is substantially the same for all the individuals comprised in the group. "Race" is a biological concept, and wherever it is applied it signifies common descent of the group from an ancestry possessed of a given specific type and transmitting the traits that mark this type, intact to all members of the group so designated. The other terms, that are currently used as interchangeable with "race," as, *e.g.,* "nation" or "people," do not necessarily imply such a biological solidarity of the group to which they are applied; although the notion of a common descent is doubtless frequently present in a loose way in the mind of those who so use them.

In this colloquial use of terms, when the distinction between these several peoples or alleged races is not allowed to rest quite uncritically on a demarkation of national frontiers, the distinguishing mark to which recourse is usually had is the community of language. So it comes about that habituation to a given type of speech has come to do duty as a conventional mark of racial derivation. A certain (virtual) uniformity of habit is taken to mean a uniformity of hereditary endowment. And many historians and publicists who discuss these matters have been led into far-reaching generalisations touching hereditary characteristics of temperament, intelligence and physique, in cases where there is in fact ground for nothing more substantial than a discriminating comparison between divergent schemes of use and wont. Such differences of use and wont as mark off one people from another may be a sufficiently consequential matter, of course; but their reach and effect are after all of quite another character, and have quite another place and bearing in the cultural growth, than differences of racial type.

The scheme of institutions in force in any given community — as exemplified, *e.g.*, by the language — being of the nature of habit, is necessarily unstable and will necessarily vary incontinently with the passage of time, though it may be in a consistent manner; whereas the type of any given racial stock is stable, and the hereditary traits of spiritual and physical endowment that mark the type are a matter of indefeasible biological heritage, invariable throughout the life-history of the race. A meticulous discrimination between the two concepts — of habit and heredity — is the beginning of wisdom in all inquiry into human behavior; and confusion of the two is accountable for much of the polemical animus, and not a little recrimination, in recent and current writing on historical, political and economic matters. And, of course, the larger the burden of chauvinism carried by the discussion the more spectacular and sweeping has been its output of systematic blunders.

If an inquiry into the case of Germany is to profit the ends of theoretical generalisation bearing on the study of human institutions, their nature and causes, it is necessary to discriminate between those factors in the case that are of a stable and enduring character and those that are variable, and at the same time it is necessary to take thought of what factors are peculiar to the case of the German people and what others are common to them and to their neighbors with whom their case will necessarily be compared. It happens that these two lines of discrimination in great part coincide. In respect of the stable characteristics of race heredity the German people do not differ in any sensible or consistent manner from the neighboring peoples; whereas in the character of their past habituation — in their cultural scheme — as well as in respect of the circumstances to which they have latterly been exposed, their case is at least in some degree peculiar. It is in the matter of received habits of thought — use and wont — and in the conditions that have further shaped their scheme of use and wont in the recent past, that the population of this country differs from the population of Europe at large.

In view of the prevalent confusion or ignorance on this head among the historians and publicists who have been dealing with these matters, it seems necessary, even at the cost of some tedium, to recite certain notorious facts bearing on the racial complexion of the German people. In so far as may bear on the question of race for the German people taken as a whole, these facts are no longer in controversy. Students of European race questions still are, and no doubt long will be, engaged on many difficult problems of local displacement, migration and infiltration of racial elements, even within the frontiers of the Fatherland; but for the purpose in hand recourse need scarcely be had to any of these matters of recondite detail. Even if more might be convenient, nothing is required for present use beyond those general features of the case on which a secure consensus has already been reached.

It is only in so far as we can make shift to conceive that

the linguistic frontiers coincide in some passable way with the political frontiers of German dominion that we can make use of the name as it is currently employed in historical, polemical and patriotic writing, without phrase or abatement. Taking the name, then, as loosely designating the Empire with its German-speaking population — *das deutsche Volk* — and overlooking any discrepancies in so doing, the aggregate so designated is in no defensible sense to be spoken of as a distinct race, even after all allowance has been made for intrusive elements in the population, such as the Jews or the Germanised Poles and Danes. The German people is not a distinct race either as against the non-German population of Europe or within itself. In both of these respects the case of this population is not materially different from that of any other national population in Europe. These facts are notorious.

Like the populations of the neighboring countries, the German population, too, is thoroughly and universally hybrid; and the hybrid mixture that goes to make up the German people is compounded out of the same racial elements that enter into the composition of the European population at large. Its hybrid character is perhaps more pronounced than is the case in the countries lying farther south, but the difference in degree of hybridisation as between the Germans and their southern neighbors is not a serious one. On the other hand the case of the Germans is in this respect virtually identical with that of the peoples lying immediately to the east and west.[1]

---

[1]For a more detailed consideration, see Supplementary Note I, p. 281 below.

In point of race the population of south Germany is substantially identical with that of northern France or the
neighboring parts of Belgium; while in the same respect
the population of north Germany has substantially the same
composition as that of Holland and Denmark on the west
and of western Russia on the east; and, taking the Fatherland as a whole, its population is in point of race substantially identical with that of the British Isles. The variations
in local detail within this broad belt of mixed populations
are appreciable, no doubt, but they are after all of much the
same character in one country as in another, and taken one
with another they run to much the same effect both east,
west and middle. When taken in the large there is, in other
words, no sensible difference of race between the English,
Dutch, Germans and the Slavs of Great Russia.

In the current expositions of national merit and nota-
bility, when a pure-bred German, Germanic or Anglo-Saxon
race is spoken for, the context presently brings into view
that what is present in the eulogist's conception, if anything in the way of a definite biological category, is the
dolicho-blond. Now it happens, unfortunately for the invidious insistence on purity of race, that this particular racial stock is less frequently to be found unmixed than either
of the other two with which it is associated. It is, indeed,
quite safe to affirm that there is no community extant, great
or small, that is made up even approximately of pure-bred
blonds to the exclusion of other racial elements.

One may even safely go further and assert that there is
not by any chance an individual to be found in the population of Europe who, in point of pedigree, is of unmixed

blond extraction. Nor is there any reasonable chance, nor any evidence available, that a community of pure-bred blonds ever has existed in any part of Europe. And the like assertion may be made, with but a slightly less degree of assurance, as regards pure-bred specimens of the other main European races.

The variation in race characters is very appreciable within each of these national populations; in the German case being quite pronounced between north and south. Whereas the differences which go to make the distinction between these nationalities taken as aggregates are of an institutional kind — differences in acquired traits not transmissible by inheritance, substantially differences of habituation. On this side, however, the divergences between one nationality and another may be large, and they are commonly of a systematic character; so that while no divergence of racial type may be alleged, the divergence in the cultural type may yet be serious enough.

The hybrid composition of these peoples affects their character in yet another bearing, which is of grave consequence in the growth of culture, at the same time that it affects the fortunes of all the peoples of Europe in much the same fashion, though perhaps not in the same degree. By consequence of their hybrid composition the individual members of these nationalities vary more widely in respect of their native capacities and aptitudes than would be the case in any pure-bred people.[1] So that these peoples each

---

[1]It is evident that under the Mendelian rules held to govern matters of heredity in hybrids it follows that the cross offspring of two (or three) distinct specific types may vary by approximately as many per-

present a much larger diversity of personalities than would be found among them if they were not cross-bred. On the physical side, in respect of such traits as can be measured and compared by mechanical methods, this great range and complexity of variations within each nationality is obvious enough, — in stature, color, mass and anatomical proportions. But it no less indubitably comprises also those (spiritual and intellectual) traits that are less amenable to anthropometrical statistics, at the same time that they are of greater consequence to the fortunes of the people among whom they are found. It is these psychological traits — spiritual and intellectual proclivities, capacities, aptitudes, sensibilities — that afford the raw material out of which any given scheme of civilisation is built up and on which its life-

---

mutations as the number of viable combinations possible between the double (or treble) range of determinants, or "factors," comprised in their double (or treble) ancestry. That is to say, while the pure-bred representatives of a given specific type may vary within the narrow limits of the type, through varying stress on the several determinants comprised in the type constitution during the growth of the filial individual (zygote); it is on the other hand contained in the premises that the cross-bred individual may vary not only by consequence of such differences of stress during its growth (what may be called variation in initially acquired characters) but also (what may be called variation in hereditary characters) by a number of new combinations of characters coming in from the two (or three) sides of his double (or treble) ancestry and amounting approximately to the square (or cube) — 1 of the number of determinants comprised in the type constitution, — barring such combinations, more numerous the more divergent the two (or three) parent types, as may not be viable, and provided always that the filial generation in question is sufficiently numerous to provide scope for so extensive a variation. The extreme variants in such a case may easily go beyond the extreme range of either parent type in any given direction, owing to the fact that a given determinant coming in from one side may be fortified or inhibited (perhaps more easily the latter) by a determinant coming in from the other side and affecting the same group of tissues.

history and the sequence of its permutations run their course. It is, of course, a trite matter-of-course that no people can work out a scheme of culture that lies beyond or outside the range of its capacities; and it is likewise a matter-of-course that a nation whose population is gifted with many and various capacities is thereby better fitted to meet the exigencies that arise in the course of its life-history, and so will be in a position more promptly to respond to any call. A larger, fuller, more varied and more broadly balanced scheme of culture will, under tolerable circumstances, be found among such a people than in a community made up of individuals that breed true with close approximation to a single specific type.

Such a hybrid population will, of course, also have the faults of its qualities. The divergence of temperament and proclivities will be as wide as that of its capacities and aptitudes; and the unrest that works out in a multiform ramification of achievements on the one side is likely to work out also in a profuse output of irritation and dissentient opinions, ideals and aspirations on the other side. For good or ill, such has been the congenital make-up of the Western peoples, and such, it may be called to mind, has also been the history of Western civilisation.

All the while it may as well be kept in mind that in this respect, as regards the range and multifarious character of their native endowment, these Western peoples are today what they once were in neolithic time. The range of variations in each and all is very appreciably wider than would be had within any pure-bred stock; but it is no wider, nor is it in any sensible degree different, among the hybrid generations that inhabit these countries today than it once was among the similarly hybrid generations that carried this Western culture in that earlier time. This wide-ranging heritage is after all a neolithic heritage; and however multiform and picturesquely varied the cultural scheme of the Western peoples in later times may seem, the stream does not, after all, rise higher than its neolithic source. The population that makes up and carries forward this civilisation is, after all, endowed with the faults of its qualities, and they are the neolithic qualities.

CHAPTER II

THE OLD ORDER

I

THE state of civilisation and of the industrial arts into which the remote ancestry of the north-Europeans may be said to have been born was the earlier neolithic, — the earliest phase of the stone age of which there is certain evidence in northern Europe. The European palæolithic does not come into the case, since it closed before the formation of that hybrid population out of which these later European peoples have sprung; besides which its traces are virtually wanting throughout the habitat in which this population of mixed race lived and moved and made good their survival. Even for Europe at large, it is held, there is no cultural continuity, and little if any racial continuity, between the palæolithic and the neolithic. The neolithic is believed to have begun independently, so far as concerns its course in Europe, having come in as an intrusive culture, presumptively at the intrusion of the Mediterranean race into Europe, probably late in quaternary time; the earlier stages of the advance that led up to the European neolithic having been worked out outside the European area and before the bearers of the neolithic penetrated that quarter of the world.

It may therefore be said that this early neolithic state of

the arts of life is in a way congenital to the north-European peoples. Whether such a statement will apply in the case of the Mediterranean race, which is held to have brought this culture into Europe, may be left an open question. It is of no immediate interest here. The like is true for the Alpine stock, which is held to have come in from the east, presumably from Asia, during the early neolithic, and which is likewise believed to have reached the neolithic stage before breaking into the European situation. Neither of these races, nor the two together, as they stood at the time of their intrusion into Europe, are to be reckoned the ancestors of the north-Europeans, in the sense of affording the ancestral type, whether physical or spiritual, of that north-European population that presently multiplies and continues to find a livelihood by help of the neolithic technology on the north-European seaboard.

Doubtless each of these races contributes its share to this ancestry; they are both present from the outset, or nearly so, in the mixed north-European population, and they have apparently always continued to account for at least one-half of the racial constitution of these peoples. But the ancestry of the north-Europeans can not be said properly to have come into effectual bearing until the dolicho-blond stock is mixed with the other two, so as to give rise to the particular hybrid strain that has continuously occupied this region since neolithic times and has peopled north Europe with the nations now living. The racial history of these peoples is the history of a population of hybrids made up of the three stocks in conjunction, not of one and another of these racial types in severalty; it can therefore not fairly be said to take its beginning until the three racial factors requisite for its constitution came into conjunction.

The selective test of fitness to survive in the climatic region of the Baltic and North Sea under neolithic conditions, and to hold that habitat against all comers, was not applied to the three constituent stocks in severalty, and so was not a conclusive test of superior fitness in either one of the three taken by itself. The test, and the conclusion to be drawn from the experiment, applies solely to the composite population into which the three enter as essential constituents. Such is obviously the case, since in the course of selective breeding through several thousands of years no one of the three constituent types has displaced both or either of the other two in any part of the region in question, nor has any one of the racial types at any point displaced the hybrid offspring of the three. The most that can be said is that while the population has continued through this long interval of time to be a hybrid mixture, the character of the mixture has come to vary from one place to another in such a way that this composite population is more blond toward the north and more brunet toward the south, at the same time that, even with an equal initial chance, the dolicho-brunet (Mediterranean) counts for less both north and south, within this special climatic region, than either of the other two constituent stocks.

For a contrast that will enforce this line of argument illustrative instances may be drawn from almost any country lying within striking distance of this Baltic-North Sea tract. The hybrid populations of this region have repeatedly, almost unremittingly, broken bounds and migrated in force into other countries and so have been mixed in by cross-breeding with these other peoples. But in no case where the experiment has had time enough to be at all conclusive have they succeeded in making over the racial constitution of the peoples among whom they so have intruded, with such effect as in any instance to supplant the indigenous population and substitute their own racial composition for what they found at the time of their immigration; at least one of the racial factors that go to make up the northern hybrids — the dolicho-blond — has in all cases presently disappeared selectively from these outlying populations into which it so has been introduced; and the composite northern population has proved itself unfit in its composite character to live outside the Baltic-North Sea tract, at the same time that its constituents have proved unfit to hold this tract except in a composite.

Nor has any intrusive population of a different racial derivation, pure-bred or composite, succeeded in displacing the northern hybrids from this habitat, whether by mass movement or by infiltration, although that experiment has also been tried on a sufficient scale, — as, *e.g.*, in the advance of the Finns (Lapps) into the Baltic country, particularly on the northern and northeastern borders of this region that has by a process of selection been proved to belong to the blond-hybrid peoples. At least in the one instance of Finland, and less assuredly elsewhere toward the north and east, the onset of the intruders was so far successful as to have displaced the language of the earlier population; but in the long run the racial composition of the inhabitants has reverted substantially to what it was before the coming of the Finns, so that there is at present no appreciable racial difference between the two shores of the Baltic.[1]

The early Baltic culture is of interest, then, as showing the state of the arts of life to which the ancestry of substantially all the north-European peoples was originally accustomed; which might, indeed, be said to be congenital to these peoples. This culture runs somewhat of an even course, as near as the evidence permits it to be seen, over a long interval, — sufficiently long to have tested the fitness of the Baltic population for the manner of life which it offered, and at the same time sufficiently exposed to contact with other racial elements or aggregates outside to prove that the characteristic hybrid mixture of these Baltic peoples was better fitted than any competing population for life on that technological footing and under the geographical and climatic conditions in which they were placed. A summary recital of the characteristic features and salient events of this cultural period, so far as the evidence permits, will substantiate the claim.[2]

In general terms the Baltic stone age may be characterised as a relatively advanced savagery, placed in a geographic situation drawn on a relatively small scale, — a small-scale system of tillage and presently of mixed farming. It may perhaps as fairly be called a relatively low stage of barbarism; there need be no dispute about the alternative terms; they both are suggestive rather than technically competent descriptive terms. And the bronze age comes under the same loose designation, with the necessary caution that

---

[1]Cf., *e.g.*, A. H. Keane, *Man Past and Present*, ch. ix.
[2]See Note II, p. 291.

it is marked, on the whole, by an appearance of greater technological efficiency and a larger accumulation of wealth, — perhaps also a more settled habit of life.

The neolithic population appear, throughout the period and throughout their territory, to have lived in open settlements of no great size, scattered over the face of the land as the available soil for tillage and pasture might decide. It is doubtful whether these settlements were grouped in villages or loosely dispersed by individual households over the open country. But in any case there is said to be no evidence of towns, or even of large villages,[1] nor is there any trace of fortifications or any evidence of a preference for naturally defensible sites. Taken in conjunction with the relative scarcity of weapons, and the total absence — in the available evidence — of any form of defensive armor, this defenseless distribution of settlements conveys perhaps an unduly broad suggestion of a peaceable habit of life. Yet with all due caution of allowance for what the material does not, and perhaps can not, show, it is impossible to set aside the circumstantial evidence that the culture was character-

---

[1] The kitchen middens — refuse heaps — that are so extraordinarily numerous and extensive on Danish ground may raise a question as to the absence of large settlements. In the earlier canvass of the matter of the kitchen middens it was somewhat naively taken for granted that their size roughly indicated the size and duration of settlements that once occupied these sites. Later and more critical handling of the question is apparently coming to the conclusion that, for much of their later accretions especially, these shell-mounds owe their formation in great part to seasonal occupation of the sites on the beach by a population whose chief interest and permanent habitations are to be looked for on the cultivated lands farther back in the country, — while it is, of course, not denied that the shell-mounds may at the same time mark the sites of permanent fishing villages.

istically a peaceable one. And it necessarily follows also, in the light of considerations already set out above, that the population will have been of a peaceable temper on the whole. The like conditions continue, and the circumstantial evidence runs on with a degree of consistency to the same effect, not only through the stone age but also through the succeeding period of bronze. In the latter period especially the distribution of the population has in several places been traced in some detail, showing that it followed the lay of the land in such a way as to take account of the most practicable fords and roadways, many of which are still in use.[1]

II

ON THE MERITS OF BORROWING

IN ONE connection and another it has already appeared that this stone and bronze-age culture of the Baltic peoples drew for its elements on other cultural regions and earlier phases of civilisation. These peoples borrowed persistently and with great facility. So far as this practice of borrowing is traceable in the stone age it is necessarily a borrowing of technological elements, since the nature of the materials in which they worked has allowed very little but industrial

---

[1]Cf., *e.g.*, Sophus Müller, *Aarböger for nordisk Oldkyndighed*, 1904, "Vei og Bygd i Sten-og Bronzealderen"; also later papers, *ibid.*, by the same author; H. A. Nielsen, *ibid.*, 1906, "Bidrag til Danmarks forhistoriske Befolknings — särligt Stenaldersfolkets — Anthropologie," and "Yderligere Bidrag," *ibid.*, 1911.

appliances to come down to the present; but as regards these technological elements the borrowing is of the most ubiquitous character. Even in the use of flint, as shown by the series of implements running through the period specifically characterised by the kitchen middens and down over the full-blown neolithic into the bronze age, — even in their use of flint they appear to have learned much of the serviceable innovations from outside, chiefly from the south. The early kitchen-midden implements are rather rudely chipped flints, and it is apparent that the grinding of flint was unknown on the Scandinavian waters in that time. Presently, when this improvement comes into vogue, it comes in along with the use of new and more serviceable forms, such as to suggest that they were worked out by help of examples drawn from the more advanced neolithic populations to the south. But along with a due recognition of this technological indebtedness it is also to be recognised that the Baltic peoples presently carried this polished (and chipped) flint technology to a perfection of workmanship and mechanical serviceability not surpassed, even if it may have been equalled, by any other neolithic culture.

Again, neither the crop plants nor the domestic animals are visibly present in the kitchen middens from the outset. As for the crop plants this may mean only a quite intelligible failure of evidence, and does not conclusively argue that, e.g., barley was not known and used from the beginning of the Baltic settlement, though the total absence of any trace is not to be set aside as having no significance. For the domestic animals, on the other hand, the negative evidence is conclusive, and it must be taken as an ascertained fact that these were introduced gradually at an appreciable interval after the beginnings of the Baltic culture had been made, and after the Baltic peoples had definitely acquired the (hybrid) racial complexion that marks them through later time. The paucity of the material, not in volume but in range, permits little more to be said in this connection for the stone age; except it be that the only other appreciable material evidence available, that of the graves and mounds, runs to much the same effect, — the use of these being also held to have been learned from outside, and developed in a characteristic manner on lines originally given by the same usage as it prevailed in other countries.

Throughout the bronze and iron periods of prehistory the same facile borrowing goes on; both the use and the material of the bronze and iron work being of foreign derivation. And as the sequence comes on down the ages and approaches historical dates, offering a progressively increasing volume and diversity of archæological material, the evidence of borrowing extends also to other than the industrial arts. As the beginning of history, in the stricter sense, is approached this borrowing shows itself ever more notoriously in the æsthetic arts; in which, at the close of the pagan era, e.g., Scandinavian art shows its indebtedness to the Irish and other Gælic culture at every turn. What is known of late Baltic (mainly Scandinavian) paganism carries the same insidious suggestion of facility for new ideas in the domain of supernatural beliefs; very much as the shifting progression of usages in sepulture in the remoter past argues that these peoples were not above learning from their neighbors, or perhaps rather were temperamentally defenseless against innovation from the outside. In the late pagan era they seem, e.g., to have borrowed, and in some degree made over, several deities of foreign extraction; and it may be recalled that the pagan era closes with the wholesale acceptance of an alien mythology and religious scheme, the improvement and adaptation of which to their own temperamental needs has occupied much of the serious attention of these peoples ever since.

None of this extensive and unremitting draught on the technological and institutional resources of other cultural regions can be called an idle borrowing. The borrowed elements have invariably been assimilated, drawn into the cultural system and so combined and shaped to its purpose as to have led to an unbroken evolution of a scheme peculiar to these (hybrid) peoples and their needs, rather than to the substitution of a scheme from outside or a piecing-out of the scheme of things into which it is intruded. In other words, the borrowing has been done in a thoroughly workmanlike manner and with a free hand.

This proclivity to borrow, and the free and easy efficiency with which borrowed elements are turned to account, is a characteristic trait of north-European antiquity, as, indeed, it is still something of a distinctive mark of these peoples. It probably marks a temperamental bent of the north-European population, at the same time that it gives a certain characteristic flexibility to their scheme of institutions. As a temperamental trait it would appear to be traceable, at least in good part, to the fact of their hybrid extraction; possibly also in part to the peculiar race characteristics of the stocks from which this hybrid population is derived.[1]

The efficacy of borrowing that so comes to light in the life-history of the Baltic culture, as also in a less notorious manner in other instances of cultural intercourse, puts up to the student of institutions a perplexing question, or rather a group of perplexing questions. Something has just been said on the question of why one people borrows elements of culture or of technology with greater facility and effect than another. But the larger question stands untouched: Why do the borrowed elements lend themselves with

---

[1]Certain other cultural regions and populations offer an instructive parallel on this head, notably the Japanese, and possibly also the Aegean peoples of antiquity. Like the Baltic peoples the Japanese are a hybrid population, a composite of two (perhaps rather three) main racial stocks, with two or three minor racial factors thrown in. Such has apparently been the composition of the Japanese population since the first beginnings of which anything can be said to be known, even if the legends of the *Ko Ji Ki* — the "Records of Ancient Matters" — be accepted at what may be called their face value. By a curious coincidence, the period of Japanese prehistory and history seems to cover loosely the same general interval of time as that of the Baltic peoples; and as with the latter, so in the case of the Japanese, the cultural life-history of the people is a history of facile and ubiquitous borrowing done in the most workmanlike manner and executed with the most serviceable effect. The instance of Japan, however, palpably suggests that this temperamental facility for the acceptance and utilisation of cultural elements from outside, whether in the Japanese or in the Baltic population, should be credited not so much to any marked racial traits of temperament in the constituents of such a hybrid people, but rather to the fact of hybrid derivation itself. It would seem to be due in great part to the exceptionally wide range of variation among the individuals of such a hybrid people, quite as much as to any presumed exceptional facility of this kind in any one of the racial types that have gone to make up the composite population. The parallel between the Japanese and the Baltic peoples in this respect can by no stretch of fantastic ethnological argument be set down to a putative community of descent.

greater facility and effect to their intrinsic use in the hands of the borrower people than in the hands of the people to whose initiative they are due? Why are borrowed elements of culture more efficiently employed than home-grown innovations? or more so than the same elements at the hands of their originators? It would of course be quite bootless to claim that such is always or necessarily the case, but it is likewise not to be denied that, as a matter of history, technological innovations and creations of an institutional nature have in many cases reached their fullest serviceability only at the hands of other communities and other peoples than those to whom these cultural elements owed their origin and initial success. That such should ever be the case is a sufficiently striking phenomenon, — one might even say a sufficiently striking discrepancy.

An explanation, good as far as it goes, though it may not go all the way, is to be looked for in the peculiar circumstances attending the growth, as well as the eventual transmission by borrowing, of any article of the institutional equipment. Technological elements affecting the state of the industrial arts, as being the more concrete and more tangible, will best serve to demonstrate the proposition. Any far-reaching innovation or invention, such as may eventually find a substantial place in the inventory of borrowed elements, will necessarily begin in a small way, finding its way into use and wont among the people where it takes its rise rather tentatively and by tolerance than with a sweeping acceptance and an adequate realisation of its uses and ulterior consequences. Such will have been the case, *e.g.*, with the domestication of the crop plants and the beginnings of tillage, or the domestication of the useful animals, or the use of the metals, or, again, with the rise of the handicraft system, or the industrial revolution that brought in the machine industry. The innovation finds its way into the system of use and wont at the cost of some derangement to the system, provokes to new usages, conventions, beliefs, and principles of conduct, in part directed advisedly to its utilisation or to the mitigation of its immediate consequences, or to the diversion of its usufruct to the benefit of given individuals or classes; but in part there also grow up new habits of thought due to the innovation which it brings into the routine of life, directly in the way of new requirements of manipulation, surveillance, attendance or seasonal time-schedule, and indirectly by affecting the economic relations between classes and localities, as well as the distribution and perhaps the aggregate supply of consumable wealth.

In the early times, such as would come immediately in question here, it is a virtual matter-of-course that any material innovation, or indeed any appreciable unit of technological ways and means, will be attended with a fringe of magical or superstitious conceits and observances. The evidences of this are to be found in good plenty in all cultures, ancient or contemporary, on the savage and barbarian levels; and indeed they are not altogether wanting in civilised life. Many students of ethnology, folk-psychology and religion have busied themselves to good effect with collecting and analysing such material afforded by magical and superstitious practice, and in most instances they are able to trace these practices to some ground of putative utility, connecting them with the serviceable working of the arts of life at one point or another, or with the maintenance of conditions conducive to life and welfare in some essential respect. Where the ethnologist is unable to find such a line of logical connection between superstitious practice and the exigencies of life and welfare, he commonly considers that he has not been able to find what is in the premises, not that the premises do not contain anything of the kind he is bound to expect. But if magical and superstitious practices, or such of them as are at all of material consequence, are with virtual universality to be traced back through the channels of habituation to some putative ground of serviceability for human use, it follows that the rule should work, passably at least, the other way; that the state of the industrial arts which serve human use in such a culture will be shot through with magical and superstitious conceits and observances having an indispensable but wholly putative efficacy.

In many of the lower cultures, or perhaps rather in such of the lower cultures as are at all well known, the workday routine of getting a living is encumbered with a ubiquitous and pervasive scheme of such magical or superstitious conceits and observances, which are felt to constitute an indispensable part of the industrial processes in which they mingle. They embody the putatively efficacious immaterial constituent of all technological procedure; or, seen in detail, they are the spiritual half that completes and animates any process or device throughout its participation in the industrial routine. Like the technological elements with which they are associated, and concomitantly with them, these magically efficacious devices have grown into the prevalent habits of thought of the population and have become an

integral part of the common-sense notion of how these technological elements are and are to be turned to account.[1] And
at a slightly farther shift in the current of sophistication, out
of the same penchant for anthropomorphic interpretation
and analogy, a wide range of religious observances, properly so called, will also presently come to bear on the industrial process and the routine of economic life; with a
proliferous growth of ceremonial, of propitiation and avoidance, designed to further the propitious course of things to
be done.

These matters of the magical and religious ritual of industry and economic arrangements among the peoples of
the lower cultures are sufficiently familiar to all ethnological
students, and probably they also are so far a matter of common notoriety that there is no need of insistence on their
place and value in these lower cultures. They are spoken of
here only to recall the fact that the large and consequential
technological elements involved in any primitive system of
industry have commonly carried such a fringe of putatively
efficacious, though mechanically futile, waste motion. These
naive forms of mandatory futility are believed to belong
only on the lower levels of culture, although it should not
be overlooked that magical and religious conceits still exercise something of an inhibitory influence in the affairs of
industry even among the very enlightened peoples of Christendom.

But aside from these simple-minded institutional inhibi-

---

[1] For illustration from contemporary lower cultures, cf. W. W. Skeat,
Malay Magic, perhaps especially ch. v.; for classic antiquity cf. Jane
E. Harrison, *Prolegomena to the Study of Greek Religion*, ch. iii. iv.

tions on industrial efficiency that seem so much a matter of course in the lower cultures, there are others that run to much the same effect and hold their place among the more enlightened peoples in much the same matter-of-course way. These are in part rather obscure, not having been much attended to in popular speculation, and in part quite notorious, having long been subjects of homiletical iteration. And since this growth of what may be called secular, as contrasted with magical or religious, institutional inhibitions on efficiency, has much to do with latterday economic affairs, as well as with the material fortunes of our prehistoric forebears, a more detailed exposition of their place in economic life will be in place.

On the adoption of new industrial ways and means, whether in the way of specific devices and expedients or of comprehensive changes in methods and processes, there follows a growth of conventional usages governing the utilisation of the new ways and means. This applies equally whether the new expedients are home-bred innovations or technological improvements borrowed from outside; and in any case such a growth of conventions takes time, being of the nature of adaptive habituation. A new expedient, in the way of material appliances or of improved processes, comes into the industrial system and is adapted to the requirements of the state of things into which it is introduced. Certain habitual ways of utilising the new device come to be accepted; as, would happen, e.g., on the introduction of domestic animals among a people previously living by tillage alone and having no acquaintance with the use of such animals under other conditions than those prevailing among purely pastoral peoples. So, again, the gradual improvement of boat-building and navigation, such as took place among the prehistoric Baltic peoples, would induce a progressive change in the conventional scheme of life and bring on a specialisation of occupations, with some division of economic and social classes. Or, again, in such a large systematic shift as is involved in the coming of the handicraft industry and its spread and maturing; class distinctions, occupational divisions, standardisation of methods and products, together with trade relations and settled markets and trade routes, came gradually into effect. In part these conventional features resulting from and answering to the new industrial factors continued to have the force of common-sense conventional arrangement only; in part they also acquired the added stability given by set agreement, authoritative control and statutory enactment.

So, in the case of the handicraft system such matters as trade routes, methods of package, transportation and consignment, credit relations, and the like, continued very largely, though not wholly nor throughout the vogue of the system, to be regulated by conventional vogue rather than by authoritative formulation; while on the other hand the demarkation between crafts and classes of craftsmen, as well as the standardisation of methods and output, were presently, in the common run, brought under rigorous surveillance by authorities vested with specific powers and acting under carefully formulated rules.

But whether this standardisation and conventionalisation takes the set form of authoritative agreement and enactment or is allowed to rest on the looser ground of settled use and wont, it is always of the nature of a precipitate of past habituation, and is designed to meet exigencies that have come into effect in past experience; it always embodies something of the principle of the dead hand; and along with all the salutary effects of stability and harmonious working that may be credited to such systematisation, it follows also that these standing conventions out of the past unavoidably act to retard, deflect or defeat adaptation to new exigencies that arise in the further course. Conventions that are in some degree effete continue to cumber the ground.

All this apparatus of conventions and standard usage, whether it takes the simpler form of use and wont or the settled character of legally competent enactment and common-law rule, necessarily has something of this effect of retardation in any given state of the industrial arts, and so necessarily acts in some degree to lower the net efficiency of the industrial system which it pervades. But this work of retardation is also backed by the like character attaching to the material equipment by use of which the technological proficiency of the community takes effect. The equipment is also out of the past, and it too lies under the dead hand. In a general way, any minor innovation in processes or in the extension of available resources, or in the scale of organisation, is taken care of as far as may be by a patchwork improvement and amplification of the items of equipment already in hand; the fashion of plant and appliances already in use is adhered to, with concessions in new installations, but it is adhered to more decisively so in any endeavor to bring the equipment in hand up to scale and grade. Changes so made are in part of a concessive nature, in sufficiently large part, indeed, to tell materially on the aggregate; and the fact of such changes being habitually made in a concessive spirit so lessens the thrust in the direction of innovation that even the concessions do not carry as far as might be.[1]

---

[1]An illustrative instance of this obsolescence of equipment on a large scale and in modern circumstances is afforded by several of the underlying companies of the United States Steel Corporation. The plants in question had been installed at a period when the later methods of steel production had not been perfected and before the later and richer sources of raw materials had become available by the latest methods of transportation; they were also located with a view to smaller markets, distributed on an earlier and now obsolete plan, which has become obsolete through changes in the railway system and the growth of new centers of population. It was technologically impossible to bring them up to date as independent industrial plants, and as a business proposition it was impracticable abruptly to discard them and replace them by new equipment placed to better advantage and organised on a scale to take full advantage of available resources and methods. The remedy sought in the formation of the Steel Corporation was a compromise, whereby the obsolete items of equipment — in part obsolete only in the geographical sense that the industrial situation had shifted out of their way — were gradually discarded and replaced with new plant designed for specialised lines of production, at the same time that the monopolistic position of the new Corporation enabled the shift to be made at a sufficiently slow rate to mask the substitution and make the community at large pay for this temporary lower efficiency due to a gradual disuse of obsolete equipment and methods, in place of such an abrupt and sweeping shift to a new basis as the altered technological situation called for.

At a later juncture the Steel Corporation found itself also face to face with a serious difficulty due to "obsolescence through improvement" of the same general kind; when it appeared that by the later improved processes steel of the first quality could be made from ore peculiar to the southern field as cheaply as from the Minnesota supply on which the Corporation's mills were in the habit of depending, and with special advantages of access to certain markets. How far the resulting acquisition of the southern coal, ore and lime by the Corporation may have resulted in a retardation of efficiency in steel production would be hazardous to guess.

It is in the relatively advanced stages of the industrial arts that this retardation due to use and wont, as distinguished from magical and religious waste and inhibitions on innovation, become of grave consequence. There appears, indeed, to be in some sort a systematic symmetry or balance to be observed in the way in which the one of these lines of technological inhibition comes into effectual bearing as fast as the other declines. At the same time, as fast as commercial considerations, considerations of investment, come to rule industry, the investor's interest comes also to exercise an inhibitory surveillance over technological efficiency, both by the well-known channel of limiting the output and holding up the price to what the traffic will bear, — that is to say what it will bear in the pecuniary sense of yielding the largest net gain to the business men in interest, — and also by the less notorious reluctance of investors and business concerns to replace obsolete methods and plant with new and more efficient equipment.

Beyond these simple and immediate inhibitory convolutions within the industrial system itself, there lies a fertile domain of conventions and institutional arrangements induced as secondary consequences of the growth of industrial efficiency and contrived to keep its net serviceability in bounds, by diverting its energies to industrially unproductive uses and its output to unproductive consumption.[1]

With any considerable advance in the industrial arts business enterprise presently takes over the control of the industrial process; with the consequence that the net pe-

---

[1]See below, pp. 136–149.

cuniary gain to the business man in control becomes the test of industrial efficiency. This may result in a speeding up of the processes of industry, as is commonly noted by economists. But it also results in "unemployment" whenever a sustained working of the forces engaged does not, or is not believed to, conduce to the employer's largest net gain, as may notoriously happen in production for a market. Also, it follows that industry is controlled and directed with a view to sales, and a wise expenditure of industrial efficiency, in the business sense, comes to mean such expenditure as contributes to sales; which may often mean that the larger share of costs, as the goods reach their users, is the industrially wasteful cost of advertising and other expedients of salesmanship.

The normal result of business control in industry — normal in the sense of being uniformly aimed at and also in that it commonly follows — is the accumulation of wealth and income in the hands of a class. Under the well-accepted principle of "conspicuous waste" wealth so accumulated is to be put in evidence in visible consumption and visible exemption from work. So that with due, but ordinarily not a large, lapse of time, an elaborate scheme of proprieties establishes itself, bearing on this matter of conspicuous consumption, so contrived as to "take up the slack." This system of conspicuous waste is a scheme of proprieties, decencies, and standards of living, the economic motive of which is competitive spending. It works out in a compromise between the immediate spending of income on conspicuous consumption — together with the conspicuous avoidance of industrial work — on the one side, and deferred spending —

commonly called "saving" — on the other side. The deferred spending may be deferred to a later day in the lifetime of the saver, or to a later generation; its effects are substantially the same in either case. There is the further reservation to be noted, that in so far as property rights, tenures and the conjunctures of business gain are in any degree insecure, measures will be taken to insure against the risks of loss and eventual inability to keep up appearances according to the accepted standard of living. This insurance takes the shape of accumulation, in one form or another, — provision for future revenue.

Like other conventions and institutional regulations, the scheme of spending rests on current, *i.e.*, immediately past, experience, and as was noted above it is so contrived as to take up the calculable slack, — the margin between production and productive consumption. It is perhaps needless to enter the caution that such a scheme of conspicuous waste does not always, perhaps not in the common run of cases, go to the full limit of what the traffic will bear; but it is also to be noted that it will sometimes, and indeed not infrequently, exceed that limit. Perhaps in all cases, but particularly where the industrial efficiency of the community is notably high, so as to yield a very appreciable margin between productive output and necessary current consumption, some appreciable thought has to be spent on the question of ways and means of spending; and a technique of consumption grows up.

It will be appreciated how serious a question this may become, of the ways and means of reputable consumption, when it is called to mind that in the communities where the modern state of the industrial arts has adequately taken effect this margin of product disposable for wasteful consumption will always exceed fifty per cent of the current product, and will in the more fortunate cases probably exceed seventy-five per cent of the whole. So considerable a margin is not to be disposed of to good effect by haphazard impulse. The due absorption of it in competitive spending takes thought, skill and time for the organisation of ways and means. It is also not a simple problem of conspicuously consuming time and substance, without more ado; men's sense of fitness and beauty requires that the spending should take place in an appropriate manner, such as will not offend good taste and not involve an odiously aimless ostentation. And it takes time and habituation, as well as a discriminate balancing of details, before a scheme of reputable standardised waste is perfected; of course, it also costs time and specialised effort to take due care of the running adjustment of such a scheme to current conditions of taste, ennui and consumptive distinction, — as seen, *e.g.*, in the technique of fashions. It has, indeed, proved to be a matter of some difficulty, not to say of serious strain, in the industrially advanced communities, to keep the scheme of conspicuous waste abreast of the times; so that, besides the conspicuous consumers in their own right, there have grown up an appreciable number of special occupations devoted to the technical needs of reputable spending. The technology of wasteful consumption is large and elaborate and its achievements are among the monuments of human initiative and endeavor; it has its victories and its heroes as well as the technology of production.

But any technological scheme is more or less of a balanced system, in which the interplay of parts has such a character of mutual support and dependence that any substantial addition or subtraction at any one point will involve more or less of derangement all along the line. Neither can an extremely large contingent of reputable waste be suddenly superinduced in the accepted standard of living of any given community — though this difficulty is not commonly a sinister one — nor can a large retrenchment in this domain of what is technically called "the moral standard of living" be suddenly effected without substantial hardship or without seriously disturbing the spiritual balance of the community. To realise the import of such disturbance in the scheme of wasteful consumption one need only try to picture the consternation that would, e.g., fall on the British community consequent on the abrupt discontinuance of the Court and its social and civil manifestations, or of horse-racing, or of the established church, or of evening dress.

But since the growth and acceptance of any scheme of wasteful expenditure is after all subsequent to and consequent upon the surplus productivity of the industrial system on which it rests, the introduction, in whole or in part, of a new and more efficient state of the industrial arts does not carry with it from the outset a fully developed system of standardised consumption; particularly, it need not follow that the standard scheme of consumption will be carried over intact in case a new industrial technology is borrowed. There is no intimate or intrinsic mutuality of mechanical detail between the technology of industry and the technique of conspicuous waste; the high-heeled slipper and the high-wrought "picture hat," *e.g.*, are equally well accepted in prehistoric Crete and in twentieth-century France; and the Chinese lady bandages her foot into deformity where the Manchu lady, in evidence of the same degree of opulence in the same town, is careful to let her foot run loose. It is only that, human nature being what it is, a disposable margin of production will, under conditions of private ownership, provoke a competent scheme of wasteful consumption.

Owing to this mechanical discontinuity between any given state of the industrial arts and the scheme of magical, religious, conventional, or pecuniary use and wont with which it lives in some sort of symbiosis, the carrying-over of such a state of the industrial arts from one community to another need not involve the carrying-over of this its spiritual complement. Such is particularly the case where the borrowing takes place across a marked cultural frontier, in which case it follows necessarily that the alien scheme of conventions will not be taken over intact in taking over an alien technological system, whether in whole or in part. The borrowing community or cultural group is already furnished with its own system of conceits and observances — in magic, religion, propriety, and any other line of conventional necessity — and the introduction of a new scheme, or the intrusion of new and alien elements into the accredited scheme already in force, is a work of habituation that takes time and special provocation. All of which applies with added force to the introduction of isolated technological elements from an alien culture, still more particularly, of course, where the technological expedients borrowed are turned to other uses and utilised by other methods than those employed in the culture from which they were borrowed, — as, *e.g.*, would be the case in the acquisition of domestic cattle by a sedentary farming community from a community of no-madic or half-nomadic pastoral people, as appears to have happened in the prehistoric culture of the Baltic peoples. The interposition of a linguistic frontier between the bor-rower and creditor communities would still farther lessen the chance of immaterial elements of culture being carried over in the transmission of technological knowledge. The borrowed elements of industrial efficiency would be stripped of their fringe of conventional inhibitions and waste, and the borrowing community would be in a position to use them with a freer hand and with a better chance of utilising them to their full capacity, and also with a better chance of improving on their use, turning them to new uses, and carrying the principles (habits of thought) involved in the borrowed items out, with unhampered insight, into farther ramifications of technological proficiency. The borrowers are in a position of advantage, intellectually, in that the new expedient comes into their hands more nearly in the shape of a theoretical principle applicable under given physical conditions; rather than in the shape of a concrete expedient applicable within the limits of traditional use, personal, magical, conventional. It is, in other words, taken over in a measure without the defects of its qualities.

Here, again, is a secondary effect of borrowing, that may not seem of first-rate consequence but is none the less neces-sarily to be taken into account. The borrowed elements are drawn into a cultural scheme in which they are aliens and into the texture of which they can be wrought only at the cost of some, more or less serious, derangement of the accustomed scheme of life and the accepted system of knowledge and belief. Habituation to their use and insight into their working acts in its degree to incapacitate the borrowers for holding all their home-bred conceits and beliefs intact and in full conviction. They are vehicles of cultural discrepancy, conduce to a bias of skepticism, and act, in their degree, to loosen the bonds of authenticity. Incidentally, the shift involved in such a move will have its distasteful side and carry its burden of disturbance and discomfort; but the new elements, it is presumed, will make their way, and the borrowing community will make its peace with them on such terms as may be had; that assumption being included in the premises.

In some instances of such communication of alien technological and other cultural elements the terms on which a settlement has been effected have been harsh enough, as, *e.g.*, on the introduction of iron tools and fire-arms among the American Indians, or the similar introduction of distilled spirits, of the horse, and of trade — especially in furs — among the same general group of peoples. Polynesia, Australia, and other countries new to the European technology, and to the European conceits and conceptions in law, religion and morals, will be called to mind to the same effect. In these cases the intrusion of alien, but technologically indefeasible, elements of culture has been too large to allow the old order to change; so it has gone to pieces. This result may, of course, have been due in part to a tempera-

mental incapacity of these peoples for the acquisition of new
and alien habits of thought; they may not have been good
borrowers, at least they appear not to have been sufficiently
good borrowers. The same view, in substance, is often formulated to the effect that these are inferior or "backward"
races, being apparently not endowed with the traits that
conduce to a facile apprehension of the modern European
technological system.

It appears to have been otherwise with the peoples of the
Baltic culture, late and early. They have been good borrowers, having borrowed persistently, ubiquitously and well.
The proof of their exceptional capacity as borrowers is the
general run of the life-history of these populations and their
culture. As a general proposition, they appear not to have
suffered a disproportionate setback in population or in productive efficiency even at those epochs when the borrowing
took on a wholesale character, as, *e.g.*, on the transition to
bronze, or later to iron, or later still in the sweeping shift
from paganism to Christianity. In each of these instances,
of course, something of a serious disturbance and impairment is traceable, at least in the two latter episodes; but
even the shift to the Christian faith appears to have involved only a relatively transient decline, and in each case
this cultural region comes out of the era of transition apparently stronger than before the intrusion of new cultural
elements took place. As would be expected, the last named,
the shift to Christianity, was the most demoralising of these
adventures in cultural borrowing; since this was, in the main
and immediately, a borrowing of immaterial, institutional
elements, without any corresponding gain in technology; so

that in this instance the shock to the cultural scheme came from factors which did not carry such an immediate and intrinsic compensation for the resulting derangement as did the technological change involved in the introduction of the metals. It is, of course, also possible to overstate both the magnitude and the abruptness of the change from the pagan to the Christian scheme in the Baltic region; indeed, it has not been unusual to do so. But when all is said the fact remains that through all their borrowing of expedients, information, institutions and ideals no collapse has overtaken this culture, such as either to reduce the population to virtual extinction — as has happened in analogous circumstances, *e.g.*, in Tasmania, Australia, various parts of Polynesia and America, in a more or less sweeping fashion — or to substitute a substantially alien cultural scheme for what prevailed before the coming of the innovation in technology or in use and wont.

Not that there have been no serious, or even alarming, conjunctures in the cultural history of the Baltic peoples; it is only that they have come through without that degree of discontinuity that would involve a substitution of a new race (or racial mixture) or a new scheme of civilisation alien to what went before. There is at least one juncture in the bronze age when the derangement of the conditions of life in the Baltic country appears to have fallen into really precarious shape, — between the second and third periods of the bronze age in Montelius's chronology, or between the "early" and the "late" bronze age as more commonly spoken of, — and there is suggestive evidence of something of a break at a later point in the sequence, before the coming of iron.[1] Something of grave import, in the way of a difficult interval, may also be surmised in the earlier half of the iron age. What may have been the nature of these episodes that so have an untoward look is at the best a matter of surmise, with little chance of reaching anything like a secure conclusion in the present state of the archæological evidence. There may have been something like hostile contact with alien peoples outside, or internal dissensions, or an epidemic disease, such, e.g., as the black death, or the plague that visited Athens in the fifth century; or it may conceivably have been nothing more serious than an interruption of trade relations with the Mediterranean and Black Sea, due to extensive raiding or to the shifting of peoples in the intervening territory. Through it all, however, the continuity of the cultural sequence is visible, as is also the efficiency of this culture, in the biological sense that the population does not seriously or enduringly fall off. The latter test is perhaps the more conclusive. So much so that the Baltic region is known to antiquity as a "cradle of nations" even before anything much else is known of it by the civilised peoples of antiquity and their writers. That it deserved that name and continued to make it good is seen in the inexhaustible barbarian migrations that continued to run outward from the Baltic center.

The presumptive characteristics of this culture, then, as one gets an impression from a study of its antiquities and by inference from the conditions of life which the country

---

[1] Cf., e.g., Montelius, *Les temps préhistoriques en Suède et dans les autres pays Scandinaves;* Sophus Müller, *Vor Oldtid,* and *L'Europe préhistorique.*

offers and from the make-up of its population, may tentatively be set down. It would be a small-scale culture, in the sense that the local units would be of no great magnitude; although it may be conceived to have covered a relatively extensive area in the aggregate and to have covered this area with a fairly dense population; it habitually stood in fairly close communication with other peoples outside, even over relatively long distances, principally by way of trade; these peoples borrowed freely, both in technological and in other institutional matters,[1] and made notably free and efficient use of all borrowed elements. The scheme of institutions, economic, civil, domestic and religious, that would fit these circumstances would be of a relatively slight fixity, flexible, loose-knit, and naive, in the sense that they would be kept in hand under discretionary control of neighborly common sense, — the continued borrowing and the facility with which borrowed elements are assimilated and turned to account goes far to enforce this conclusion. Altogether its most impressive traits are a certain industrial efficiency, particularly efficiency in the mechanic arts, and its conduciveness to the multiplication of its people; whereas its achievements in political organisation or in the domain of art and religion are relatively slight. It is a civilisation of workmanship and fecundity rather than of dynastic power, statecraft, priestcraft or artistic achievement.

---

[1] In methods of burial, art motives, etc.

III

The Pagan Anarchy

No contemporary, or nearly contemporary, record is to be had of the culture of the Baltic peoples prior to their conversion to Christianity and their consequent entrance into the history of Christendom. Consequently no direct evidence is at hand as to the institutions of that culture, except such as shows the state of things in retrospect, as seen by writers who had, in a good measure at least, left that culture behind and saw it as more or less an alien state of society. Any presentation of the state of the Baltic culture in prehistoric times, in any but the material respect, therefore, must be of the nature of a reconstruction on the basis of insufficient documents and circumstantial evidence. Yet such is the need of a perspicuous conception of this prehistoric state of society, for any endeavor to understand the long-term bent and hereditary genius of the English and German peoples, considered as an offshoot of the Baltic civilisation, that it seems necessary to accept the hazard of the adventure and make the most of the resources available to this end. At its best the material leaves much to be desired; but any inquiry into human institutions will in such a case have to fall back on the aphorism that "The best is always good enough," and so make the most of what is to be had.

Looking back through the perspective given by the late-pagan culture of the Scandinavian countries, then, a reconstruction of the prehistoric state of society on the Baltic seaboard may be attempted, in rough outline and in a provisional way, as seen against the background afforded by the archæological material of this region. The purpose of such a tentative delineation is to present, as near as may be, the scheme of life and the state of the industrial arts to which the north-European peoples of today are, by hereditary temperament and capacity, presumably best suited; to which, in other words, they are adapted by birth, and into which they would fall, if circumstances permitted, as their "state of nature"; and from which they have been diverted only by force of habituation under pressure of a later state of the industrial arts that requires a different manner of life, essentially alien to the north-European blond-hybrid population.[1]

In the civil organisation all power vests finally in the popular assembly, made up, in effect, though not by strict formal specification, of the freehold farmers; including under that designation the able-bodied male citizens of substantial standing, but not formally excluding any part of the free population, and perhaps not even with absolute rigor excluding all women.[2]

This deliberative assembly exercised the powers, such as

---

[1]See Note III, p. 302.

[2]The restriction of the franchise to able-bodied men at arms, and the requirement of coming to the assembly under arms, such as is to be observed among the predatory bands and warlike communities of these barbarians during and after their incursion into the older civilised countries of Europe, does not appear to have been in force in Scandinavian antiquity; it would rather appear that all that matter was left loosely in the option of the citizens, although there was at least an occasional prohibition of weapons at the assembly. Practice appears to have varied.

were exercised, of legislation, executive (extremely slight), and judiciary. There is little, if any, police power, though there are established conventions of police regulations; and there is no conception of the "King's peace," outside the king's farmyard; nor is there any conception of a "public peace" to be enforced by public authority of any kind, outside the precincts of the popular assembly. What stands out all over this civil fabric is the evidence of its resting on the assumption of neighborhood autonomy, and that within the self-sufficient neighborhood the individual is depended on wholly to take care of his own interest, with the backing of his kin and within such loose limits of tolerance as may be implied in the eventual formation of a vigilance committee in case any individual or group should develop into an insufferable public nuisance.

This civil system might be described as anarchy qualified by the common sense of a deliberative assembly that exercises no coercive control; or it might, if one's bias leads that way, be called a democratic government, the executive power of which is in abeyance. All of which does not imply, in any degree, the absence of a legal system, of a conception of legality, or of specific, and even minute, provisions of law covering all conjunctures likely to arise in such a society.

While such a quasi-anarchistic scheme of social control resting on insubordination can be installed only on the basis of a natural propensity in its favor — an ethical or æsthetic sense of its equity — its practicability is conditioned by certain mechanical circumstances. The scheme depends on personal contact within the group, and the group over which its rule will extend must be limited by the bounds of such personal and informal contact. It is in the nature of things a neighborhood organisation, and is not applicable beyond the effectual reach of neighborhood relations. It is practicable, therefore, only so long and so far as the necessary industrial relations do not overpass the possibilities of such neighborly contact; and with any appreciable advance in the state of the industrial arts, such as will unduly increase the scale of industrial operations or of the consequent economic relations, the anarchistic scheme of society grows increasingly precarious.

Sooner or later the discrepancy grows too great, between what is mechanically practicable, or rather unavoidable, in the extension of the industrial community on the one hand, and the farthest practicable stretch of the anarchistic system of neighborly common-sense surveillance on the other hand. So that the old order is manifestly due to break down under the impact of cumulative change that entails a scale of organisation effectually exceeding the working limits of that undifferentiated consensus of sentiment that conditions its efficiency. By the same token, a people which has proved its eminent fitness for this scale and measure in the arts of life, by carrying forward a culture of this character under varying circumstances through several thousands of years, should presumably be unable to find itself equally at home under the conditions imposed by a state of the industrial arts that greatly overreaches these moderate bounds, and should so be unable, under these new conditions, to achieve anything like the same measure of cultural balance and grace, of popular comfort and content, or of wholesome commonplace fecundity.

With an advance in the industrial arts such as to require a larger material equipment, or such as will permit enterprise of a larger scope, the possessor of the requisite means comes into a position to extend his enterprise beyond the bounds within which neighborhood surveillance is effective. What he undertakes beyond these bounds does not, under the anarchistic rule, concern his neighbors who live within them. Indeed, in any enterprise outside he will have the moral support of his neighborhood group under the rule of Live and let live, since it is right and good that he should live as good him seems, so long as the traffic in which he engages does not impinge in a disastrous way on his neighbors; and in case of need he will have their active backing, to a reasonable extent, so far as the common-sense animus of group solidarity may carry them. Gain at the cost of other communities, particularly communities at a distance, and more especially such as are felt to be aliens, is not obnoxious to the standards of home-bred use and wont.

At the same time such gains add to the standing of the man who makes them, as all pecuniary gains do in a culture that makes much of property. And all gains coming to any of its members from outside are felt to be gain to the community, by award of the uncritical but ubiquitous sense of group solidarity.[1]

---

[1]This sense of group solidarity is a trait of race psychology that may not be readily explained by perspicuous reasoning. But it will doubtless have to be accepted as an opaque hereditary fact of human nature; and it is readily enough to be explained by the logic of selective survival, since any racial type devoid of this propensity, or insufficiently furnished in this respect, must infallibly have disappeared in the biological competition with such types as included this trait, — inasmuch as human life

The good repute and the added power to be gained by such enterprise acts as an incentive to its pursuit on the one hand and as a sanction to the practice on the other hand; until it becomes a commonplace of use and wont that the competitive pursuit of gain by the use of all available means is an inalienable right, and that gain at the cost of outsiders is more to be commended than serviceability to the home community. By some obscure trick of psychological sophistry that is explicable in perspicuous analysis neither for prehistoric nor for historical times, but that is well authenticated by ancient and modern usage and that may be rated as an hereditary infirmity or an hereditary advantage, the sense of group solidarity coalesces with the pride of achievement to such effect that the members of the group at large are elated with the exploits of any member of the group in good standing. So far will this sentimental sophistry carry, that the community not only looks with approval and elation on the successful self-aggrandisement of a given individual member at the cost of outsiders, but it will also unreflectingly further such enterprises at a palpable cost to itself and with the certainty of getting no gain from the venture, — as, *e.g.*, in exploits of loyalty.

So it is quite safe to say not only that the citizens in the small-scale kingdoms of the Old Order had no material

has been carried on only by groups, at least through that segment of the life-history of mankind that touches the races here in question.

The effectual presence and uncritical efficiency of this propensity is well seen in the attitude of modern nations on questions of international trade; where the trade is carried on for the gain of the business men immediately concerned, and where the benefit presumed to accrue to the community at large from such gains coming to the home-bred business men will bear no scrutiny.

interest in extending the boundaries of the realm, or in adding a second kingdom to the patrimony of their prince, but that, on the contrary, their interest palpably lay in avoiding any such outcome. By sound logic they should have taken measures to defeat the ambitions of the crown; whereas in point of fact they went to considerable lengths to further such projects of dynastic aggrandisement. Such, of course, has also been the history of dynastic war and politics ever since. The claims and perquisites of the prince appear under the old order of petty neighborhood kingdoms to have been extremely slight and irregular; but so soon as the king's dominions increased to such a size as to take him personally out of range of an effectual surveillance by neighborly sentiment — that is to say, so soon as the realm increased beyond the extent of a single rounded neighborhood — the crown would be able to use the loyalty of one neighborhood in enforcing exactions from another, and the royal power would then presently find no other obstacle to its continued growth than the limit placed upon it by the state of the industrial arts. This limit was determined primarily by the disposable means of communication, and secondarily by the productive efficiency of the community on which the crown drew for the supplies of men and means consumed in extending and controlling his wider dominions. Habituation, enforced and authenticated by the royal countenance, engendered the virtue of loyalty; until in the end — the end of the Old Order — the rule of Live and let live passed over into the rule that the king is to live as good him seems and the common man is to live as the king of his grace will grant him. The predisposition to group solidarity coalesced with the bias of approval for the aggrandisement of their accredited spokesman, to such effect that abnegation in his favor became the prime virtue of the new order, in place of the insubordination and initiative which, together with a neighborly tolerance, had formed the pillars of the house under the old.

Enterprise at this point appears to have followed two main lines, distinct but both leading in the end to much the same outcome: (a) local kings set about extending their dominions, displacing and disinheriting such royal lines as fell short in the struggle for empire, and imposing a more despotic rule on the communities that so coalesced into a larger realm; (b) restless young men, and older men to whom the increasing pressure of royalty was intolerable, set out in companies at adventure, fought their way to a new footing outside or ran to waste in the turmoil. Those bands of marauders that overran and subjugated what is now the Fatherland appear to have been of this class. An occasional one of these hordes, as, *e.g.*, the Heruli, may have been led by some scion of royalty; though such appears commonly not to have been the case. But in any case the outcome is much the same, in that the old order of quasi-anarchistic autonomy presently gave place to irresponsible authority and subjection.

CHAPTER III

THE DYNASTIC STATE

WHAT befel the Germanic peoples through the ages that lie between prehistoric paganism and the late-modern period, whether within their ancient habitat on the Baltic seaboard, or abroad in those seats of conquest and immigration that have since come to be spoken of as the Fatherland, — all that does not concern this inquiry. Just as the particular fortunes of these peoples in prehistoric antiquity have also no interest in this connection, except as the recital may serve to show what is the hereditary racial bent of this population that so lived and thrived under that archaic state of culture. That they did so live and thrive goes to prove that that archaic culture, and the state of the industrial arts in which it was grounded, were suited to their temperamental bent. This hereditary type of human nature, so shown in the working-out of this characteristic culture of pagan antiquity, is of interest in this connection because it is the same human nature with which these peoples today go to their work of getting a living under the conditions offered by the technology of today.

A summary paragraph in the way of a conspectus may therefore be in place. By and large, all these north-European peoples that live within the climatic region of the Baltic-North Sea littoral are of one racial complexion, irrespective of language or nationality. They are all of a composite derivation, a hybrid population made up of some three (or more) racial stocks, with minor contingents thrown in sporadically; the composition of this population varying only by negligible differences from west to east, and varying north and south after a systematic fashion, in respect of the relative proportion in which the several racial constituents enter in the hybrid mixture, — always with the reservation that for the immediate purpose this characterisation need apply only within the climatic region of the Baltic and North Sea. The population of these countries has, therefore, the wide range of individual variability that belongs to a hybrid stock. But even this wide variability, which goes far to give a facile adaptiveness of the people to novel and even to alien conditions, runs after all within certain broad, selectively determined lines, and does not set aside the effectual long-term assertion of a certain, flexible but indefeasible, general drift or generic type of human nature that runs through the whole of these populations, — the tone-giving traits of this type of human nature being those that show themselves in that archaic civilisation which the Baltic peoples worked out during that early period of their racial life-history when they made good their survival. This period of prehistory has been the only phase in the experience of this population that has lasted long enough under passably stable conditions to exert anything like a definitively selective effect, and so to test what they are fit for and what is fit for them. This archaic culture, which so may be said, by selective test, to be congenital to the north-Europeans, will, on its technological side, typically have been of the character of the neolithic, rather than anything else that can be given a specific name; while in point of its domestic, social and civil institutions it may be called a conventionalised anarchy, in the sense that it lacks formal provision for a coercive control, and is drawn on a sufficiently small scale to make it workable by exercise of a tolerant neighborhood surveillance. The like characterisation applies also to the religious cult, and presumptively to the underlying religious conceptions, so far as the available evidence goes. When the polity of this pagan culture finally broke down after many vicissitudes, its place was taken by a predatory organisation that developed into the feudal system among those warlike and piratical migrants that settled in the outlying countries of Europe; while among the population left at home in the Baltic-Scandinavian countries it was presently replaced by a coercive scheme of government of somewhat the same character, constructed in imitation of feudalism.

Particular attention has here been directed to the hybrid derivation of these peoples, and to the fact that the racial composition of this population has not varied in any serious degree since the initial settlement of the Baltic-North Sea littoral in neolithic times; with the possible qualification that the infusion of the brachycephalic-brunet stock into the mixture may have taken effect after the first settlement, although its coming falls also in neolithic times. It results from this state of their racial composition that there is today substantially no hereditary difference between different nationalities within this climatic region, or between the dif-

ferent social classes that make up any one of these nationalities.

Their hybrid composition gives also an extremely large
facility for the acceptance of novel ideas from outside, together with a wide range of adaptation in all the arts of life,
both in technological matters and as regards the scheme of
civil and social institutions and the currency of religious
and intellectual conceptions. At the same time the same
individual variability of the hybrid acts to hinder any
given scheme or system of accepted use and wont from attain-
ing a definitive stability; in such a population no system of
knowledge, belief, usage, or control can achieve that degree
of authenticity and fixity that will make it break rather
than bend under the impact of new exigencies that may arise
out of technological changes or out of contact with an alien
culture; in so much that no scheme of usage and convictions
can be devised which will, even with a reasonable margin of
tolerance, fall nicely in with the temperamental bent of all,
or virtually all, the individuals comprised under it. Therefore, in a population of this character, any comprehensive
scheme of use and wont, of knowledge and belief, will in
effect necessarily be in some degree provisional; it will
necessarily rest on acceptance (in some part concessive acceptance) by a majority of the individuals concerned, rather
than on a uniform and unqualified spontaneous consensus
of the entire population that lives under its rule. The acceptance accorded such a standard scheme by this effective
majority is also necessarily in some appreciable measure
an acceptance by consent rather than by free initiative.

That such is the case is evident in any one of the revolutionary changes that have passed over the peoples of Christendom during the historical period; as, *e.g.*, in the growth of feudalism and in the later development of a dynastic state, together with the subsequent shift to a constitutional basis, where that change has been carried out; so also in the gradual acceptance and subsequent growth of the Christian cult and its ecclesiastical dominion, together with the many incidental adventures in religious dissent, and in the variegated outcome of them.

This latter category, the adventures of the religious cult among the north-Europeans, affords perhaps the most felicitous illustration available of the working of such temperamental variability, and of the consequent rise, dominance and decay of successive systems of knowledge and belief. This is, of course, in its own right, a department of the arts of life that is full of polemical asperities and charged with frictional heat. Yet it lies sufficiently aside from the main line of interest involved in the present inquiry to admit of its being drawn on for illustrative material without its engendering heat in the main argument.

In the successful departures in the domain of faith, as well as in those enterprises of devotion that have run a troubled course to an inglorious end, it will be seen that any such novel or aberrant scheme of habits of thought touching the supernatural, uniformly takes its rise as an affection of a certain small number of individuals, who, it may be presumed, have been thrown into a frame of mind propitious to this new fashion of thinking by some line of discipline, physical or spiritual, or rather both, that is not congruous with the previously accepted views on these matters. It will ordinarily be admitted by all but the converts that such pioneers in the domain of the supernatural are exceptional or erratic individuals, specially gifted personalities, perhaps even affected with pathological idiosyncrasies or subject to magical or præternatural influences; that is to say, in any case, erratic variants of the commonplace racial type, whose aberrant temperamental bent has been reënforced by some peculiar discipline or exceptional experience, and so does not fall in with the currently received habits of thought in these premises. The resulting variant of the cult will then presently find a wider acceptance, in case the discipline exercised by current conditions is such as to bend the habits of thought of some appreciable number of persons with a bias that conforms to this novel drift of religious conceit. And if the new variant of the faith is fortunate enough to coincide passably with the current drift of workday habituation, the band of proselytes will presently multiply into such a formidable popular religious movement as to acquire general credibility and become an authentic formulation of the faith. *Quid ab omnibus, quid ubique creditur, credendum est.* Many will so come into line with the new religious conceit who could not conceivably have spun the same yarn out of their own wool under any provocation; and the variant may then even come to supplant the parent type of cult from which it first sprang.

If it should be fortunate enough, again, to fit neatly into the scheme of use and wont in secular matters, as that scheme is being shaped by the current exigencies, the new cult may then become the only true faith, and so may become mandatory on all alike; particularly is this likely to happen if at the same time it lends itself to the ends of a ruling class who possess or can find the means of enforcing its observance. This last proposition may also be turned about; if the animus embodied in the new cult is effectually borne up by the discipline of current workday experience at large, persons strongly imbued with the bias of the cult are likely to be thrown up by popular acclaim into responsible offices of discretion, and so come to combine the promptings of their own interest with their pious convictions in its support and bring it to the mature phase of a self-evident and intolerant infallibility.

In the engendering and growth of habitual ideals and convictions touching matters of use and wont at large, or in any given connection, the run of events is not of a character essentially different from the circumstances that surround the inception and spread of these religious verities. The changes that alter the face of national life have small beginnings; the traceable initial process having commonly set in with some overt act on the part of a small and distinctive group of persons, who will then presently be credited with insight and initiative in case the move proves itself by success. Should the movement fail of acceptance and consequent effect, these spokesmen of its propaganda would then prove to have been fanciful project-makers, perhaps of unsound mind. To describe the course of such a matter by analogy, the symptoms of the new frame of mind will first come in evidence in the attitude of some one individual, who, by congenital proclivity and through an exceptional degree of exposure, is peculiarly liable to its infection. In so far as the like susceptibility is prevalent among the rest of the population, and so far as circumstances of habituation favor the new conceit, it will then presently find lodgment in the habits of thought of an increasing number of persons, — particularly among those whom the excursive play of a hybrid heredity has thrown up as temperamental variants peculiarly apt for its reception, or whom the discipline of life bends with exceptional rigor in the direction of its bias. Should the new idea also come to have the countenance of those in authority or in a position to claim popular deference, its vogue will be greatly helped out by imitation, and perhaps by compulsory observance, and so it may in a relatively short time become a matter of course and of common sense. But the reservation always stands over, that in such a hybrid population the same prevalent variability of temperament that so favors the infiltration and establishment of new ideas will at the same time render their tenure correspondingly precarious.

The point may be illustrated by the rise and decline of warlike ideals from time to time among modern nations; though it is the rise and rule of these ideals, rather than their decline, that will best illustrate the point. The decline of such ideals, and of the patriotic animosity in which they find outward expression, would appear to be a matter of reversion through neglect rather than of aggressive indoctrination through propaganda and suitable discipline. The cause of peace and amity appears not to be served by polemical propaganda, any more than by a strenuous warlike preparation for "keeping the peace."

There is always an appreciable warlike animus present in these modern nations; necessarily so, since their governmental establishments are necessarily of a coercive character and their ruling classes are animated with dynastic ambitions. In this matter the republican states uncritically imitate the dynastic ones so effectually as to make no grave exception from the rule. The historical tradition and precedents run that way. So that the ferment is always at hand. But in the absence of special provocation the commonplace body of the population, being occupied with other interests and having no natural bent for fighting in order to fight, will by easy neglect drift into peaceable habits of thought, and so come habitually to think of human relations, even of international relations, in terms of peace, if not of amity.

Temperamentally erratic individuals, however, and such as are schooled by special class traditions or predisposed by special class interest, will readily see the merits of warlike enterprise and keep alive the tradition of national animosity. Patriotism, piracy and prerogative converge to a common issue. Where it happens that an individual gifted with an extravagant congenital bias of this character is at the same time exposed to circumstances favoring the development of a truculent megalomania and is placed in such a position of irresponsible authority and authentic prerogative as will lend countenance to his idiosyncrasies, his bent may easily gather vogue, become fashionable, and with due persistence and shrewd management come so ubiquitously into habitual acceptance as in effect to throw the population at large into an enthusiastically bellicose frame of mind. Such is particularly apt to be the consequence in case of a people whose historical traditions run in terms of dynastic strategy and whose workday scheme of institutions is drawn on lines of coercion, prerogative and loyalty.

It is only with the new departure of 1870 that Germany has come to take its place in the general apprehension as a singularly striking, not to say unique, instance of exuberant growth. The history of its unfolding power, of course, is not contained in this brief interval that lies within the memory of men still living; but the new departure by force of which the life-history of the German nation has come to diverge so notably from the commonplace run of events in modern Europe can after all not be pushed back far beyond that epoch. Anyone who seeks a precise period from which to date this epoch of German history will have difficulty in deciding on any given point earlier than the year named. And what had taken place in the way of an unfolding of national forces before that date is of great significance only for its bearing on what has taken place since then.

The visible achievements of the German people during this historical period, so far as they are amenable to statistical statement, are a gain in population, in industrial efficiency, and in military force. Other gains are claimed, perhaps even of greater moment in the apprehension of the spokesmen, and there is no inclination here to discount or minimise their achievements outside of this material domain; but the magnitude of the advance in these other lines is in some degree a matter of estimate and opinion, which may in that degree be influenced by sentiments of self-complacency or of depreciation, whereas the gains in the material respect spoken for above are beyond cavil. But judged by these physically measurable marks of excellence, the historical period within which this modern onset of the German people runs will have to be dated somewhat back of the French-Prussian war. In each of the three respects named the advance was well under way before that date. It is, however, safe to say that this beginning of the current era falls within the second quarter of the nineteenth century.[1] It is also safe to say that the prime mover among these factors of the nation's unfolding power has been its increased industrial efficiency, rather than either of the other two. While their increasing efficiency has doubtless been conditioned by the growth in population, the initiative, as between these two, has doubtless vested in the former rather than in the latter. In the correlation between industrial advance and population the primacy belongs to the former. The like is true, of course, as regards the growth in military strength. Also, doubtless, a large place among the causes of growth and efficiency is believed to be due to a wise governmental policy and a shrewd administration, but opinion counts for much in the appraisal of this governmental policy, and opinion on such a matter is liable to partiality, for or against. The unfolding of warlike power has unequivocally been a work of governmental policy, and the same policy has unquestionably sought to further the industrial advance; the question that presents itself in the latter

---

[1]Cf., *e.g.*, W. H. Dawson, *The Evolution of Modern Germany*, ch. iii.; also more at large, von Sybel, *The Founding of the German Empire*, vol. i.; and Sombart, *Die deutsche Volkswirtschaft im XIX. Jahrhundert*, bk. ii.

connection is not as to the faithful intentions and endeavor of the government — or "State," to use the German concept — but only as to the probable degree of efficacy of these good intentions and endeavor; and on this head opinions will not coincide, and the proposition will therefore best be left out of the premises.

As is well known, the practical movement for German union, which came to a successful issue in the eventual formation of the Empire, owed its beginnings and its earlier success to the economic needs of the German countries, — or it may be said to have been provoked by the grievous burden of artificial evils created by the governments of the small states among which the country was divided. So, as a practical measure, it begins with the formation of a Tariff Union, designed to remove certain of the obstacles which the particularist policies of these states had erected. And this union and uniformity of economic policy within the Empire is still one of the chief assets of its strength, particularly the absence of internal tariff restrictions.

The place and relation of Germany to the industrial development of modern Europe, therefore, will necessarily be the point of departure for any inquiry into the fortunes and achievements of the German people in this modern era. On this head, then, its natural resources available for modern industrial use are of the same kind and range as those found in the neighboring countries; there is substantially nothing to distinguish the German lands from those of north Europe at large, unless it be that the resources of the country are slightly under grade in quality and slightly scant in quantity, at least as compared with the most fortunate of the neighboring countries. Again, in point of native proclivity and aptitude the German population is virtually identical with its neighbors. In respect of hereditary endowment — racial character — it is the same people as the population of the neighboring nations, — more particularly identical with the Dutch, Belgian and British. By virtue of its hybrid extraction it is, like these others, gifted with a large capacity for acquiring and turning to account a wide range of technological knowledge; and by virtue of the same hereditary bias of workmanship that animates these others it is, like its neighbors, assiduously and sagaciously addicted to industry and thrift. What chiefly distinguishes the German people from these others in this connection, and more particularly from the British, is that the Germans are new to this industrial system; and the distinctive traits of the German case are in the main traceable to this fact that they are still in their novitiate.

When the current era in the life-history of the German people began, in the second quarter of the nineteenth century, Germany was far in arrears, as compared with its neighbors to the west, but more particularly as contrasted with the British. This is historical commonplace, of course. It may be taken with such allowance and qualification as may seem needful; the main fact remains, that in certain decisive, or at least substantial, respects Germany was in an anachronistic state, particularly as seen from the station occupied by the English-speaking peoples.

There is no call to depreciate the merits of the German culture of that time in those respects in which it excelled, as there would also be no use in attempting an under-valuation of it; it is too large a fact in the heritage of man-kind to suffer seriously from an assault of words. However, those genial respects in which the civilisation characteristic of Germany excelled, — in which, indeed, Germany tri-umphed, — were not in the line of efficiency that counted materially toward fitness for life under the scheme of things then taking shape in Europe. It may have been better or it may have been worse than what came to take its place, but in any case it was not an articulate part of the working scheme; as is proven in the sequel, which was worked out with only negligible contributions from the accumulated wisdom of the German people.

Germany was in arrears in the industrial arts and in its political institutions, as well as in such features of its civil and domestic scheme of life as come intimately into cor-relation with, or under the dominant influence of, these fundamental agencies in the scheme of institutions. This is the visible difference between the case of the German and of the British peoples at the time, apart from superficial peculiarities of usage and the idly decorative elements of culture. In industrial matters Germany was still at the handicraft stage, with all that is implied in that description in the way of institutional impedimenta and meticulous standardisation of trifles. Measured by the rate of progres-sion that had brought the English community to the point where it then stood, the German industrial system was some two and a half or three centuries in arrears — some-where in Elizabethan times; its political system was even more archaic; and use and wont governing social relations in detail was of a character such as this economic and political situation would necessarily foster.

The characterisation so offered applies to the industrial organisation as a balanced and comprehensive working system. It does not overlook the fact that many alien details had been intruded into this archaic system by force of Germany's unavoidable contact with the more modern industrial communities of western Europe. But it was not until the second half of the nineteenth century that the alien elements seriously began to derange the framework of the archaic scheme.

Politically much the same will hold, except that fewer modernisms had found their way over the frontiers in this domain, nor had such modernisms effected an equally secure and disturbing lodgment in the tissues of the body politic, Germany being still consistently organised on the pattern of the "territorial State," — a peculiarly petty and peculiarly irresponsible autocracy, which has come to its best maturity only among the Germanic peoples, and which has held its place with remarkable tenacity within the limits of the Fatherland.

The territorial State, or its less finished replica under another designation, has not been unknown elsewhere in the north-European country, but it passed out by obsolescence some time ago among the other north-European peoples; so that even the Scandinavian countries, which would appear by geographical necessity to have been designed for petty things, had lost this archaic fashion of state policy and political control by the time when the question of its supersession began to attract an (ineffectual) speculative interest in Germany. The territorial State is in effect a territorial aggregate, with its population, conceived as an estate belonging in usufruct to a given prince; the concept is visibly of feudal derivation, and the habit of mind which makes it a practicable form of political organisation is the feudal habit of personal subservience to a personal master. In such a polity subordination, personal allegiance, is the prime virtue, the chief condition precedent to its carrying on; while insubordination is the fatal vice, incompatible with such a coercive system.

As seen from the standpoint of the political interests in such a State, the spirit of abnegation is by apologetic euphemism spoken of as "duty," while insubordination is called "contumacy." The former is the habit of mind engendered by continued and consistent suppression, and is the basis of a servile political organisation, such as the territorial State; the latter, if allowed a free course will eventuate in an anarchistic autonomy, such as appears to have been the constitution of Germanic society in the prehistoric ages before the barbarian invasions established a coercive rule in what is now the Fatherland. The latter appears to coincide with the natural bent of these peoples; but the former has that secure hold on their spirit that results from fifteen centuries of submission to a masterful discipline of coercion. The spirit of "duty" in these people is apparently not "nature," in the sense of native proclivity; but it is "second nature" with the people of the Fatherland, as being the ingrained traditional attitude induced by consistent and protracted experience.

In speaking of these things in the terms current among

modern civilised men it is nearly impossible to avoid the appearance of deprecating this servile or submissive attitude of "duty"; particularly will this difficulty beset anyone using the English language, — the fringe of derogatory suggestion carried by the available words and phrases is appreciably less embarrassing, e.g., in German, although even there the commonplace vocabulary lends itself with greater facility to the dispraise of servility and irresponsible rule than to the commendation of these elements of modern patriotism. That such should be the case is doubtless due to the drift of institutional development in western Europe in modern times, which has on the whole set somewhat consistently in the direction of a gradual loosening of the grip of dynastic autocracy. This drift has perhaps not so much created or initiated the growth of an anarchistic (that is to say, non-servile) spirit, but rather has permissively harbored it, and so has allowed the native anarchistic bent of these peoples to reassert itself in a measure, by force of the indefeasible resiliency that characterises all hereditary proclivities.[1]

---

[1] As already suggested in an earlier passage, the folk-tales, and other folklore, of Germany testify to the tenacious hold which this archaic, small-scale scheme of neighborhood autonomy still has on the spirit of the German people. These folk-tales have lived obscurely in the hand-to-mouth legendary lore transmitted through generations of illiterate and commonplace idealists held in subjection, and doubtless in loyal allegiance, under the coercive rule of the dynastic territorial State; but the ideals to which they give expression still are those of that quasi-anarchistic neighborhood life that has not come within the horizon of these peoples' experience, or even of their narratives of reality, since long before the close of the pagan era. This state of the folk-tales is all the more remarkable in view of the fact that the tales have undergone a fairly complete revision in all that relates to the religious cult, where the church,

Any, even a very cursory, scrutiny of the historical growth of free, or popular, institutions in modern Europe should satisfy all parties in interest that this growth has come about, not because the authorities vested with discretion and power have not taken thought to defeat it wherever a chance has offered, but because the conditioning circumstances have not enabled them to discourage it sufficiently. And by virtue of the close and facile communication of ideas among modern peoples the anarchistic penchant has, by channels of education and neighborly intercourse, come to infect even the subject populations of the better preserved territorial States; so that even there, under the shadow of the masterful system, the current vocabulary shows a weakness for free institutions and the masterless man.

While the exigencies of the language, therefore, almost unavoidably give a color of deprecation to any discussion of this surviving habit of abnegation in the people of the Fatherland, there is no intention here to praise or to blame this spirit of subordination that underlies so much of German culture and German achievement. It is one of the larger factors that have gone to the creation of the modern era in that country, and this era and its "system" will have to count with whatever strength or weakness this animus

---

the cross, the priest and the monk come in with all the air of being well at home. These "cult objects," as one might call them, are of the mediæval, or even of the modern pattern; whereas the social and political life and apparatus still is typically idealised after the pre-Christian fashion. The preservation of this homely folklore of the archaic type has been the work of the submerged classes. The corresponding legendary lore of the ruling classes is of an other and later spirit, though this, too, is archaic as tested by comparison with current actualities, turning to the mediæval rather than to the modern scheme in its ideal creations.

of feudalism contributes to the outcome. Now, it happens that this surviving feudalistic animus of fealty and subservience has visibly been a source of strength to the German State hitherto; as it presumably also has to the economic system, apart from the political ends to be served by the community's economic efficiency. This is to be recognised and taken account of quite apart from any question as to the ultimate merits of such a popular temper in any other connection, or even as to its ulterior value for the ends of the State. For all that concerns the present inquiry it may or may not appear, as doubtless would appear to the mind of most English-speaking persons, that this spirit of subservient alacrity on which the Prussian system of administrative efficiency rests is beneath the human dignity of a free man; that it is the spirit of a subject, not of a citizen; that except for dynastic uses it is a defect and a delinquency; and that in the end the exigencies of civilised life will not tolerate such an anachronistic remnant of mediævalism, and the habit of it will be lost. For all that can be made to appear today, it may also be true that it has only a transient value even for the uses of the dynastic State; but all that does not derange the fact that hitherto it has visibly been a source of strength to the German State, and presumably to the German people at large as an economic body.

In the second quarter of the nineteenth century there began a complex movement of readjustment and rehabilitation in German affairs. At least on its face this movement is primarily of an economic character, the immediate provocation to practical activity being the needs of trade and of the princely exchequers. Much genial speculation, of an academic kind, and much edifying popular exposition and agitation of national ideals ran along beside these practical measures, and this intellectual and spiritual disturbance may have had more or less to do with the measures taken and with the general drift of national policy. It is not easy to say whether this spiritual disturbance is to be rated as a cause or a concomitant of the practical changes going forward during this period, but it should seem reasonable to give it place on both of these grounds.

The fashion among historians of the period, particularly among patriotic historians, has been to construe this complex movement of forces, material and immaterial, that makes German history through the middle half of the century, as a movement of the German spirit, initiated by the exuberant national genius of the race. Such is the tradition, but the tradition comes out of the Romantic era; out of which no tradition of a more matter-of-fact character could conceivably come.

A matter-of-fact view of such an historical movement will necessarily look to the factors which may have had a part in shaping habits of thought at the time, and here there are only two lines of derivation to which the analysis can securely run back, — discounting, as is the current fashion, any occult agencies, such as manifest destiny, national genius, Providential guidance, and the like. There is no call to undervalue these occult agencies, of course; but granting that these and their like are the hidden springs, it is also to be called to mind that it is their nature to remain hidden,

and that the tangible agencies through which these presumed hidden prime movers work must therefore be sufficient for the work without recourse to the hidden springs;
which can have an effect only by force of a magical efficacy.
Their relation to the course of events is of the nature of
occult or magical efficacy, not of causal efficiency; and under
the modern materialistic prejudice in these matters of scientific inquiry, the causal sequence in which an explanation
of events is sought must be complete in all elements that
touch the motivation and the outcome, without drawing on
any but tangible fact, on matters that are of the nature of
"data." To the modern preconception in favor of efficient
cause, as contrasted with the Romantic postulate of efficacious guidance, any attempt to set up a logical finality in
any terms other than matter-of-fact is quite nugatory. It
may be a genial work of futility, and it may have its value
as dramatic art or homiletical discourse; but in the house
of scientific inquiry such premises, and generalisations in
such terms, are but as sounding brass and a tinkling cymbal.

There are two lines of agency visibly at work shaping
the habits of thought of the people in the complex movement of readjustment and rehabilitation spoken of above.
These are the received scheme of use and wont, and the
new state of the industrial arts; and it is not difficult to see
that it is the latter that makes for readjustment; nor should
it be any more difficult to see that the readjustment is necessarily made under the surveillance of the received scheme
of use and wont. The latter is modified in the course of this
new range of habituation enforced by the new state of the

industrial arts, but the changes taking place in use and wont are, here as elsewhere, made in the way of tardy concession under the impact of exigencies that will tangibly not tolerate usage that has passed out of date.

The complex movement in question is a movement of readjustment in the arts of life to meet the requirements of new technological conditions, and of rehabilitation of the received scheme of princely policy to make it workable under the new technological conditions. The changes which appear in the outcome, therefore, come about on the initiative of the new technological advance, and by expedient concessions and shrewd endeavors on the part of the constituted authority to turn the new-won efficiency to use for its own ends; the conscious directive management in the case being under the hands of the governmental organisation and directed to such a rehabilitation of the territorial State as would enable it to do business on the increased scale imposed by the new state of the industrial arts, and adequately to handle the forces which the new industrial system so placed at its disposal.

Much had already been done during the preceding hundred years to take advantage of technological improvements, so far as these improvements contributed directly to the military strength of the prince, and much had been done, incidentally to the extension of territorial control and of fiscal administration, in the way of improved means of communication and intercourse; but the modern industrial system, as such, and except as an outside and essentially alien factor, had not seriously touched the German population, particularly not those Prussian dominions which take the central place in the rehabilitation of Germany in the nineteenth century. But the industrial state of Germany was after all mediæval rather than modern, and the state of the industrial arts, therefore, still continued, on the whole, favorable to the maintenance of the old régime; particularly since this old régime was securely lodged in the interests and traditional ideals of the dynastic rulers and of the privileged classes.

There is a side line of influence from the technological side in the growth of German culture prior to its modernisation, which requires to be noted in any attempt to realise what has taken place in the unfolding of the modern era. The art of printing and the consequent use of printed matter had always been at home among the German people, ever since that technological advance first was made. From the outset and down into the nineteenth century the printer's art was a handicraft process, and was well developed in Germany. But the institutional consequences, the effect on use and wont, of the habit of consuming printed matter need not therefore be of the handicraft order. A free consumption of printed matter means a free intercourse of ideas, and it therefore entails an exposure of the consumers to contact with ideas current beyond the circle of their immediate personal contact.

The habitual consumption of print has much the same order of disciplinary effect as habituation to the wide-reaching standardisation of the arts of life brought on by the machine industry; but it goes without saying that the effect so wrought by the use of print will not extend much beyond the class of persons addicted to it; the illiterate, and the classes who make little use of print anyway, will not be seriously or extensively disturbed, — what may be called the extravasation of printed literature is not a matter of large consequence, although it is not to be denied that the diffusion of ideas conveyed by print, among the illiterate, will always amount to something. Whereas the disciplinary value of life under the standardising régime of the machine industry touches the illiterate perhaps more immediately and intimately, and almost as comprehensively, as it touches the classes who habitually read.

It is worth noting in this immediate connection, although it is also a proposition of general validity, that in the nature of the case no profound or massive revolutionary disturbance of the established order, in any respect, can be carried through by the medium of printed matter alone, or in the absence of other, materially more exacting and peremptory, factors of habituation working to the same general effect. So in the case of Germany, although that fraction of the population that was given to reading had long been in contact with the intellectual movement in Europe at large and had, indeed, from time to time, taken effective part in the shaping of current ideas, yet this fraction made up so small a class, was so little in touch with the mass of the population, and held its intellectual convictions on such "academic" tenure — that is to say, so uniformly without reënforcement from its own experience of mechanical fact — that with the best intentions it never succeeded in infecting the people at large with its own ideals of a new order, or in disturbing the incumbents of office in their tenure and usufruct of the old order.[1]

At the same time printed matter is a highly efficient

---

[1]The disturbances of 1848 may serve to show how things run on this head. The enlightened conceptions and impulses of the literate minority here joined hands with the irritation of the illiterate due to intolerable conditions of physical discomfort, with a transient appearance of success, and with the net result that in the end both parties to the misunderstanding were convicted of contumacy.

By the same token, the meticulous vigilance of the keepers of political antiquities in such an archaic state as Russia, *e.g.*, should be rated as supererogation, particularly as regards the circulation of obnoxious literature that purveys excessively modern ideas. In spite of all efforts the diffusion of the ideas that come in by way of print scarcely extends beyond the readers of the printed matter; and of these, again, it is only a fraction that are seriously deranged by what they read; and the readers are, fortunately, but a negligible percentage of the mass. The alien ways of thinking that come in in this way, without treading the ground of the workday routine of industry, may flutter the birds of plumage that roost in the upper branches of the tree of knowledge, but all the disturbance will go on over the heads of that multitude the usufruct of which is of value to the ruling class. The habits of thought of the latter are made by the workday routine, and provided the routine of the system is not seriously deranged these will continue in the same frame of mind, such that any goose-girl can still lead them contentedly to the plucking-sheds. On the other hand the substitution of a new industrial system, enforcing a workday routine of a different trend, might easily breed mischief. But, judging by the German example as an object lesson, the wiser precaution against a fatal derangement of the system of irresponsible mastery would apparently be so far to engender the habit of reading as to make the assimilation of the new industrial order an easy matter, resulting in a marked advance in efficiency and physical comfort, and then to temper coercion with a well-conceived cajolery.

The cultivation of illiteracy and the exclusion of obnoxious literature with a view to maintenance of the *status quo* in religious concerns may be quite another matter. The derangement to be hedged against in this case being of a somewhat superficial kind — a change in the color-scheme of current superstitions — it is conceivable that heretical teachings might work mischief even in the absence of discrepancies of a technological kind.

vehicle for the spread, assimilation and standardisation of habits of thought that are otherwise consonant with the workday exigencies of the arts of life; and then, too, the habit of reading is a nearly indispensable auxiliary of that machine technology that invaded the German community in the nineteenth century, — less so, of course, at that date (middle of the century) than at any later time, but sufficiently so even then to count seriously in the outcome.[1] Now, literacy, both in the higher potency of "learning" and in the homelier fashion of ability fluently to read print, was relatively common among the German people at the time when the new era came on; and the movement for improving and extending the means of popular education was already in good practicable shape, so that deficiencies in this respect could be made good as fast as they visibly required a remedy. It used to be one of the stock aspersions on the German community that it was top-heavy with a redundance of learned men. Fault-finding on this score has ceased since the latter part of the century, the learned class having been found useful and the demand for men proficient in the sciences having fully caught up. Meantime the character of this learning, or rather the direction of it, has changed somewhat, the change resulting on the

---

[1] It should need no insistence or amplification to gain assent to the proposition, e.g., that illiteracy is a serious, perhaps the decisive, obstacle to the present reorganisation of the Russian community (or communities) on the lines of the modern industrial system; nor need there be any doubt entertained that the higher percentage and higher range of literacy among the Germans or the English-speaking peoples accounts for much of their superior industrial efficiency. Under the old régime of handicraft and household industry, illiteracy was by comparison a trivial deficiency if any.

whole in a pronounced shift toward those branches of knowledge that have some technological or commercial value.[1]

As regards the logical relation between the modern industrial advance and the modernised dynastic State in Germany, it may be held that the makers of this State, the policy of the Hohenzollern dynasty from Frederick the Great to William II, have made use of all available technological improvements to extend the dominion and improve the efficiency of the State; or it may be held, on the other hand, that the technological advance which enforced a larger scale of industry and trade, as well as a larger and more expensive equipment and strategy in the art of war,

---

[1]The supererogatory character of German learning under the old régime is doubtless connected with the absence of a large-scale technology of such a kind as to obtrude questions of wide theoretical bearing. The organisation of social life on class lines and the standardisation of it in terms of putative worth and authenticity, birth and antecedents, will also have contributed to a bias in favor of putative theoretical constructions and an interest in the lore of intrinsic, that is to say metaphysical, creatures and characters rather than in matter-of-fact. While those classes whose conventional standard of propriety would not admit their employment in useful or gainful occupations were prevented by their ubiquitous poverty from going consistently into a life of sports and standardised dissipation, at least on such a scale and with such generality as to take up the slack of the respectable classes; learning, being a form of dissipation within the reach of this very numerous and very impecunious gentry, came in for a larger share of attention at their hands, and came to be rated more confidently as a mark of gentility than in England, *e.g.*, or even in France. But learning that is or may be gainful, or that concerns itself with matters germane to the quest of a livelihood or to the ways and means of vulgar industry, can not well be genteel, more particularly in a community where industry typically is of the vulgar nature of manual labor, and where manual labor is conventionally tabu to a gentleman.

also drove the dynastic State to reorganisation on a new and enlarged plan, involving an increased differentiation of the administrative machinery and a more detailed and exacting control of the sources of revenue.

Either view appears to be equally true. German students of the case have commonly adopted the former, somewhat to the neglect of what force there is in the latter view. It should be evident that the minuscular territorial State of the high tide of German particularism, with its crepuscular statesmanship, would have no chance of survival under the conditions prevailing in Europe in the nineteenth century. It is equally evident that those dynastic statesmen within this circle of particularism who, either by force of insight or by force of special exigencies and tentative expedients, were led to take advantage of the larger and mechanically more efficient devices of the new age would enjoy a differential advantage as against their conservative neighbors, and would in the end supplant them in the domain of statecraft and presently take over their substance, — the dynastic State being necessarily of a competitive, or rapacious, character, and free to use any expedient that comes to hand. It is a case of selective survival working out through the competitive manœuvres of those who had the administration of the one and the other policy in hand.

When the state of the industrial arts had so extended the physical reach of civil administration and political strategy as definitively to make a large-scale national organisation practicable, the old order of self-sufficient petty principalities became impossible. This change reached the German territories at a later date than the rest of western

Europe, and it did not take effect in a reorganisation of national life until so late a date that the retardation is a matter of surprise in spite of all the explanations offered by the historians. But in consequence of this retardation the magnitude of the reorganisation, when it came, was also such as to leave the historians somewhat at a loss to account for it without recourse to race characteristics imputed *ad hoc* as well as to the magical effects of a nepotic predilection on the part of Providence.

By wise management on the part of the dynastic statesmen who have had the direction of policy and the control of the administrative machinery, the rapidly increasing material efficiency of the German community, due to the introduction of the modern state of the industrial arts, has successfully been turned to the use of the State, in a degree not approached elsewhere in western Europe; so that in effect the community stands to the Hohenzollern State somewhat in the relation of a dynastic estate, a quasi-manorial demesne or domain, to be administered for dynastic ends, very much after the fashion of the cameralistic administration of fiscal affairs in the territorial states of Germany a hundred years ago. This subservience of the community to dynastic ends and dynastic management has been secured in the gross by a policy of warlike aggression, and in detail by a system of bureaucratic surveillance and unremitting interference in the private life of subjects.

It goes without saying that there is no secure ground for such a scheme of dynastic usufruct and control except in the loyal support of popular sentiment; and it likewise goes without saying that such a state of popular sentiment can be maintained only by unremitting habituation, discipline sagaciously and relentlessly directed to this end. More particularly must the course of habituation to this end be persistent and unwavering if it is to hold the personal allegiance of a body of subjects exposed to the disintegrating discipline of modern life; where the machine industry constantly enforces the futility of personal force and prerogative in the face of wide-sweeping inanimate agencies and mechanical process, and where the ubiquitous haggling of the price system constantly teaches that every man is his own keeper. It is a matter of common notoriety that all this has been taken care of with unexampled thoroughness and effect under the Prussian rule.[1]

Chief of the agencies that have kept the submissive allegiance of the German people to the State intact is, of course, successful warfare, seconded by the disciplinary effects of warlike preparation and indoctrination with warlike arrogance and ambitions. The attention deliberately given to these concerns is also a fact of common notoriety; so much so, indeed, that the spokesmen of the system have come to take it for granted as a matter of course, and so are apt to overlook it. The experience of war induces a warlike frame of mind; and the pursuit of war, being an exercise in the following of one's leader and execution of arbitrary orders, induces an animus of enthusiastic subservience and unquestioning obedience to authority. What is a military organisa-

---

[1] Perhaps the most concise and yet the most illuminating presentation of this Prussian economic policy, typically as pursued by Frederick the Great, is that of Professor Schmoller, *The Mercantile System*. (Translation reprinted in *Economic Classics*, ed. Ashley.)

tion in war is a servile organisation in peace. The system is the same, and the popular animus requisite to its successful working is the same in either case. It reaches its best efficiency in either case, in war or peace, only when the habit of arbitrary authority and unquestioning obedience has been so thoroughly ingrained that subservience has become a passionate aspiration with the subject population, where the habit of allegiance has attained that degree of automatism that the subject's ideal of liberty has come to be permission to obey orders, — somewhat after the fashion in which theologians interpret the freedom of the faithful, whose supreme privilege it is to fulfil all the divine commands. Such an ideal growth of patriotic sentiment appears to have been attained, in a tolerable degree of approximation, in the German case, if one is to credit the popular encomiasts, who explain that "duty," in the sense indicated, combined with "freedom," makes up the goal to which the German spirit aspires. "Duty," of course, comprises the exercise of arbitrary command on the part of the superior as well as the obedience of the inferior, but such arbitrary authority is exercised only in due submission to higher authority, until it traces back to the dynastic head, — who, it would appear, in turn exercises only a delegated authority, vested in his person by divine grace.

The phrase, "dynastic State," is here used in preference to "patrimonial State," not because there is any substantial difference between the two conceptions, but rather because the later German spokesmen for the German State, as it is seen at work during the Imperial era, appear to have an aversion to the latter term, which they wish to apply to the

territorial State of the pre-Imperial time, in contradistinc-
tion to the State as rehabilitated in the adoption of a constitution comprising a modicum of representative institutions and parliamentary forms. The designation "dynastic"
is still applicable, however; and in effect the constitutional
rehabilitation has not taken the German State out of the
category of patrimonial monarchies. The difference resulting
from the Imperial constitution is in large part a difference
in form and in administrative machinery; it does not greatly
circumscribe the effectual powers, rights and discretion of
the Imperial crown; still less does it seriously limit the powers of the Prussian crown, or the dynastic claims of suzerainty vested in the Prussian succession. Even under the
constitution it is a government resting on the suzerainty of
the crown, not on the discretion of a parliamentary body. It
is, in other words, a government of constitutionally mitigated absolutism, not of parliamentary discretion tempered
with monarchy.

In the shift from particularism to the Empire no revolutionary move was made, comparable with the change
initiated in the United Kingdom by the revolution of 1688;
if such a shift to a democratic constitution is to overtake
the German State, that move lies still in the future. The
changes introduced with the constitution of the Empire, in
so far as they have been effectual, were such as were made
necessary by the larger scale on which the new national
jurisdiction was required to work, and involved only such
a modicum of delegated jurisdiction to parliamentary and
local organisations as would be expedient for the control
and usufruct of territory and resources, population, trade

and industry, that exceed the effectual reach of the simpler bureaucracy characteristic of the small territorial State. The economic policy of the Imperial era has still continued to be a "cameralistic" policy, with such concessive adaptations as the modern scale and complexity of economic affairs necessitate. It is true, under the administration of Bismarck there was a perceptible drift in the direction of those "liberal" preconceptions that subconsciously biassed the endeavors of all European statesmen through much of the latter half of the century; but this drift, which showed itself in the Bismarckian policies of trade, colonies, and incipient ministerial responsibility, never came to anything conclusive under his hands; nor had it gone so far as in any appreciable degree to embarrass the endeavors of the later emperor, directed to the complete revendication of the Imperial suzerainty. The paramount authority, under the Imperial constitution, vests in the crown, not in any representative body, although this holds with even less qualification in the Prussian than in the Imperial government; but Germany has, in these respects, been progressively "Prussianised" during the Imperial era, while Prussia has not been drawing toward the lines of that democratic autonomy that holds the rest of north and central Europe, at least on a qualified and provisional tenure.

Imperial Germany does not depart sensibly from the pattern of Prussia under Frederick the Great, in respect of its national policies or the aims and methods of government control, nor do the preconceptions of its statesmen differ at all widely from those prevalent among the dynastic jobbers of that predaceous era of state-making. The difference touches mainly the machinery of politics and administration, and it is mainly of such a character as is dictated by an endeavor to turn the results of modern industry and commerce to account for the purposes that once seemed good to the pragmatists of that earlier era.

That such is the case need give no occasion for dispraise. At least there is nothing of the kind implied here. It may be an untoward state of things, perhaps, though sufficient proof of such a contention has not yet come in sight. It is specifically called to mind here because it is one of the main factors in the case of Imperial Germany considered as a phase of the development of institutions within the Western culture.

This modern state of the industrial arts that so has led to the rehabilitation of a dynastic State in Germany on a scale exceeding what had been practicable in earlier times, — this technological advance was not made in Germany but was borrowed, directly or at the second remove, from the English-speaking peoples; primarily, and in the last resort almost wholly, from England. What has been insisted on above is that British use and wont in other than the technological respect was not taken over by the German community at the same time. The result being that Germany offers what is by contrast with England an anomaly, in that it shows the working of the modern state of the industrial arts as worked out by the English, but without the characteristic range of institutions and convictions that have grown up among English-speaking peoples concomitantly with the growth of this modern state of the industrial arts.

Germany combines the results of English experience in the development of modern technology with a state of the other arts of life more nearly equivalent to what prevailed in England before the modern industrial régime came on; so that the German people have been enabled to take up the technological heritage of the English without having paid for it in the habits of thought, the use and wont, induced in the English community by the experience involved in achieving it. Modern technology has come to the Germans ready-made, without the cultural consequences which its gradual development and continued use has entailed among the people whose experience initiated it and determined the course of its development.

The position of the Germans is not precisely unique in this respect; in a degree the same general proposition will apply to the other Western nations,[1] but it applies to none with anything like the same breadth. The case of Germany is unexampled among Western nations both as regards the abruptness, thoroughness and amplitude of its appropriation of this technology, and as regards the archaism of its cultural furniture at the date of this appropriation.

It will be in place to call to mind, in this connection, what has been said in an earlier chapter on the advantage of borrowing the technological arts rather than developing them by home growth. In the transit from one community to another the technological elements so borrowed do not

---

[1] It applies with at least equal cogency to the case of Japan, and indeed the Japanese case is strikingly analogous to that of Germany in this connection. Cf. "The Opportunity of Japan," in the *Journal of Race Development,* July 1915.

carry over the fringe of other cultural elements that have grown up about them in the course of their development and use. The new expedients come to hand stripped of whatever has only a putative or conventional bearing on their use. On the lower levels of culture this fringe of conventional or putative exactions bound up with the usufruct of given technological devices would be mainly of the nature of magical or religious observances; but on the higher levels, in cases of the class here in question, they are more likely to be conventionalities embedded in custom and to some extent in law, of a secular kind, but frequently approaching the mandatory character of religious observances, as, *e.g.*, the requirement of a decently expensive standard of living.

Chapter IV

THE CASE OF ENGLAND

Propounded in this explicit fashion, the view that a given technological system will have an economic value and a cultural incidence on a community which takes it over ready-made, different from the effects it has already wrought in the community from which it is taken over and in which it has cumulatively grown to maturity in correlation with other concomitant changes in the arts of life, — when so stated as an articulate generalisation this proposition may seem unfamiliar, and perhaps dubious. But apart from its formal recognition as a premise to go on, the position has long had the assured standing of commonplace. Where such an instance of borrowing comes up for attention among historians and students of human culture, the people that so has taken over an unfamiliar system of industrial ways and means will commonly be characterised as "raw," "immature," "unbalanced," "crude," "underbred"; the spokesmen of such a community on the other hand are likely to speak of its being "youthful," "sturdy," "unspoiled," "in the prime of full-blooded manhood." The meaning in either case, invidious emotions apart, being that such a people has on the one hand not acquired those immaterial elements of culture, those habits of thought on

other than industrial matters, that should, and in due
course will, come into effect as the necessary correlate of
such an advance in technological efficiency, and on the other
hand that the people with the new-found material efficiency
has not come in for the wasteful and inhibitory habits and
fashions with which in the course of time the same technological assets have come to be encumbered among those
peoples who have long had the use of them. There is no
need of quarrelling with either view. Seen as a phenomenon
of habituation, and so of the growth of use and wont, the
two supplement one another. They are two perspectives of
the same view. And the difference between the case of Germany and that of the British, and indeed of the other industrially advanced peoples of Europe, is of this nature.
The German people have come in for the modern technology without taking over the graces of the modern industrial culture in which this technology belongs by right
of birth; but it is at least equally to the point to note that
they have taken over this technological system without the
faults of its qualities.

Wherein the case of Germany falls short of the measure
of experience and cultural maturity that has come to the
English-speaking peoples, or in other words what the Germans have escaped in having stood to one side of the current of material civilisation in the West, is best to be seen
in contrast with the case of the English people through the
period of this technological growth. The racial derivation
of the two peoples is the same, and their cultural antecedents are identical through antiquity, down to a late
period in the pagan era. Even in the Middle Ages the ex-

perience of the two does not differ so widely as to give a notably different cultural outcome. It is only from the close of the feudal age that the divergence begins to be pronounced, and it is within the interval since the beginning of modern times, as counted by the English chronology, that the technological situation has taken on that modern character which until recently distinguished the British industrial system from the German. So it is also in modern times that the British pattern of culture in other respects has sensibly diverged from the German.

Differences of detail, such as should, of course, receive attention in any careful historical survey, come in sight quite early; and these early differences may well be called to mind here, since they are much the same in kind as the later difference in situation between the two peoples, so far as concerns the general lines of cultural development. From the period of the Migrations the invaders of the British Isles have been exposed to a different character of circumstances from those that shaped the fortunes of their congeners who invaded what is now the Fatherland. The pagan invaders of Britain found a Christian and Romanised population before them; which would mean that the people whom they conquered, and for the continued subjection of whom their governmental organisation was first installed, were a people that had already learned submission and an orderly life under the mastery of the Roman Peace and of the priests of the church. The barbarians who settled in Germany, on the other hand, appear to have found a population less tractable and presumably of less economic value; at the same time the various bodies of barbarians in the

German territories continued more unremittingly at war among themselves on the one side and in continued hostile contact with the Roman Empire and its successors on the other side. So that, in spite of the absolutely tumultuous state of Britain in the Anglo-Saxon period, the situation in the Island was after all relatively tranquil by contrast with the state of blood and wounds, rapine, slavery and oppression, that made up the scheme of life in Germany through the dark ages. Yet the two countries came through the experience of the feudal age without differing in so general and profound a manner in their mode of life that the two could then be said to follow two divergent lines of cultural development.

At the transition from mediæval to modern time the English people were in arrears, culturally, as compared with the rest of west and central Europe, including west and south Germany; whether that epoch is to be dated from the close of the fifteenth century or from any earlier period, and whether the comparison is to be made in industry and material civilisation or in immaterial terms of intellectual achievement and the arts of life. But during the succeeding century the English community had made such gains that by its close they stood (perhaps doubtfully) abreast of their Continental neighbors. This British gain was both absolute and relative, and was due both to an accelerated advance in the Island and a retardation of the rate of gain in much of the Continental territory, although the retardation is more visible on the Continent during the seventeenth than even toward the close of the sixteenth century. Relatively, by comparison again with the state of things among the rival states on the Continent, the English community at this time experienced a respite from political, military and religious disturbances; though this respite is a matter of mitigation, not of surcease. It doubtless has much to do with the advance of the new trade, industry and learning of that classic age, particularly in the increased security of life which it brought; and it is at the same time noteworthy as the initial period of that British peace that has held since then, at times precariously, no doubt, but after all with sufficient consistency to have marked a difference in this respect between the conditions of life offered in the Island and those that have prevailed on the Continent. So that, with reservations, the arts of peace have claimed the greater attention throughout modern times. It may be doubtful whether one can with equal confidence say that the arts of war and of dynastic politics and religion have claimed the chief attention of the Continental peoples during the same period; but in any case the contrast in this respect is too broad to be overlooked, and of too profound a character not to have had its effect in a divergent growth of the institutions and preconceptions that govern human relations and human ends.

For the purpose in hand this modern period of British life may best be divided into two phases or stages, contrasted in some respects; the earlier phase running from an indefinite date in the early sixteenth to somewhere in the early seventeenth century, while the later begins loosely in the later seventeenth and runs to the historical present. The former phase, of course, comes to its most pronounced manifestation in the Elizabethan era; although its cultural consequences are more fully realised at a later date. The high tide of the latter is marked by the Industrial Revolution, conventionally so called, and leaves its mark on British culture chiefly in the nineteenth century.

The criteria as well as the reasons for so subdividing British modern time are chiefly of a technological or industrial nature and bearing. The earlier of these two periods is the high tide of English borrowing and assimilation in the industrial arts, and so corresponds in some sense with the Imperial era of Germany; the latter period is to be remarked as in a special sense a creative era in English life, which has engendered the current technological system, characterised and dominated by the machine industry; and which has no counterpart in the life-history of the German people hitherto. There would accordingly appear to be an interval of, loosely, some three or four hundred years' experience included in the life-history of the English community, but omitted from the experience that has gone to make the national genius of the German people.

Left in this unqualified shape this proposition doubtless would amount to an exaggeration. The necessary qualifications to be made are obviously forcible, but they are by no means easily reducible to a formal statement; particularly would it be difficult to introduce qualifications that could be stated in quantitative terms, whether of time or of any other dimension. And so far as bears on the point here in question — the contrasted previous experience and consequent contrasted habitual bent of the two communities — the discrepancy is not to be reduced by calling to mind that while the English have been exposed to the discipline of life under this gradually modernised régime the German population has been gathering more and sterner experience of the ancient line.

Here, again, to avoid possible misapprehension, it seems necessary to enter the caution that in so pointing a contrast between the experience, and therefore the resulting habituation, that has fallen to the share of the two contrasted peoples, no invidious comparison is intended. Except as rated for some specified purpose, on some conventionally agreed basis of merit or expediency, it does not follow that the one is better or worse than the other; the whole point sought to be exhibited is that "there is a discrepancy there." Of course, seen from the point of view of the modern Occidental culture, as it runs in the advanced industrial countries, this discrepancy will have to be rated as an arrested spiritual development on the German side of the comparison; nothing in the way of atrophy or of heritable defect, of course, but simply an habitual bent at variance with the ideals, aims and animus of latterday civilised mankind, as seen among those peoples that have drifted farthest from mediævalism; it is not a trait of human nature in the substantial sense, but only the second nature of habit and tradition. Such farther drift from the holding-ground of the mediæval mind will be rated as gain or loss, of course, very much according as one may have the grace to see it; so that it resolves itself into a question of taste, concerning which there is no disputing.

Modern writers who have handled this segment of English history from a large and genial outlook are apt to look on Elizabethan England as a self-contained cultural epoch, which made its own growth out of vital forces comprised within its own historical limits; and such is doubtless a competent view of that exuberant season of British achievement in so far as touches the exploits of the new learning, the warlike and commercial enterprise of the period, and the swift and sure advance of its literature, provided one confines one's attention to these works of fruition and their immediate ground in the wealth of unfolding energy that created them. But Elizabethan England is not an episode that happened by the way; no more than Imperial Germany. Like the Imperial era in Germany the Elizabethan era grew out of and carried out a new situation, a new posture of the material forces that conditioned the life and endeavors of the community. And like the corresponding German case this new posture of economic forces is in great part an outcome of new acquisitions in the industrial arts, largely drawn from abroad.

Earlier Tudor times that led up to the Elizabethan period proper began the movement for bringing English industry abreast of the neighboring countries on the Continent; which was continued through the greater part of Elizabeth's reign. This movement is chiefly occupied with borrowing processes, devices, workmen and methods, and with adapting all these things shrewdly to the needs and uses of the island community. In so borrowing, the English had the advantage that comes to any borrower in like case. They took over what approved itself, and took it over without the conventional limitations that attached to the borrowed elements in the countries of their origin. These

conventional elements were those characteristic of the handicraft system, with its gild and charter regulations and the
settled usages, routes and methods of the petty trade that
went with that system. Among the new gains a not inconsiderable item is what the English learned from the Dutch,
of ship-building and navigation.

An immediate though secondary effect of the new departure in the industrial system — a departure which is better expressed in terms of improvement and innovation
than in those of a new start — is the (virtual) discovery of
resources made available in the new posture which industrial forces were taking, and the consequent freedom with
which these new resources were turned to account. New
and wide opportunities offered, by contrast with what had
been the run of things before, and these opportunities for
enterprise, then as ever, played into the posture of affairs as
provocations to enterprise; which then as ever brought on
its cumulative run of prosperity. The wealth in hand increased in utility under the stimulus of new opportunities
for its gainful utilisation, and the men in whose hands lay
the discretion in industrial matters saw opportunities ahead
which their own faith in these opportunities enabled them
to realise through adventurous enterprise inspired by the
new outlook itself.

It is the tale familiar to all students of periodic prosperity
in trade and industry — periods of cumulatively increasing
confidence, speculative advance, enhanced buoyancy, expansion, inflation, or whatever term is chosen as the antith-
esis of depression — the chief distinguishing trait of this
particular period of prosperity being that it grew out of the

acquirement of a new efficiency, due to what was in effect a discovery of new technological resources backed by a concomitant discovery that the natural resources at hand were acquiring an increased industrial value through their larger use under the new industrial régime; together with the further characteristic feature that this virtual discovery of powers went forward progressively over a considerable space of time, so that no stagnation due to an exhaustion of the stimulus overtook this era of prosperity and enterprise within the lifetime of the generation which first caught the swing of its impulsion.

In this respect the case of Imperial Germany shows a parallel, although the greater scale and rate of their acquiring the new industrial system, as well as the swifter pace of modern trade and industrial enterprise, has so foreshortened the corresponding experience of the Germans as to compress within a lifetime the rounded movement from initiative to climax that would correspond with what occupied the English for more than a century. This very different tempo grows out of the different character of the machine technology, as contrasted with the handicraft system and its petty trade.

There is another, extraneous, feature of the case, that also sets off this English period of enterprise in contrast with the German case. Whereas the unfolding of the new economic régime in Germany has taken place during a half century of peace and advancing industrial enterprise throughout the nations of Christendom, barring essentially trivial and ephemeral disturbances, so that German enterprise has had to make its way under the competition of other industrial countries that already had the lead; Elizabethan England has the differential advantage given it in the matter of enterprise that the rest of Christendom then was presently involved in destructive wars, and so was caught in a protracted season of industrial incapacity and economic decay, which, fortunately for the English industrial community, fell with exceptional severity on the most capable of their industrial and commercial rivals. There followed the extended period of state-making on the Continent, which involved Christian Europe, with the partial exception of the British Isles, in interminable warfare and political intrigue, brought on the collapse of the great era of south-German business enterprise, and closed in a collapse of exhaustion. This progressive, scarcely interrupted, economic decay of Continental Christendom gave the English such a progressively sustained differential advantage in trade and industry that, in spite of all the disturbances fomented at home, the island population retained the lead which the peculiar circumstances of the sixteenth century had thrown into their hands; and so in spite of minor checks — some of great absolute magnitude — the prosperity that set in with the Elizabethan era may be said to have run on at a lower tension through the succeeding two hundred years, and to have been continuous with the new era brought on by the Industrial Revolution of the eighteenth century.

Much of this interval of commonplace material success, it should be admitted, is to be set down less to the credit of the English than to the discredit of their Continental neighbors. The great advantage of the English was their easily defensible isolation, which left them in comparative peace;

and the dynastic ambitions and patriotic and religious fervor of the Continental states, which brought them to the extremities of economic confusion and industrial decay, and so left the English free to make a doubtfully efficient use of an unparalleled and irretrievable opportunity. In respect of their economic interests and the advancement of technology, the interval from the accession of Elizabeth to the close of the Napoleonic era may, for the peoples of Continental Christendom, be set down under the rubric of, The Years that the Locust hath Eaten. For the English the middle half of the same interval is occupied with a sluggish advance by inertia.

But the time so allowed the English for the acquirement of the technological wisdom of Continental Christendom, and for the unimpeded usufruct of it, exceeds the corresponding time allowance of Imperial Germany by some sixfold, and the enforced rate of utilisation and transition to a new scheme would be correspondingly temperate. The new scheme of habituation in the material arts of life would accordingly have a more adequate chance to work out its consequences in the way of a revision of the community's habits of thought on other heads; the technological institutions so taken into the scheme of life would enforce their discipline upon the population that so became addicted to this new economic situation, and would bend their thinking on other matters in consonance with the frame of mind inbred in the industrial system.

The system which the English borrowed and worked out into its farther consequences was the system of handicraft and petty trade, and the frame of mind native or normal to this industrial system is that which stands for self-help and an equal chance.[1] All this pervasive discipline of the industrial occupations and of the scheme of interests and regulations embodied in this system worked slowly, with a temperate but massive and steady drift, to induce in the English people an animus of democratic equity and non-interference, self-help and local autonomy; which came to a head on the political side in the revolution of 1688, and which continued to direct the course of sentiment through the subsequent development of a scheme of common law based on the metaphysics of Natural Rights.

An effect of the English forward move into the early modern régime of handicraft and self-help, therefore, was, among other things, the collapse of autocracy and the decay of coercive surveillance on the part of self-constituted authorities. With the redistribution of discretion and initiative in economic matters, consequent on and enforced by the new industrial system, the ancient animus of insubordination again took effect in the affairs of the community, threw the material interests and initiative of the individual into the foreground of policy, changed the "subject" into a "citizen," and went near to reducing the State to a condition of "innocuous desuetude" by making it a bureau for the administration of the public peace and the regulation of equity between private interests. All this drift of things away from the landmarks of the ancient dynastic régime has

---

[1]Cf. Werner Sombart, *Der moderne Kapitalismus*, bk. i. ch. v. vi. vii., *Der Bourgeois*, "Einleitung," ch. ii.; W. J. Ashley, *English Economic History and Theory*, bk. ii. ch. vi.; and authors referred to by these writers.

never reached a consummate outcome, — the proliferation of English Natural Rights has never matured into a system of regulated anarchy, after the prehistoric pattern, although a speculative excursion in that direction has made its appearance now and again. Neither the large scale and intricate organisation of modern industry and trade, nor the ever-present shadow of international discord, has permitted such an eventuality.

All this has taken time. Time has been required for the discipline of this industrial and commercial régime to take effect in the rehabituation of the people and the gradual readjustment of legal and moral conceptions to the working conditions of the new scheme. The readjustment doubtless took place in part advisedly, by a set endeavor to make statutory specifications and authoritative regulations fit the exigencies of the new industry and commerce, to standardise civil and political relations in such terms as should fit the new exigencies. These endeavors were not altogether successful. They proceeded in great part on preconceptions carried over from the earlier régime, rather than on habits of thought instilled by the discipline of the new. Nor were these earlier endeavors of the constituted authorities to standardise and regulate the new economic situation either of commensurate practical value or of permanent effect.

More is to be said for such later statutory and administrative measures as presently grew out of the new situation in the way of what may be called a psychological precipitate of the new discipline. And still greater substantial value attached to the revised outlook on matters of moral, legal or intellectual interest, which in great part has taken effect in current use and wont and current standards and canons of valuation in these lines, without necessarily being embodied in statutory or other authentic form. So in religion, art — especially literature, — philosophy, science and the canons of propriety and loyalty.

Such a growth takes time. It is a matter of habituation and of the gradual displacement of received habits of thought. Principles of valuation and of conduct, of this class, are not to be acquired or to be put away in one generation; nor are they to be suddenly imposed by ordinance, although doubtless a strenuous and well-conceived authoritative management may appreciably accelerate the process of habituation through which they are to be acquired or displaced. But the best-conceived authoritative surveillance is relatively impotent to further the growth of free institutions or of what may be called free thought, such as characterises the English development during the period in question. These things, being a product, by resilience, of the ancient spirit of insubordination and initiative, are not fostered by coercive direction.

It is unnecessary, and it would even more be tedious, here to set out in any articulate fashion what has happened to the religious cult and its underlying theological conceptions under the protracted discipline of this modern régime of work and self-help. The results have varied through all degrees of devout authenticity, short of the high dignity from which the new departure diverged, and the patchwork of dissentingly autonomous and obstreperous variants is such as no person of cultivated taste in the devout proprieties

could willingly dwell on. Philosophy has followed in the
wake of the retreat of religion, as should properly happen,
since philosophy at its best is the handmaid of theology; so
that the characteristic English philosophical work in modern
times has been of a skeptical temper on the whole and has
leaned greatly on principles of self-interest and serviceability to human use, with its moral premises and precepts
strongly impregnated with utilitarian and pragmatic, not to
say materialistic, conceits.

The spirit of loyalty has suffered a like reduction to lower
terms. Not that the British subject in modern times has not
been loyal to the commonwealth, and even on occasion to
the sovereign and the dynasty; but it has more than once
become painfully evident, both within the Island and in
the more considerable colonies — as, *e.g.*, in the thirteen
that formed the United States — that the British subject's
loyalty to the reigning monarch or to the crown is conditioned on the serviceability of such allegiance to his own
material interests. A loyalty which raises the question, What
for? comes far short of the feudalistic ideal and of that spirit
of enthusiastic abnegation that has always been the foundation of a prosperous dynastic State. British loyalty is not
precisely to be stigmatised as "fair-weather loyalty," but as
seen from the standpoint of dynastic politics, neither is it a
good merchantable article in its class. It is too far tempered
with insubordination. At this point, again, the English case
diverges from that of Imperial Germany.

This difference of temper in respect to loyalty to the
dynasty, or even to the State, as between the English and
the German people, appears in the main to be a short-

coming on the English side. The English fall short in point of self-sacrifice and abnegation for the sake of dynastic politics and the advancement of the reigning house and its patrician bureaucracy. By contrast with the naive patriotic solidarity of the German people, the allegiance of the English might even be called a mitigated insubordination rather than loyalty tempered with self-interest. Yet it is more a difference in degree than in kind. The English appear to have lost something in the course of these centuries, which the Germans have retained or even reënforced, — something in the way of an habitual abandon of deference to the majesty of the State and the pretensions of the sovereign. There is less devotion in the habitual outlook and temper of the English. There is, no doubt, a good and serviceable residue of this honorable obsequiousness still left in the frame of mind habitual among the English; but it has the appearance of having been left over, in some sense by oversight, and even what there is left over of it is subject to a limit of tolerance imposed by an afterthought of self-interest.

The shortcoming of the English as compared with the Germans, in respect of dynastic solidarity and subservience, arises out of a divergence of growth, due to more than a single factor. When the lines began to diverge, at the transition from the mediæval to the modern régime, the English were already less well furnished in this respect than their friends on the Continent. Mediævalism never was as well developed in England, and its development in the German territories was of a particularly harsh and militant order. Since the new departure, loyalty to dynastic ideals and subservience to the pretensions of the sovereign have lost ground in England, due to the comparatively peaceable conditions prevailing there; at the same time all this habit of mind has, on the whole, gained rather than lost in Germany, particularly in respect of the cruder and more truculent forms of loyalty to the person of the ruler, due to the continued and strenuous discipline in petty and personal warlike enterprise to which those peoples have been subjected,[1] — more especially true of the North, where personal mastery and servile allegiance have, under less settled conditions, suffered less encroachment from conventionalisation of the rights of tenure by prowess.

But the most striking feature of the English culture in modern times, and at the same time the most characteristic point of difference between the English and the German scheme throughout the modern period, and down to the middle of the nineteenth century, is after all the English preoccupation with material realities. "Reality," in English, means materiality, whenever and in so far as the person using the term does not advisedly take thought of its wider extension; by neglect rather than by aggressive intention the concept has suffered this narrowing of its connotation at the hands of the modern English-speaking peoples. This materialistic bias in the English frame of mind culminates in the "mechanistic conception," as it has been called by men who have had occasion analytically to attempt a preciser definition of this habit of thought. The mechanistic

---

[1] "The centuries have raised to high relief the elemental Teutonic qualities of hate, greed, courage and devotion." — H. O. Taylor, *The Mediæval Mind.*

conception and mechanistic point of view are, of course, of a visibly technological nature and bearing. It comes on by degrees of approach throughout the modern period, and the culmination has been reached only in the historical present, — if it is fairly to be said that the culmination of this movement has yet been reached, and not rather that what appears in our perspective to be the culmination, appears to be such only because it is the farthest point yet arrived at along this line. Throughout the few centuries of this modern era the drift in this direction has gone on with such a degree of consistency that, as seen from the point arrived at in its later phases, the mechanistic conception has the appearance of a goal toward which the discipline of modern life has tended.

In all this drift of modern intellectual life toward a materialistic basis of valuations and recourse to a mechanistic logic in the handling of phenomena, the German peoples have not shared in any sensible degree, nor have they borne any part in or contributed at all appreciably to it. An exception to this broad denial is doubtless due as applies to the south-German peoples through the earlier half of the modern era, but this exception holds good only with progressively lessening force even during the period when it applies at all; and seen simply in its own light, not viewed from the standpoint of the ulterior culmination which it never reached, it would scarcely be so rated at all. Except for this earlier modern phase — say, loosely, the sixteenth and perhaps the seventeenth century — the intellectual drift among the German peoples has been rather away from the materialistic animus, though perhaps not in any pronounced degree. Within the general confines of the Fatherland the discipline of workday life through these centuries has on the whole been of that personal character that throws immaterial qualities and relations into the foreground of habitual attention and leads to valuations of differential authenticity, dignity, caste, class, precedent and precedence; it has in an exceptional degree been the discipline of court, camp, bureaucracy and police, rather than that of the town-meeting, the open market and the open road, — still less has it taken its bias from the machine shop and the large industry. The intellectual bent and the principles of systematic thinking induced by such discipline do not lie parallel with the mechanistic conception, but rather fall in with that higher range of habits of thought that are spoken of as idealistic, spiritual, transcendental; that lead into generalisation and subsumptions under immaterial and ulterior categories, — transcendental in the sense of seeking precision and finality by recourse to conceptions that transcend the actualities of sense perception.

It is not that there is a sheer contrast between English and German, through this earlier formative period of modern times, in respect of the habituation that has gone to shape the intellectual life of Christendom. They both lie within the cultural confines of Christendom and within the range of modern as contrasted with mediæval cultural interests, at least in the main. But they represent the two extreme terms (or terminals) within this cultural complex, so far as regards the intellectual life of Christendom and so far as regards those elements of culture, particularly, that have much to say in the current shaping of modern institutions. As there has already been occasion to remark, the difference is one of degree, of the different stress that falls on one or another of the several factors that enter in the life of both; but such a difference is most conveniently handled in terms of contrast, in so far as the point of inquiry is the difference rather than the identity of the two.

Except for intrusive factors that had little more than a transient and superficial effect, then, and except for the earlier segment of modern times, the intellectual life of the German peoples has taken the direction given by the discipline of life in the Fatherland as characterised above. Relatively little attention, with relatively very slight effect, has been given to the material sciences or to technological lore of the mechanistic kind, — until such a date as English (and French) results achieved in these lines began finally to take a hold by way of borrowed gains, about the beginning of the nineteenth century. German speculation and inquiry took what has been called a profounder character, in that attention turned habitually to ulterior and transcendental systematisations of the knowledge in hand and to a quest of realities in the domain of the spirit, that is to say, in rationalised terms of personal force and spiritual congruity; the rationalisation taking its color from the régime of mastery and submission, orderly subservience to an authentically imposed scheme of conventional values. The culmination, of course, is German metaphysics of the Romantic school; drawn on lines of logical congruence rather than of efficient causation, and reaching its ultimate in the quasi-pantheistic over-ruling dominance of a transcendental personality. German speculation culminates in a (qualified) pantheistic scheme of logical categories and moral necessities; while the corresponding English movement, in so far as touches the point here in question, has tended strongly to an atheistic and unmoral scheme of opaque and impersonal matter of fact. This work of the human spirit as it has come into play under the German habituation is spoken of as "nobler," "profounder," — a point not to be disputed, since such discrimination is invidious and is an affair of taste and perspective.

Yet the characteristic bent of the intellectual life among the peoples of modern Christendom, as distinguished from what has prevailed elsewhere and in other times, is the animus that shows itself in the mechanistic conception. This may be little to the credit of modern Christendom, but the fact remains that only at this point has the culture of modern Christendom outrun the known civilisations that have gone before. It is also to be noted that this animus has come into such a position of dominance in modern intellectual life only by virtue of its practical efficiency, its congruence with matter of fact; as it is likewise to be noted that it is at the hands of the English-speaking peoples, primarily, that the mechanistic conception has been given its dominant place in the logic of modern thinking; which comes to saying that it is an outcome of the course of habituation to which the English community has been subject since modern times began. The conception is plainly of the technological order, and this fact marks the modern culture in which it prevails as a civilisation whose substantial core is the state of the industrial arts, even more obviously and immediately than such a proposition would apply to any other known civilisation. But its technological counterfoil is found in the late-modern state of the industrial arts, such as it has prevailed since the Industrial Revolution, rather than in the industrial system of modern times prior to that epoch.[1]

The manner in which this correlation between technological use and wont on the one side and the preconceptions of scientific inquiry on the other runs through modern intellectual life, as well as the apparent sequence of cause and

---

[1]What may appear to be an undue insistence on the priority of the English-speaking peoples in this matter of initiative and creative lead in the exact sciences does not overlook the work of scientists belonging to other nationalities and with other linguistic affiliations. It is not a matter of linguistic or national affiliation, still less is it a matter of race. The point of the argument is only that this lead in the exact, and particularly in the material, sciences is closely bound up with the state of the industrial arts — and the cognate institutional conceptions — among the Western peoples; and that the peculiar geographical distribution of the modern technological advance has brought a freer growth and fuller maturity of the mechanistic bias that underlies modern science in the Island than elsewhere, particularly during the later eighteenth and earlier nineteenth century. At the same time, and owing in chief to the use of print, the culture of these Western countries, all through the modern period, has had a cosmopolitan character; and the share — a very consequential share — in the scientific development, due to Italian, Dutch, south-German, and even Scandinavian specialists, and peculiarly and especially to the French, is not to be undervalued by comparison with the English contingent. (See pp. 189–193.) These others, for the most part, came earlier in this field, just as they have on the other hand borne a slighter share in the onward movement during the period of its more consummate modernisation under the more finished mechanistic discipline.

In all of this, as in so much else that touches the apex of growth in Western civilisation, the French community, of course, stands out as an apparent exception to any general characterisation that may apply to the Continental peoples at large. That the French have continued throughout the course of modern civilisation to occupy a position of hegemony does not disturb the analysis attempted above, which is directed more immediately to the divergence between the English and the German case, considered as extreme types of the culture current among the peoples lying within the climatic area of the Baltic-North Sea littoral.

effect in the case, has already been set out elsewhere in sufficiently full outline for the present purpose;[1] and no useful
end would be served by repeating it all here. The discussion referred to shows the general run of the facts in the
case, as a phase of the Western culture at large, but does
not touch especially on those circumstances of the case that
have made this development a work of the English-speaking peoples as distinct from the rest of Europe. So that
there is still something due to be said of the particular circumstances of the English case which brought on this development in the Island rather than elsewhere, and which
influenced the manner of its growth in the Island.

The chief and decisive circumstance, the *causa causans* of
the other circumstances bearing on the case, is the insularity
of the Island. From this insular position of the English
community it followed that the feudal system was not as
well established or as well matured in England; the "dynastic State" was not maintained in so coercive and workmanlike a fashion, nor did it last as well or linger as long as
on the Continent, since it lacked in some degree the necessary provocation and opportunity afforded by recurrent foreign warfare; the industrial situation, including the handicraft system, was in a backward state at the transition to
the modern régime; and the handicraft system, having
a shorter term of life in the Island, never reached the
same degree of elaboration, particularly in respect of its
gild regulations. The whole political, civil and industrial
organisation was of a looser texture and so offered a

---

[1]Cf. *The Instinct of Workmanship and the State of the Industrial Arts*,
ch. vi. and vii.

readier field of change and a freer field for individual initiative. It is notorious that insubordination and indivi- dual self-assertion showed themselves somewhat more read- ily and on slighter provocation in the Island than on the Continent in early-modern times, as also that concessions in that direction from the side of authority were more habitual. In the further course this insular situation con- tinued to affect the concerns of the community in the same sense; the chief fact being a relatively peaceable manner of life, leading to a further gradual weakening of personal government and a decline of bureaucratic surveillance, with a drift of interest and attention away from militant pa- triotism and dynastic policy and toward the arts of peace, a growing preoccupation with industry and trade in the place of war and politics.

The industry which so engaged the everyday speculations of the common man was of the order of handicraft, of course, in England as elsewhere at that time. But in the absence — relative absence or slighter pressure — of other, higher and more idealistic canons of logic and categories of generalisation, the commonplace Englishman — and they were mostly commonplace, like other people — speculated on whatever engaged his curiosity by help of the categories which habitually lay in his mind and by use of the logic which his workday occupations had taught him the force of. These categories, enforced by the workday routine of getting along by self-help under a system of handicraft, would be the categories of workmanship, and the logic which he habitually carried about with him by force of the same homely experience was the logic of the industrial

process and of the give and take of the petty trade. By failure of due discipline in discriminate conformity to conventions of immaterial dignity and invisible splendor, he had
lost much of that compelling sense of distinction where there
is no sensible difference that has remained one of the orna-
ments of his Continental congener. He fell, in the course of
commonplace generations, into a materialistic habit of mind,
and his materialism took form from the industrial operations that touched his routine of life, and from the goods
upon which his interest in his livelihood centered, as well
as from the meticulous figures of weight and tale and price
about which he grew excited in the "higgling of the market." These matters, and matters of this kind, he could
understand; and the logic of them was, by unbroken indoctrination, good logic to apply to whatever came within the
horizon of his interest; and few things came within this
horizon unless they came in the guise of material data, or
at least of data capable of statement in sensible terms of
weight and tale and of something that would serve as a
price valuation.

In such a frame of mind, one sees the sequence of events
as a concatenation of sensible data, in which action at a distance has no place or force and in which it is bootless to look
for a "sufficient reason" that will not bear formulation in
sensible terms of weight and tale. Indeed, in such company
argument on intangible grounds of sufficient reason is less
convincing than a wager, — the latter being at least susceptible of statistical formulation in standard units of the
realm. But the logic of workmanship runs on good and
sensible ground of manual contact and tangible alteration

of the materials on which the work is spent; a cause which sensibly "works" a tangible effect is something within the metaphysical horizon of the most commonplace material- ist. It is against this background of handicraft, and in the dry light shed by the statistics of commercial accountancy, that the scientists of the new era see the phenomena that pres- ently begin to engage their curiosity and require them to find a framework for the systematisation of their knowl- edge. So it comes about that when scientific inquiry gets under way in the English community it seeks efficient causes, and finds these causes in a shape that continually suggests craftsmanlike workmanship.

Not that this is a new and unprovoked discovery of the English; the like is present in all earlier systematisations of knowledge; but in the nobler or more idealistic systems that run back to the personal grounds of theology, meta- physics, magic, and the like, — as *e.g.*, the systematisations of the schoolmen and the later (German) mystics[1] and the alchemists of early-modern times,[2] — this principle (habit of thought) of workmanlike efficient cause is present only obscurely and in good part unavowedly, though pervasively throughout the argument. Nor is it that the new era under the English auspices claims right of priority in this matter; these latterday seekers after physical causes seek support wherever it is to be had and find it in many places; for the principle is itself one of the most ancient and incorrigible metaphysical habits of the race. It is only that in this new era under commonplace English auspices this metaphysical

---

[1]Cf., *e.g.*, Jakob Boehme, *The Signature of All Things.*
[2]Cf. Robert Boyle, *The Sceptical Chymist.*

postulate of workmanlike causation edges its way into the foreground of inquiry, and by default of higher principles through neglect it is left standing as the sole and self-sufficient category of conclusive systematisation in the domain of knowledge. The Italians in their day, when handicraft and private initiative had bred habits of materialistic inquiry among them, and before ecclesiastical persecution and partisan warfare had again brought that community in under the dim, religious light of orthodoxy and loyalty, — the Italians had gone out on the same homely quest and brought home staple goods merchantable in the same market; so had also the French, Dutch and south-Germans, in the times when analogous conditions induced a similar orientation of the idle curiosity in those communities. Now, when the turn came for the English they had the use of what had been done — and what still was being done — elsewhere, though circumstances decided that the English community presently fell into the lead.

Presently, by insensible degrees, a further new departure was initiated, or initiated itself, when the handicraft technology overpassed the bounds of its own characteristic methods and began to loosen the texture of its own peculiarly workmanlike habits of thought. Somewhere along about the beginning of the eighteenth century the recourse to such technological expedients as involve extensive and comprehensive physical processes, "labor-saving devices," and mechanical prime movers, begins to take on such proportions as to introduce engineering of a sort into the technological scheme; and then presently to install this new line of approach to questions of industrial efficiency as an intrinsic element in the state of the industrial arts. This new factor, or rather this old factor which now begins to take on proportions that make it count toward the shaping of the technological system and of the intellectual outlook induced by and subservient to that system,[1] — this new factor comes into view in such connections as the increasing size and mechanical elaboration of shipping, together with a systematised and calculable art of navigation; the improvement of highways (and waterways) and vehicles, and the consequent reduction of the ways and means of communication and transport, to more of a mechanically systematised affair; the increasing use of water-wheels, windmills, and similar mechanical prime movers; the extension and systematic determination of agricultural processes, together with a rationalised and deliberate attention to improvement of the breeds of domestic animals.

It is, however, not until well along in the century that this incursion into the industrial system of elements alien to the simpler spirit of handicraft proper reaches such proportions as visibly to affect the state of the industrial arts and to suggest that something in the way of a new range of

---

[1] The new factor in the technological scheme brought in by increased recourse to mechanical ways and means will count as a substantial contributory agent in the situation at large only if it rises above a certain "threshold" of proportional magnitude or intensity, relatively to the concert of agencies bearing on the same point. This is particularly true as regards the several factors of habituation in any given case; such as are present in relatively slight measure may easily become negligible. The case is analogous to what happens in therapeutics, where a drug administered in less than the "minimal dose" has no effect, — unless it may be, in the case of certain drugs that are peculiar in this respect, persistent repetition of the minimal dose may in time work a cumulative effect. Therapeutics, it should be remarked, is also a field of habituation.

principles of efficiency is beginning to take the place of the old, so that the "mechanic arts" is no longer securely synonymous with workmanship. But somewhere in the third quarter of the century the primacy among the habits of thought that made up the technological scheme may be said to have passed from workmanship to engineering, — at least so it appears when the matter is seen in the perspective given by the later development along the same line; it may be doubtful if anyone would have assented to that proposition simply in view of the situation as it then stood, and un-influenced by the later course of events in the mechanical industries.[1] It is only by afterthought that this epoch has been named the Industrial Revolution, and even so the revolution has conventionally been appraised in terms of "labor-saving devices," as being a system of ways and means for "facilitating and abridging" the manual operations of handicraft. But as seen in the light of what has come of it, the technological character of this industrial revolution is not to be mistaken, except wilfully. The efficiency of it is not that of specialised craftmanship but of a process in which mechanical factors engage.

Yet at the outset, or more properly in the initial phases of the era of the machine industry, the preconceptions with which the designers and projectors of the new expedients went to their work were plainly of the handicraft order. In the early designing of machinery their conscious aim was, by mechanical means, to reproduce craftsmanlike manual

---

[1]Adam Smith, *e.g.*, did not so see the matter, although his preoccupation with economic questions that turned on the efficiency of the industrial process would logically place him at an advantage in this respect.

operations on an enhanced scale, scope or pace. This will not hold, of course, in such matters as ship-building, navigation, roadway engineering or cattle breeding; but while these matters now find their place in the broader scheme of the machine technology as seen *ex post facto,* and are seen to come under the dominion of the mechanistic conception, they were not then apprehended as ramifications of the technology of the machine era. The technological innovations which first, and for a long time alone, commended themselves as such and, as making the difference between the old and the new, were the devices spoken of as machinery in the narrower sense, — the designing of these new contrivances was first actuated by preconceptions of craftsmanship, and it was only gradually, insensibly, that the inventors and designers swung free from these personalised conceptions of industrial processes and came to work out their mechanical problems in the logic of the mechanical factors and processes at work in the case, rather than in that of the manual operations which these processes had displaced.

As always, habituation took time; and it was apparently necessary that the generation at whose hands the decisive move into the world of mechanical process had taken place should pass, before the logic of the mechanistic conception could gain a secure lodgment in the habitual thinking even of the men who were occupied with the concrete details of mechanical process. The norms and categories of science, according to which the current body of knowledge was to be systematised, being remoter derivatives from the discipline of workday life, would suffer transmutation more tardily than the preconceptions of the technologists; but being derivatives of the same workday routine, the transmutation would necessarily overtake them also, provided only that this workday routine held its character consistently enough and long enough for its discipline to take conclusive effect. So it will be found that the men who did the scientific work of the generation or two following the Industrial Revolution, still continue to conceive of their systematisation in terms of efficient causes that look much like abstractions from the typical handicraftsman dealing with a parcel of raw materials and turning out a piece of wrought goods, — and there is even more than a passing suggestion of the ancient gild regulations in the irrepressible framing of Natural Laws to govern the sequence of cause and effect in the theoretical speculations of those early generations of scientific men.[1]

But slowly, irresistibly, and irresponsibly, this mechanistic conception that so makes the efficient spiritual core of the modern industrial arts has also been insinuating its logic into the domain of knowledge at large; first and most obviously, of course, in the field of material science, but presently also among those inquiring spirits who speculate on higher things. Very much in the same measure and with the same degree of generality as the machine technology has displaced handicraft and diverted interest from the concerns of ritual observance and coercive rule, so has also the

---

[1]Indeed, except for the fear of giving annoyance, one might find survivals of the gild-regulation concept of natural laws in the work of scientists still living, particularly perhaps in those sciences that lie farthest afield from the technological domain and so come least in touch with the logic of mechanical engineering, as, *e.g.*, in economics.

mechanistic conception supplanted the preconceptions of the college of divinity and of the college of heraldry in the logic of scientific theory. Always with the reservation, of course, that the latter movement is consequent upon and conditioned by the former, and will therefore show a marked degree of retardation in moving along the same line.

In all this analysis of the English case it has been assumed with unwarranted freedom that the state of the industrial arts has worked unhampered toward a comprehensive habituation in materialistic and mechanistic terms; and that it so has brought about a passably universal animus of self-help and mechanistic logic, with no remnant of deference to the authentic conventions of the ancient régime of prerogative, and with no respect of persons. Such is manifestly not the case, of course, but by contrast with what has befallen the German people during the same historical interval, such as these have after all been the more salient features of the distinctively British culture, and indeed of the civilisation of all the advanced industrial countries. But in all these communities, and perhaps not least in the British case, there have stood over out of the past very substantial survivals, at least, of that scheme of use and wont that antedates the coming of the machine technology and that are not its offspring or of its kind. Church and State and Nobility are still present in effectual force; but it is unnecessary here to look closer into the play of these factors in modern British life, inasmuch as history is by ancient convention still written in the terms afforded by these

categories of a transfused antiquity, and common notoriety
will supply all necessary reminder and reference to their
share in the outcome. Their share in the cultural drift has in
the main been of the conservative kind.

On the other hand there has grown out of the new industrial régime itself, in part by direct consequence of its
technological character and in greater part by way of use
and wont conditioned by the industrial efficiency of the
new régime, a broad fringe of usages, conventions, vested
rights, canons of equity and propriety, that are no part of
the new state of the industrial arts, but that are after all
not easily to be separated from it or from its usufruct by
the community whose work it is. In good part these conventions and canons have the effect of hindrances to the
working of the industrial system, or of deductions from its
net efficiency.

In the English case, as in the rest of Europe, from time
immemorial the rights of ownership have had the sanction
of law and custom; and in England less than in much of
the rest of Europe these rights have been weakened by the
State's arrogation of a superior right of usufruct. In the
days of the handicraft system as well as, even more pronouncedly, since the machine industry came in, industry
has been carried on on a pecuniary basis and for pecuniary
gain. But with the advance in industrial efficiency and the
increasing scale of operations and of market relations, the
pecuniary enterprise which began in the shape of a "petty
trade" and served as a handmaid to handicraft, has in the
course of time become the master of the industrial system,

owner of the industrial equipment, and potentially the sole beneficiary of the community's technological efficiency, with full discretion to direct the operations of industry for its own pecuniary ends. So that the technological knowledge and proficiency gained by the community in the course of modern times primarily serves, by right of ownership, the pecuniary gain of the business men in control, and only secondarily contributes to the welfare of the population. This state of things, of course, is not peculiar to the English case, except in the fuller measure and security of discretion which legally and customarily vests in the owners, and except for the relatively large and long continued industrial efficiency of the English community, which has given time and scope for a larger growth of subsidiary consequences in this country than elsewhere.

These subsidiary consequences of the English industrial system as managed for private gain fall under two general heads: those which affect industry (production), and those which affect the consumption of the product; the former belong under the principle of competition, the latter under that of conspicuous waste — also called the standard of living. A third factor, the inertia of use and wont, comes in powerfully to affect both of these two, most usually to fortify them, at the same time that it has serious effects of its own upon the efficiency of the industrial system, — particularly in the way of hindering initiative and delaying innovations in industrial ways and means. In all of these several directions there is something of a systematic growth, conditioned by the opportunities of the case and requiring time for mature results, as well as for the discontinuance of the practices in question in case such a course should become urgently expedient.

The industrial effects of business management, or rather what may be called its "organic" effects on the industrial system, are not all hurtful to its productive efficiency, though nearly all of those that require time and habituation for their adequate development are of that nature. These are well known, in a general way; indeed they are a matter of common notoriety, but they are also so intimately bound up with the immemorial rights of ownership and with the price system that they are — and perhaps rightly — accepted as a matter of course that lies in the nature of the economic situation. Most obvious, perhaps, is the systematic working at cross-purposes due to competition in the market, the purpose of each contestant being to divert gain to himself, and perhaps incidentally to serve the material welfare of the community. Under given, but not infrequent, circumstances this situation may take such a turn that the pecuniary gain of the business men in control will best be served by devices that are detrimental to the community's material well-being, — as, e.g., in the use of adulterants and disingenuous substitutes, such as shoddy; the production and sale of unwholesome nostrums and beverages; of unsafe and insanitary habitations, roadways, vehicles, and contrivances for household use; the employment of dangerous machinery and poisonous ingredients and processes in industry, and the like. These dubious expedients of gain will be worked into the industrial and commercial scheme more fully and pervadingly in the course of time; much ingenuity is spent on these matters and much businesslike industry in the course of time comes to have a vested interest in the maintenance and the tolerant oversight of these "abuses," as they are sometimes called.

Next in order of notoriety, if not of importance, are the frequent seasons of idleness, unemployment or half-employment of the equipment and working force due to exigencies of the market. These difficulties are increased through the growth of the industrial community and its market relations into a large and complex system in which there prevails a very large measure of interdependence of the various parts and agents, due, in the last analysis, to the specialisation and subdivision of the industrial processes under the rule of the machine technology, and to the more immediate and decisive fact that the several industries are managed with a view to private gain in terms of price. Unemployment of this kind is always due to considerations of price. From the like competitive considerations of price, and of gain in terms of price, it has come about that the interests of the employer are not at one with those of the workmen. This divergence of interest has been volubly denied, and some credit should doubtless be given to such volubility. The run of the facts, however, is notorious; on the one hand the workmen have no whole-hearted interest in the efficiency of the work done, but rather in what can be got for it in terms of price; on the other hand the employer has none but a humanitarian — said to be quite secondary — interest in the well-being, or even in the continued efficiency, of the workmen. From which follow on the one hand inhibitory trades-union rules, strikes, lock-outs, and the like disturbances of the industrial process, and on the other hand an exploitation of the human raw material of industry that has at times taken quite an untoward scope and direction, in the way of over-work, under-pay, unsafe and unwholesome conditions, and so forth. In the English case, specifically, these "abuses" have notoriously gone far, and they have, also notoriously, taken time for their full development and will require time and effort for their correction. So, as one illustration out of an abundance, and merely dispassionately to exemplify the working of this competitive principle in the employment of hired labor, it is sufficiently established that during the initial one hundred years or so of the new industrial régime in England the conditions of work, pay and livelihood ran competitively to such a character as to produce an appreciable population of "depauperate" workmen, sufficiently damaged in their physique to transmit their debilities to their offspring and leave them doubtfully fit for any efficient use, "unto the third and fourth generation."[1]

---

[1]"Depauperate" is here used in its technical sense, without any designed implication of praise or dispraise for the businesslike management that so led to the establishment of a generation of "depauperate" Englishmen. It is a fact of some consequence as bearing on the continued efficiency of the industrial system, more particularly when this system is brought into competitive relations with that of another community which has not undergone a protracted experience of the character that gives rise to a depauperate working population. A "depauperate" population, or generation, of any species is one that has been subject to conditions of life differing so widely from what has selectively been proved normal to the specific type as to stunt the growth, derange the anthropometric proportions of the frame or the functional work of the viscera, and enfeeble the vital functions beyond the limits of recovery within the generation so subjected to these untoward conditions of climate, sanitation, nutrition, or strain.

Such a depauperate variation from the specific type will be heritable,

Connected with the competitive system of businesslike management is the modern enterprise in salesmanship. The extension of salesmanship goes forward in correlation with the extension of business management in industry; indeed, in the late-modern development and in such lines of enterprise as come largely into the market, as most industrial undertakings on a business footing do, salesmanship will frequently come in for one-half or more than one-half of the effort and funds expended by any given business concern. The cost of salesmanship, including advertising and similar adventures in notoriety, will not infrequently rise to appreciably over one-half of the price of the goods to the consumer, and will now and again reach three-fourths, nine-tenths, or even within a shadowy interval of one hundred

---

in effect, so long as the conditions to which it is due continue, and through an uncertain period or number of generations after return to normal conditions. For the present purpose it amounts to a transient variation of the type, due to "untoward" conditions, and does not touch the question of permanence of the racial type spoken of in an earlier passage.

Variations of the same untoward or unwholesome character may doubtless be had by an untoward or unwholesome variation of the conditions of life in the direction of over-feeding, excessive shelter from the elements, or excessive sensual indulgence and insufficient strain of the faculties, such as is to be seen now and again among the wealthy or privileged classes, as, *e.g.*, the royal, noble or hereditary rich. While etymology will not permit untoward variants due to excess of this kind to be called "depauperate," there appears to be no other term that has the sanction of technical usage. In effect, these consequences of over-indulgence among the privileged classes come to very much the same as what is accomplished by under-feeding and over-work among the indigent. It may also be noted that the two kinds of untoward variation will commonly be found together in the same community, conditions which produce the one commonly also inducing the other. England, *e.g.*, has had its quota of both, as a by-product of the era of business and industry, peace and prosperity, brought on by the technological advance in modern times.

per cent. The larger, more complex, more adequately capitalised (in the sense of being managed with sufficient means, on such a scale as to allow due specialisation of functions within the given business concern), in short the more maturely modern the business situation becomes, the larger a proportion of the aggregate expenditures will on the whole go into salesmanship.

Expenditure on salesmanship is nearly net waste, as rated in terms of serviceability to the material welfare of the community at large. How nearly all waste it may be would be hazardous to guess, but the deduction to be made for salesmanship that serves a useful purpose at large will in any case be a negligible quantity. Yet competitive salesmanship and the other strategic expedients of competitive business are of the essence of the business management of industry, and the limits of their growth are set only by what the traffic will bear — given time for a mature growth along this line. What the traffic will bear is, in the last resort, a question of how many men and how large an investment of funds can be supported at what are called "living" rates of wages and profits on the margin between the subsistence minimum for the men and equipment employed in productive industry and the total output of the same industry. Given a living rate of profits on the capitalisable value of the equipment and a living wage for the workmen employed, there is nothing but the time required for the adjustment, that stands in the way of salesmanship absorbing whatever is left over. But the necessary adjustment takes time, and as the technological scheme, and consequently the material equipment, are continually changing, and as the volume and distribution of the population who are to serve as a market for the marketable output are also changing, it is only in relatively old industrial countries that the enterprise and investment in salesmanship can with any tolerable degree of approximation be brought to the limit of what the traffic will bear; and even here, even in such a highly commercialised community as the United Kingdom, the enterprise in salesmanship has never yet come up to this limit, although it has doubtless come very appreciably nearer to it here than in any of the other, industrially newer, countries that now live within the sweep of the machine technology. The contrast with the late-coming German case is sufficiently evident.

"Depreciation by obsolescence" is a rubric of some importance in modern corporation accountancy, and also a source of irritation and perplexity to business men who have to do with industrial plant. Its first and simplest incarnation is seen in the competitive displacement of a serviceable appliance or process by a more serviceable one. Discussions of such depreciation frequently get no farther than this point in the analysis of obsolescence, although the more interesting as well as the more perplexing and disastrous cases lie beyond that point and come of causes that have a wider reach than details of mechanical invention. Detail obsolescence through technological innovation, such as alters the differential advantage enjoyed by one business concern as against its competing neighbors in the same line of industry, has commonly no detrimental effect on the industry as a whole or on the efficiency or welfare of the community at large; the depreciation is a competitive one only and takes effect only as a decrease in the pecuniary gains of one business concern as against another. The community at large, or the particular line of industry, gains in efficiency by virtue of the innovation. The like is not true in cases of what may be called "systemic" obsolescence, which may come of a change of circumstances due to the growth of the industrial community (or, also, due to its decay), or to changes in the work to be done, or in the distribution of the population to be served or employed.[1] Obsolescence of this kind is an affair of growth and is always in progress in any community where the state of the industrial arts is undergoing any appreciable degree of change, and the longer the growth of the technological situation has continued the more unavoidable is such depreciation.

An industrial system which, like the English, has been long engaged in a course of improvement, extension, innovation and specialisation, will in the past have committed itself, more than once and in more than one connection, to what was at the time an adequate scale of appliances and schedule of processes and time adjustments. Partly by its own growth, and by force of technological innovations designed to enlarge the scale or increase the tempo of production or service, the accepted correlations in industry and in business, as well as the established equipment, are thrown out of date. And yet it is by no means an easy matter to find a remedy; more particularly is it difficult to find a remedy

---

[1] The Cinque Ports afford an historic illustration of such depreciation through "systemic" obsolescence due to the growth of the industrial system and changes in the distribution of population; whereas the Roman Road in England shows how the like obsolescence may come of the decay or decline of the state of the industrial arts.

that will approve itself as a sound business proposition to a community of conservative business men who have a pecuniary interest in the continued working of the received system, and who will (commonly) not be endowed with much insight into technological matters anyway. So long as the obsolescence in question gives rise to no marked differential advantage of one or a group of these business men as against competing concerns, it follows logically that no remedy will be sought. An adequate remedy by detail innovation is not always practicable; indeed, in the more serious conjunctures of the kind it is virtually impossible, in that new items of equipment are necessarily required to conform to the specifications already governing the old.

So, *e.g.*, it is well known that the railways of Great Britain, like those of other countries, are built with too narrow a gauge, but while this item of "depreciation through obsolescence" has been known for some time, it has not even in the most genial speculative sense come up for consideration as a remediable defect. In the same connection, American, and latterly German, observers have been much impressed with the silly little bobtailed carriages used in the British goods traffic; which were well enough in their time, before American or German railway traffic was good for anything much, but which have at the best a playful air when brought up against the requirements of today. Yet the remedy is not a simple question of good sense. The terminal facilities, tracks, shunting facilities, and all the ways and means of handling freight on this oldest and most complete of railway systems, are all adapted to the bobtailed car. So, again, the roadbed and metal, as well as the

engines, are well and substantially constructed to take care
of such traffic as required to be taken care of when they
first went into operation, and it is not easy to make a piece-
meal adjustment to later requirements. It is perhaps true
that as seen from the standpoint of the community at large
and its material interest, the out-of-date equipment and organisation should profitably be discarded — "junked," as
the colloquial phrase has it — and the later contrivances sub-
stituted throughout; but it is the discretion of the business
men that necessarily decides these questions, and the whole
proposition has a different value as seen in the light of the
competitive pecuniary interests of the business men in control.

This instance of the British railway system and its shortcomings in detail is typical of the British industrial equipment and organisation throughout, although the obsolescence will for the most part, perhaps, be neither so obvious
nor so serious a matter in many other directions. Towns,
roadways, factories, harbors, habitations, were placed and
constructed to meet the exigencies of what is now in a degree
an obsolete state of the industrial arts, and they are, all and
several, "irrelevant, incompetent and impertinent" in the
same degree in which the technological scheme has shifted
from what it was when these appliances were installed.[1]
They have all been improved, "perfected," adapted, to

---

[1] Even in such an all-underlying and specifically British line of work
as the iron industry, observers from other countries — *e.g.*, German, Swedish or American — have latterly had occasion to find serious and sarcastic
fault with the incompetently diminutive blast-furnaces, the antiquated
appliances for moving materials, and the out-of-date contrivances for
wasting labor and fuel.

meet changing requirements in some passable fashion; but the chief significance of this work of improvement, adaptation and repair in this connection is that it argues a fatal reluctance or inability to overcome this all-pervading depreciation by obsolescence.[1]

All this does not mean that the British have sinned against the canons of technology. It is only that they are paying the penalty for having been thrown into the lead and so having shown the way. At the same time it is not to be imagined that this lead has brought nothing but pains and penalties. The shortcomings of this British industrial situation are visible chiefly by contrast with what the British might be doing if it were not for the restraining dead hand of their past achievement, and by further contrast, latterly, with what the new-come German people are doing by use of the English technological lore. As it stands, the accumulated equipment, both material and immaterial, both in the way of mechanical appliances in hand and in the way of technological knowledge ingrained in the population and available for use, is after all of very appreciable value;

---

[1] An interesting contrast with this state of things in businesslike industry is to be seen in the British navy, where nearly every item of equipment, as well as the greater part of the systematic organisation and control of personnel and strategy, have grown obsolete within the past decade. There is much compromise and many makeshifts in the endeavors directed to bring this naval establishment up to a satisfactory efficiency according to current technological standards, but the measure of retardation put up with in consequence is, after all, highly inconsiderable as compared with what passes for well enough in the concerns of British industry. The industrial efficiency of the community is of prime consequence, the naval establishment is of secondary importance, or something less; but industrial affairs are conducted on motives of competitive business enterprise.

though the case of the Germans should make it plain that
it is the latter, the immaterial equipment, that is altogether
of first consequence, rather than the accumulation of "production goods" in hand. These "production goods" cost
nothing but labor; the immaterial equipment of technological proficiency costs age-long experience.

This is, of course, not intended to apply to what is currently spoken of as accumulated capital, that is to say funded
wealth invested in industrial business. That has relatively
slight significance to the community at large. Capital in this
sense, business capital, in the aggregate means little else
than a pseudo-aggregate of differential claims on the usufruct of the industrial equipment, material and immaterial.
And it will doubtless hold true for the British, as for any
other of the advanced commercial countries, that the aggregate of capitalised wealth shown by the records very
greatly exceeds the aggregate market value of the material
items to which, in the last resort of the accountant, these
"book values" are presumed to constitute a claim. Such is
necessarily the case in any country that makes extensive use
of credit and of corporate organisation in its conduct of
business.

The discipline of the machine industry, simply in its direct incidence, has a certain character of impersonality, and
will apparently not conduce to the stability or extension of
personal government. It inculcates due appreciation of the
sweep of mechanical processes, impersonal, and in that
sense equitable, rather than subordination to the discretionary call of a personal superior. In so far as concerns the rela-

tions between the body of workmen and the technological elements with which their work associates them, the habit of mind induced by addiction to the modern methods of industry should favor an individualistic bias in civil relations and an impatience of authoritative government; and such appears on the whole to have been the net effect of the training enforced by modern industrial life, until a comparatively recent period. But so soon as a businesslike control of industry takes extensive effect and becomes the chief factor in the organization and management of industrial occupations, personal discretion again comes prominently into the case. The authority of ownership, enforced by pecuniary pressure, takes on a coercive character that grows more comprehensive and unavoidable as the scale of industry and investment grows larger. Under latterday large-scale conditions, this authority of ownership has the harsh aloofness of irresponsible tyranny, but it has none of the genial traits that may relieve even a very ruthless despotism. The subordination which it enforces is of a sullen, unenthusiastic character, tending more and more to a grudging disloyalty, as the scheme of business control grows more comprehensive and settles into more rigid lines. So in the English case the alienation between the two classes, the workmen and their owners, is nearly complete in all that bears on the conduct of the industrial system.

Yet the result is after all a discipline in subordination of a kind, and in concerted action and solidarity within class lines. And this training in concerted action and community of interests and convictions leaves the population by so much the more amenable to control in the mass, and more capable of being swung in a body to the support of a national authority and the aggrandisement of those in whose interest the constituted authority is administered. In England, the sense of national solidarity, and the support of national policies that have no material value to the common man, are in a visibly better state of repair the last two or three decades than formerly was the case, when business corporations of the joint-stock order on the one side and labor organisations on the other had only begun to contribute their discipline toward the shaping of popular sentiment.

It appears from this English case that the habits of thought induced by the discipline of a given economic situation are not necessarily such as conduce to the best working of the system in force, or to the best material interest of the community which gets its living by use of this system; in other words, the principles and canons of conduct that emerge out of the working of any given system of ways and means, any given scheme of life, are not such as will necessarily contribute either to the efficiency of the system or to the prosperity of the population. All that is a matter of fortuitous coincidence, as some slight reflection on the nature of habituation will easily show. There is, all the while, somewhat of a chance, much of the time a very reasonable presumption, that the principles (habits of thought) inculcated, say, by life under a given state of the industrial arts will be somewhat at cross-purposes with the conditions of life afforded by this given state of the industrial arts, — save only such habits of thought as are of a technological nature, these being part of the state of the industrial arts itself.

The broad exception to this proposition will be found where the technological scheme in question, and its concomitant scheme governing the other arts of life, have been proved suitable to the given population by the selective test of their prospering under these cultural conditions in the early phases of the life-history of this population, when it made good its survival as a specific type of man. For the British population, as for the other peoples of the Baltic-North Sea region, this would mean that the growth of habits (principles, institutions) induced by modern life is presumably of an untoward character, except in so far as its drift is toward a rehabilitation of the cultural scheme prevalent in north Europe in neolithic times; and it would appear to be the more untoward, on the whole, the more it diverges from that line.

While there has been a growth of use and wont governing the system of production, with preconceptions, vested interests and an industrial equipment now of a somewhat archaic character, there has similarly gone forward a growth of use and wont in consumption, with usages, standards, prejudices that are no less settled and exacting than the conventions which govern industry and business. These conventions of consumption may be classed together under the rubric of a standard of living, as is commonly done in the terminology of the economists; although in its technical use the term does not refer to a standard of physical well-being, as its etymological value might lead one to expect. It means rather the standard of consumption, on whatever grounds the consumption has been standardised, and it will commonly include items that bear no relation, or at least no designed relation, to the consumer's physical well-being. A large proportion, perhaps the greater part, of what is included under the standard of living for any class, whether rich or poor, falls under the theoretical category of Conspicuous Waste,[1] which comprises the consumption of time and effort as well as of substance.

It is a familiar bit of aphoristic wisdom that want of morals may be condoned but a lack of breeding can not. The canons of propriety, that is of conformity to convention, are as the law of the Medes and Persians, — they yield not, and admit no extenuating circumstances. As has often happened in the case of a simple and rigid code, the penalty for transgression is outlawry, which may or may not involve, as a duty incumbent on all *gens de bien*, the pursuit and extirpation of the offender.

Ordinarily, in the common run of neighborly amenities within the community, the resulting schedule of ostracism eventuates in a social stratification, in which individuals find their place by force of a "consciousness of kind" that draws them into contact and coöperation with those of a like habit in point of breeding and on a like level in point of current expenditures, as also by force of exclusion from those pecuniary levels on which they do not belong. The general result is nothing much more serious than a prevalence of irritation and envy between classes and of emulation and disparagement between individuals. In case the

---

[1]For a more detailed exposition of this principle and its place in modern life, see *The Theory of the Leisure Class*, especially ch. ii.–vii. and xii.

discrepancy of use and wont in respect of this consumption of time and substance, and of the attendant details of manner and breeding, is considerable and consistent, and runs between culturally distinct communities, the outcome is a state of aliency between the two, which may on slight provocation rise to the pitch of manslaughter and seek relief in international hostilities. It is on this sentimental ground of offended and offensive conventionalities that patriotic animosities commonly rest. The most capable dynastic statesmen and the shrewdest strategists of commercial patriotism would be helpless to bring about a state of international manslaughter among civilised men except for the quasi-moral animosity that arises out of such discrepancies of "culture."

Now, it happens that this growth of use and wont in respect of what is apprehended to be decent and commendable in the consumption of time and goods, and in the demeanor and observances duly to be included in the ritual of such consumption, has in the British community, and even in the English-speaking communities at large, in modern times, run to a visibly different effect from the contemporary outcome in this respect among the Continental peoples; and especially different from what has been worked out among the German peoples, who have in this particular as in so much else retained more of the conventional virtues inculcated by a more archaic phase of material civilisation. Hence a discrepancy in "culture" that has become irreconcilable.

But what is of more immediate interest here is the bearing of this growth of consumptive use and wont on the net industrial efficiency of the British community. As a matter of common notoriety the standard of living is and has long been higher in the United Kingdom, and particularly in England, than in the generality of Continental countries, and this standard has been rising, with interruptions, of course, throughout the modern period, and more notably since the Industrial Revolution. This advance in the current requirement of living has affected all classes and conditions, but has had the greatest relative effect on the higher pecuniary levels. And as, in these matters of conventional necessity, the example of the upper classes largely guides the growth of use and wont among the lowlier, the code of (pecuniarily) right and honest living among the well-to-do comes to have a far-reaching significance for the fortunes of the community at large.

In the beginning, when England began to take up the slack and set out on that course of insular economic policy that has created the modern industrial situation, the English pecuniary scale of reputability was somewhat under the Continental standard. Even in the Elizabethan days of flush and swagger the English leaders of fashion were following Continental models; and indeed were following the Continental exemplars at such an interval that those who approached nearest to the Continental standards of expensiveness and splendor were currently disparaged as being effeminate wasters.[1] That they were wasters, in the technical sense of the term, is of course a proposition not open to

---

[1] Cf., *e.g.*, Harrison's description of *Elizabethan England*, where much acrid speech is spent on those English scions of gentility for reaching out after the exotic perfections of Italy.

correction or amendment, — that being their place and use in the economy of nature; and it is to their credit as gentlemen that they so efficiently filled the "station in life in which God had placed them." Seen from the collective standpoint of the national culture, a gentleman is an article of *virtù*, the value of which lies in its consummate workmanship and its conformity to the canons of a refined taste. That a gentleman is a wasteful affair is of the essence of the case; how wasteful the standard or staple gentleman thrown up as the type of reputable waste in any given culture will be, is in effect a question of how wide a margin the current scheme of production and distribution devotes to conspicuously wasteful consumption.

The development of the perfect gentleman (and of the perfect gentlewoman) in any given case takes time. As an institution, the perfect gentleman (or gentlewoman) is a complex affair of usages, distinctions, cultivated tastes, worked out under the general surveillance of the principle (habit of thought) of conspicuous waste, against a background of critical sentiment that will tolerate only the most economical use of the materials employed. In this connection this canon of economy requires that the conspicuously wasteful consumption of the gentleman must not incidentally or by leakage conduce in any degree to the physical well-being, or to the pecuniary gain, of anyone else. Judged on these marks of excellence it will be admitted without argument that the staple product of the pecuniary culture in England in the way of gentlemen (and gentlewomen) is as good as human infirmity will permit. The volume of output is also as large as might fairly be

expected; indeed, and as a matter-of-course, it is as large as
the traffic will bear, for the English community has grown
slowly and symmetrically to the highest and most substantial maturity attained by the pecuniary culture within the
bounds of Christendom. The other English-speaking peoples have been doing well, but they have come into their
heritage too late to have yet worked out this knotty problem of how to dispose of their disposable margin of goods
and energies without leaving a materially serviceable residue. As in so much else their best efforts are directed to the
conservation and heightened efficiency of the institutions
handed down from English leadership in these premises.

So soon as the great *élan* of the Elizabethan *juventus
mundi* had given the English their start on the road to the
economic hegemony, the expensiveness of English well-to-
do persons began to attract the attention of Continental
critics. The English took to travel — an expensive usage —
and it has been a conventionally accepted criticism of English travelers ever since, that they are strikingly wasteful
in their expenditure.[1] This criticism by Continental observers will commonly carry a note of envy, though its
most obtrusive count is the uneconomical character of this
British bill of expenses — uneconomical under the canon
of economy applicable in these matters, as indicated above.
Doubtless, the English today lead the Christian world both
in the volume of their gentility and in its cost per unit.
This cost comes out of the margin of production, and re-
duces the net margin by that much. The figures represent-

---

[1]Exceeded, perhaps put in the shade, latterly by their American followers.

ing the net current cost of British gentility in the aggregate may be drawn with some confidence from the schedules of incomes; taxable incomes may safely be included under the caption of Net Conspicuous Waste, to the extent to which they are not exempt under the law, — any possible error arising from this rating will be at least offset by items of wasteful expenditure of the same class drawn from other sources, such, *e.g.*, as operating expenses of railway and steamship passenger traffic, hotels, various places of amusement, etc.

Sports have been a very substantial resource in this gradually maturing British scheme of conspicuous waste. And sports have the advantage that they afford a politely blameless outlet for energies that might otherwise not readily be diverted from some useful end. Sport, on the scale, and with the circumstance attending its cultivation in the United Kingdom, can not be incorporated in the workday scheme of life except at the cost of long and persistent training of the popular taste. It is not to be done by a brusque move. It is quite beyond the reach of imagination that any adult male citizen would of his own motion go in for the elaborate futilities of British shooting or horse-racing, *e.g.*, or for such a *tour de force* of inanity as polo, or mountain climbing, or expeditions after big game. The deadening of the sense of proportion implied in addiction to this round of infantile make-believe is not to be achieved in one generation; it needs to have all the authenticity that tradition can give it, and then its inculcation in the incoming generation must be begun in infancy and followed up throughout the educational system. Nor would it all be tolerated by popular sentiment if it were not that popular sentiment has gradually been bent to the same bias by slow habituation.[1] Yet so far has the habituation done its work that the community at large not only tolerates these things, but all this superfluity of inanities has in the course of time been worked into the British conception of what is right, good and necessary to civilised life.[2]

All this, and the like, may be good material for homiletical discourse, but its value in that respect is not in question here. What is to the present purpose is the bearing of these ingrained wasteful usages on the net industrial efficiency of the British community, the net serviceability to the community at large, of their usufruct of this modern state of the industrial arts that they have had the fortune to bring forth.

In further illustration — lest the items of sports should be left standing in apparent isolation as a single and disconnected count — mention may be made of the wasteful consumption incumbent by usage on the wealthy British in the

---

[1] Cf. Graham Wallas, *The Great Society*, perhaps especially ch. iii. and v.

[2] In the disturbance of British life due to the German war, *e.g.*, associations have been formed to care for the dogs whose owners have been drawn into the army, and to keep them undiminished against the return of their owners. British newspapers of the most sober character have been printing most Britishly sober advice and admonition on how best to further this necessary work of dog-maintenance. There is no avoiding the impression that all this agitation about the due maintenance of the soldiers' sporting equipment is really not a parcel of whimsical tomfoolery. It is rather an illustration of the dominion which habit may come to exercise over common sense.

matter of habitations and domestic establishments. A gentleman of appreciable wealth should have more than one habitation, residence, or whatever term may best cover a construction of which the sole ostensible occupant can not
occupy more than an inconsiderable fraction. How many
residences, in town and country, are mandatory on any
given gentleman of any given pecuniary rating can of course
not be stated in set terms; it can only be said that, in general terms, he should have more than he can conveniently
make use of, even ostensibly, and as many and as large as
he can afford to keep up. The visible economic effect of
this system is to keep a corps of servants and care-takers for
each establishment out of useful employment, and at the
same time to keep the common man from making use of the
grounds attached to each establishment, which should be
as extensive as may be, — that is to say, the practice serves
to reduce the net available land surface of the Island by
that much.

Further details of the menial establishment and of the
ceremonial routine incumbent on persons of genteel standing in this community need not be recited. Common notoriety will supply enough to enforce the point that, by use
and wont, much has gone into the category of conventional
necessaries, and that the margin between aggregate productive capacity and net available surplus has thereby been very
appreciably narrowed, as well as the further point that even
if, or when, the exigencies of a competitive situation should
require this community to make the most of its available
forces it would be a work of time, stress and perplexity to

bring the effectual efficiency nearly up to the theoretical efficiency of the community.[1]

This conventionally standardised waste at the hands of the conventionally accredited wasters is a sufficiently consequential handicap in itself, but the indirect consequences of it, in the direction it has given to popular tastes and the spread of like usages by imitation, are doubtless of graver consequence. As was noted above, the standard of living in the British community at large is higher than in the Continental countries and has on the whole been advancing throughout the modern period. This higher standard is in part a higher standard of physical comfort; it is frequently spoken of in terms implying that it is altogether of that character. Yet incidents of the order of the dog-feeding

---

[1] Of course, this wasteful expenditure is not rated as wasteful by the wasters, nor is the systematic diversion of wealth into these channels by the financial strategists so rated in popular apprehension. What may be called the economic theory of the vulgar on this head is well seen in the following pronouncement; which may or may not be veraciously reported, but which is none the less true to life:

" 'The foundations of our real society rest upon money, and it is only the workers who attain wealth.

" 'Take the Carnegies and Fricks, for instance,' continued Miss Morgan. 'They have enormous riches and it was amassed by prodigious labor. Those who work rule the destinies of the social as well as the business world. . . . Society and its ramifications depend upon the expenditure of money for their existence. Who have the necessary money to spend upon entertainments and the social functions that annually give employment to thousands of tradesmen? It is the men of money. Could the business world for one minute exist on the money that is placed in circulation by the thousands of men who compose the working element? By no means. Business is kept alive by the thousands of dollars that are spent by "high society." That is an item that statisticians would do well to investigate.' "

charities just mentioned are likely to raise a doubt. But it would be a work of graceless vexation to scrutinise the petty fopperies and uncouth dissipations of the British working classes with a view to appraise their economic value.

Certain facts of no questionable taste may, however, be brought in to point a comparison between British and Continental customs bearing on the industrial efficiency of the community at large. It has, *e.g.*, become improper, not to say immoral, for English women to do field work; whereas in Continental countries, and perhaps especially in German countries, women work in the fields without such a moral restraint. It is not a question of physical hardship; work in the fields being no more irksome and doubtless more wholesome than work indoors, as is borne out by the visible effects. The north-European population is by heredity no less an outdoor people than any other, perhaps more so than many others, and the women are as much affected by this heredity as the men. Various arguments are advanced for the "exemption" of women from outdoor work. So far as these arguments are fit to survive scrutiny they turn out to be considerations of conventional propriety. They appear to be of the nature of an impulsive imitation of that exemption of well-to-do women from all useful work, that constitutes one of the chief infirmities of the English social code and one of its chief exemplifications of the principle of conspicuous waste. The economic value of these reputable exemptions is considerable, both in that they directly lessen the available industrial force, and in that they indirectly lower efficiency by lowering the vitality of that portion of the population that comes under the rule.

The difficulty is traceable to the industrial efficiency of this community, which has been high enough to afford the waste, or at least to afford it in those upper, quasi-leisure-class circles where these exemptions appear first to have found a lodgment. In a community where class distinctions and class exemptions run chiefly on pecuniary ground, wasteful conventions spread with great facility through the body of the population by force of the emulative imitation of upper-class usage by the lower pecuniary classes; so that an exemption of this kind, which is an easy means of distinction among the well-to-do, will presently find its way among the indigent as a necessary mark of reputable living.

So also in the consumption of goods, much has come to be required as a matter of decency that was once a matter of superfluity, and these decencies, of apparel and household apparatus, *e.g.*, have come to be no less necessaries of life and included in the standard of living, than the requisites of physical comfort. There is visibly more of this mandatory expenditure on decencies, physically superfluous and commonly æsthetically obnoxious, among the working classes in the United Kingdom than on the Continent, and more than there was in the Island at any earlier date.[1] So, again,

---

[1] Adam Smith remarks, *e.g.*, that in his time shoes had become an article of everyday decency, included in the standard of living as a necessary item of expense, among the English working classes, although their Scottish congeners had not at that time come into the necessity of protecting their good fame by this means. The illustration is good in that it is typical, and the comparison will hold with the same force at present as between the Island and the Continent. Although the particular item of shoes is open to a specious objection, in that the modern technology has, incidentally, made shoes something of a physical necessity, — a change which has come on since Adam Smith's time. Metals, glass, brick, pottery,

as a last illustration of the growth of insidious inhibitions brought on by the growing efficiency of this modern industrial system, addiction to sport of one kind and another and preoccupation with sportsmanlike interests and values has spread from the levels of gentility down through the body of the population, until this category of dissipations has become almost the sole ground of common interest on which workingmen meet or hold opinions. It is safe to say that one-half the volume of printed matter daily put out for popular consumption is devoted to sports; a classification aiming to include all ramifications of the sporting interest would probably rate the proportion somewhat higher.

The mere, direct waste of time and substance involved in this ubiquitous addiction to sports and their adoration need perhaps stir no one's apprehension. That much of dissipation may nowise exceed the salutary minimum; though persons with a predilection for artistic and intellectual dissipations may be moved to deprecate addiction to dissipations of this crude and brutalising nature. What is more to the point here, however, is the fact that this preoccupation with the emulative and invidious interests of sportsmanship unavoidably has an industrially untoward effect on the temper of the population, bends them with an habitual bias in the direction of trivial emulative exploits and away from that ready discrimination in matters of fact that constitutes

---

stone and concrete pavements, and the like refractory substances, are so ubiquitous in modern life that the unprotected human foot is at a disadvantage. The resulting necessity of a hard and heavy protection for the feet, by the way, is a typical case of the systematic handicaps which this state of the industrial arts carries along as an unavoidable deduction from its gross efficiency.

the spiritual ground of modern technological proficiency. It is not so much that this pervasion of the British population by sportsmanlike preoccupations wastes the products and the energies of the industrial system, as that it perverts the sources from which the efficiency of the industrial system is to come. Its high consequence as a means of destruction lies in its burning the candle at both ends. Again it is to be noted that the generation and establishment of such a pervasive and stubborn habitual bent takes time, and that to get rid of it would also require time, stress and experience.

CHAPTER V

IMPERIAL GERMANY

As is true of the Elizabethan era in England, so the Imperial era in Germany can not be said to have begun abruptly at any specific date. It may defensibly be dated from the formation of the Zollverein, or from the North-German Confederation, or from the accession of William I (and Bismarck), or from the coronation at Versailles; at any rate a later date would not be acceptable. Its beginnings are to be sought earlier than the earliest of these dates, especially in so far as these beginnings are looked for in the material situation of the German peoples rather than in their diplomatic history; but in any case this modern period in German history lies this side of the Napoleonic era. The modern industrial and commercial situation begins seriously to affect the state of the German peoples only after that date, and even then it is only gradually that the Fatherland is drawn into this modern system of trade and industry to such an extent as to feel the exigencies of the new economic situation. It is toward the west that the new conditions first take visible effect, and it is apparently in commerce and the improvements in transportation that contact with the more advanced countries of the west first provoke movements of adjustment to the new state of things.

When Germany so comes into the complex of commercial and industrial Europe in the nineteenth century it is under the lead of the Prussian State, not under that of the south-German or Austrian peoples; and the lead of Prussia is wholly of a political character and is directed to political ends. Prussia contributed nothing else than a political (warlike) force and political ambitions. German cultural elements, other than warlike and political, come from the countries farther to the south and west. But this contribution from the Prussian side has been very consequential.

That the Prussian State so came into the hegemony in this Imperial era is of course neither an accident nor an afterthought of Providence. It has not unusually contented the German historians, and laymen, to ascribe the leadership of Prussia to the wisdom and other political virtues of the Hohenzollern, from the Great Elector, through Frederick the Great, to the present incumbent; just as those who incline to a romantic interpretation of history have also been content to find in Bismarck the chief cause of the eventual formation of the Empire on those practicable lines on which its great history has run. Doubtless the personal characteristics of these great figures of history have had much to do with the shaping of events, and the present state of the German nation owes much of its peculiar complexion to the work of these great men. Yet it is not precisely that the German peoples have been as wax in their hands, nor need it follow that the outcome would have been substantially different in any essential respect in the conceivable absence of these personages from the history of the past two centuries. In their absence their room would probably have been so nearly filled by convenient understudies that none but a very critical historical audience would have detected a false line or gesture. The greatness of these historic figures lies in their eminent fitness for the place into which they fell, each and several, in the unfolding of events. So great and unfailing is the degree of this fitness of each for his rôle, that the question unavoidably suggests itself: Did not the rôle create the personage out of commonplace plastic material, rather than the personage create the rôle? Seeing that the personages in question proved themselves quite commonplace in other bearings than those immediately involved in the action of the historical drama in which they played their part, and seeing that the conjuncture of events would scarcely have tolerated a different line of action in case the players had been quite commonplace also in those respects in which they are greatest.

It is true, there runs through this line of Prussian statesmen a certain characteristically callous disingenuousness, such as would in many another setting properly have been rated as of heroic stature; but then, the cordial and unqualified commendation of this trait in their typical statesmen argues that the Prussian community should have been able at any time to meet any reasonable demand for a supply of statesmen eminent in just this quality. In a way, this appears also to be a commonplace trait in the circles from which these great statesmen were drawn and on which they drew. One is induced to believe that this distinguishing trait of Prussian statecraft is a product of habituation, and so a trait of Prussian civilisation, rather than a peculiar obliquity occurring sporadically in a few extreme variants of that population. It would probably be putting the estimate too high to say that the supply of Bismarckian statesmen and Hohenzollern sovereigns possible to be drawn from the Junker population of Pomerania and Prussia is merely a special case of the Malthusian law of population, but at the same time such a view could scarcely be considered an unpardonable exaggeration. Prussian diplomacy and administration has never yet lacked for material of this nature, and at the same time the habitual bent shown in these personages whom the chance of history has thrown up into prominence is precisely what one expects to come out of the circumstances whose creatures these personages are.

Prussia came to take over the hegemony of the Empire, not because her statesmen were what they were, but because by long tradition and habit the Prussian community, or at least its ruling class, were of such a temper as was put in evidence by these statesmen; not because these personages were exceptions, but because they were not. This peculiar fitness and efficiency of Prussia for its place as the sovereign state of the Empire was given by the previous experience of the Prussian people, both in their political life and in that social life that underlay and made possible the political career of the Prussian State. It may have been a difference of degree, mainly, but there was enough of a difference between the Prussian North and the German South and West to decide that neither Austria nor Bavaria became the engineer, arbiter and pattern for Germany in the Imperial era.

Many a well-meaning apologist for the German people, since trouble and boundless odium have broken over that community, has been at pains to recall that Prussia is not Germany, and that the German spirit of the South especially, in the traditional seats of the characteristic German culture, is of a very different and more genial kind than that which animates the community of Junkers in the North; these Germans of the South and West, from Austria all across to the confines of the Low Countries, have, it is said by the apologists, in late-modern time and especially in the nineteenth century, shown an inclination to live and let live; or as seen from the higher habitual levels of Prussian efficiency, they have been a slack-twisted lot.

For an imperial State after the dynastic fashion, destiny had no other choice within the confines of the Fatherland. Had it, on the other hand, been a question of commercial hegemony on lines of peace and thrift alone, it is as unmistakably the South and West that must have been thrown into the foreground. However, speculation on such an impracticable might-have-been can have only a speculative interest. With Prussia in the ring a German Fatherland bound in solidarity by other connective tissue than blood and iron, and animated with other than dynastic ideals, was impracticable from the start.

While the kingdom of Prussia in the nineteenth century comprised much else than the original territories of Brandenburg, the Prussias and Pomerania, these territories still continued to be the substantial core of the Hohenzollern dynastic State. Although much of the material resources of the State were drawn from its later acquired and economically more valuable possessions to the west and south, the dynastic spirit of Prussia and its statesmen, as well as its more responsible personnel, was the spirit and personnel of the territories facing the Baltic littoral. By force of the Prussian rule, Prussian ideals in great measure came to permeate the other, outlying territories and peoples of the kingdom, and the center of diffusion of the peculiarly Prussian variant of German culture continued to be the Prussian-Baltic lands that had once constituted the original patrimony of the Prussian crown and the material foundation of its political power. By and large, Prussia was then, as it has after all continued to be since then, the ancient lands of the Baltic littoral, with more and more extensive territorial ramifications into the south and west; these ramifications being in effect subject and subsidiary territories, useful for the purposes of the dynasty, but contributory rather than participating members in the resultant dynastic State; they have only gradually and in an uncertain measure been outgrowing their status of stepchildren, and, it may perhaps be added, only in the measure in which they have gradually been trained into a share in the dynastic genius of the Prussian State. The process of assimilation has on the whole been pronouncedly one-sided, so that these outlying acquisitions of the kingdom have in great measure taken on the Prussian complexion, and not conversely. The like holds true in its degree for the rest of the German states since the period of their coalescence into an empire under Prussian hegemony.

The cultural pedigree of this Prussian community, therefore, becomes a matter of immediate interest to any inquiry into the work which this community has effected in the rehabilitation of the Fatherland. The official —

Almanach-de-Gotha — pedigree of its reigning house and its ruling families has, of course, no particular interest in this connection; these matters are at the most bubbles in the scum that marks the drift of the current. It is otherwise with that cultural pedigree of the community by consequence of which the reigning house and the ruling families are enabled to reign and rule after the particular fashion in which these matters are here conducted. That the Emperor and King rules by divine grace rather than by choice of his subjects is not due to any idiosyncrasy in the sovereign, nor does it come of any hereditary taint that might be conceived to incapacitate the German people for an exercise of discretion in these premises. With so much else that characterises the Prussian-German State, it comes of the peculiar line of habituation to which the German people, and particularly the communities toward the northern and eastern seaboard, have been subjected in the recent historical past.

Taking the term to apply in its larger sense, Prussia as a cultural area will comprise the German-speaking lands of the Baltic littoral from the Russian frontier to the general neighborhood of Lübeck, or perhaps to Kiel,[1] and extending irregularly inland to include whatever has felt the effects of occupation by the Teutonic Order. This stretch of country, especially eastward from the region of the Oder, is the youngest of the German lands; that is to say it is the portion of the Fatherland that comes last in the sequence of reduction to Christianity and German rule. It was made

---

[1] Cf. Meitzen, *Siedelung und Agrarwesen*, vol. ii. pp. 36–40 and Atlas, "Uebersichtskarte."

over into the pattern of feudalistic Christendom at a later date than the rest, later by some six or eight centuries than the more cultured lands of the South. The conquest of the Wendish, Lithuanian and Esthonian peoples by the Teutonic Order in the thirteenth century, and their reduction to Christianity, is the last great episode in the predatory settlement of the Fatherland by German-speaking invaders, and the immediate consequences of the invasion and settlement were of much the same character here as elsewhere. There followed a protracted period of ruthless exploitation, terror, disturbances, reprisals, servitude, and gradual habituation to settled allegiance, irresponsible personal rule, and peaceable repression.

The raid came at the time when the feudal system had reached its final development as a fighting organisation; and since the conditions, essentially predatory, which so were established in the lands reclaimed from paganism were favorable to continued exploitation on a predatory footing, the feudal spirit also continued in good vigor in this outlying region longer than elsewhere in Europe, and in a much better state of preservation. So soon as habituation to the servile state had induced in the subject population a passably stable spirit of allegiance to their noble masters,[1] so as to permit the forces of the community to be turned to account for external aggression, these countries, or rather the body of feudalistic squires in whom vested the usufruct of these lands and their population, made their entry into the po-

---

[1] This feudal allegiance was greatly helped out by the change of faith. By their conversion to Christianity the subject populace shortly acquired a sense of solidarity with their Christian masters.

litical concert of Europe in the service of the dynastic ambitions of the Hohenzollern. With the predatory animus and the servile allegiance of the feudal tradition still intact, and imbued with the spirit of chicane and effrontery that comes of a predatory settlement, this body took rank from the outset as a highly efficient engine of dynastic aggression. And in as much as this career of dynastic aggression has never ceased, and has seldom suffered protracted interruption since it first got under way, the discipline of everyday life has conserved in admirable preservation the range of habits of thought with which these peoples first entered on the stage of modern Europe. They are the best-preserved remnant of mediævalism in Europe of sufficient mass and commanding sufficient material resources to make them formidable in international politics.

At their first emergence on this stage, and with gradually lessening effect for a long time after, this community of squires and followers showed a troublesome spirit of insubordination under the leadership of their overlords; and, indeed, something of this brittle quality is still to be seen in the support which the agrarian squires accord the crown, — their support is still to be had only on conditions, only so long and far as the body of squires is persuaded that the crown is a consistent partisan of their particular material interests. They are the indispensable refuge and strength of the dynastic statesman, but they are also difficult and exacting. In the course of time, with continued discipline in following after dynastic ideals, working out the imperial destiny of the sovereign State and strengthening the powers of the crown, — all this consistent experience has greatly reduced the capricious particularism of the Junkers, and has in great part brought a sentimental loyalty to the State into the first place in their affections. The same course of discipline has, of course, given the same general drift among the people at large, whether in the Prussian territories or in the Empire.

The entrance of Prussia into modern Europe was a very different affair, in all its circumstances, from the fortunes of Elizabethan England and the subsequent incidents of English national life. Prussia came in with no cultural traits other than a mediæval militarism resting on a feudally servile agrarian system, and made its way forcibly as a political power of ever-increasing potency among an aggregation of small and feebly quarrelling neighbors. The new nation was surrounded on all sides by jealous and unscrupulous rivals, with whom it unavoidably, as well as by inclination, was constantly brought in contact in a ceaseless contest of dynastic chicane and predation; a situation which forever provoked the conversion of all available resources to political and warlike ends, and furthered the growth of a centralised and irresponsible autocracy, such as best comports with the pursuit of dynastic wars.

About the same time England, on the other hand, withdrew, or perhaps rather was forcibly withdrawn by circumstances, from the concert of nations, and confined to its island in enforced peace, with no reasonable chance for an aggressive national policy, and affording no chance of prolonged life for a dynastic State. So that while the Hohenzollern extended their dominion by war and diplomacy and increased their powers, the Stuarts went reluctantly down to final abnegation, and the dynastic State was replaced by a commonwealth in which royalty ceased to be anything but a pious legend and a decorative bill of expense. In the one case a feudalistic body of agrarian squires has continued, in spite of adverse economic circumstances, to be of decisive weight in national policy and to control the administrative machinery, while in the other the barons and feudalistic gentry, after a well-contested fight for peace, were supplanted by the spokesmen of business enterprise, whose interests dictated peace, industry and a qualified return to the rule of Live and let live.

Not that British popular sentiment and collective ambition has ever fully declined to the level of pecuniary quietism implied in this characterisation, nor that Prussianised Germany sees no end in life beyond the power of the State and the subservience of the subject, but the contrast so pointed between the two will hold after all, with due qualification. With due qualification it will hold that in the reflections of the British citizen the United Kingdom is conceived as a "commonwealth," while in the speculations of the German (Prussian) subject the Fatherland is a "State."

It is as difficult for the commonplace Englishman to understand what the German means by the "State" as it is for the German to comprehend the English conception of a "commonwealth," or very nearly so. The English still have the word "state" in their current vocabulary, because they once had the concept which it is designed to cover, but when they do not in current use confuse it with the notion of a commonwealth, as they commonly do in making it serve as a synonym for "nation," it is taken to designate an extensive tract of land; on the other hand, the Germans, having never had occasion for such a concept as that covered by the term "commonwealth," have no corresponding word in their vocabulary. The State is a matter not easily to be expounded in English. It is neither the territorial area, nor the population, nor the body of citizens or subjects, nor the aggregate wealth or traffic, nor the public administration, nor the government, nor the crown, nor the sovereign; yet in some sense it is all these matters, or rather all these are organs of the State. In some potent sense, the State is a personal entity, with rights and duties superior and anterior to those of the subjects, whether these latter be taken severally or collectively, in detail or in the aggregate or average. The citizen is a subject of the State. Under a commonwealth, as in the United Kingdom, the citizen is, in the ritual sense of heraldic rank, a subject of the king — whatever that may mean — but this relation of subjection is a personal relation, a relation of mutual rank between two persons. The terms to the relation are necessarily personal entities, and they enter into this relation only by virtue of their character as persons.

"The State is the people legally united as an independent power." So says one who speaks with authority in these premises. But then, also, "The State is in the first instance power, that it may maintain itself; it is not the totality of the people itself, — the people is not altogether amalgamated with it; but the State protects and embraces the life of the people, regulating it externally in all directions. On principle it does not ask how the people is disposed; it demands obedience." "The State is power," says the same authority, and "it is only the State that is really powerful that corresponds to our idea." It might perhaps exceed the scope of the premises to follow him farther and find that "power" here means "military power." Plainly, government by consent of the governed is not a State. The sovereignty is not in the people, but it is in the State. Failure to understand this conundrum is perhaps the most detestable trait of unreason that taints the English-speaking peoples, in the apprehension of intelligent Germans.

The German ideal of statesmanship is, accordingly, to make all the resources of the nation converge on military strength; just as the English ideal is, *per contra*, to keep the military power down to the indispensable minimum required to keep the peace. This personal — in English one is tempted to say quasi-personal — entity, impersonate perhaps in the sovereign as its avatar, is a conception and an ideal which the English-speaking peoples appear to have missed, through its not lying within the horizon of their materialistic and pecuniary cultural outlook; they appear to have lost it in losing the spiritual perspective peculiar to the mediæval mind. Rated in terms of the English cultural sequence, the conception would seem to be an archaism, an insight atrophied through disuse. It should seem also that it might be recovered in case the British nation should have the fortune to fall under the personal dominion of an autocratic prince, and so set up a dynastic State after the pattern preserved in the working constitution of Prussia.

The part played by this conception of the State in the rehabilitation of Germany is so considerable, and the difference it has made between the German scheme of right and honest living and that which prevails elsewhere, among the other contemporary branches of the north-European culture, is so characteristic and consequential that it should merit more detailed scrutiny, both as to its logical and sentimental contents and as regards its derivation and its bearing on the material fortunes of the race.

In point of its sentimental content, as regards the native propensities which find expression in this concept of the State, its chief ingredient is doubtless the ancient sense of group solidarity, expanded to take in a nation seen only in fancy, instead of the original neighborhood group known by personal contact and common gossip. This group solidarity is seen somewhat baldly at work in the small communities of the lower cultures and in the local pride and loyalty of neighborhoods and hamlets, clubs and congregations, among the more naive and commonplace elements of the civilised populations. It has been construed by the utilitarian philosophers, in their time, as a calculated outcome of material self-interest resorting to coöperation, — doubtless an inadequate if not groundless account of a propensity that is frequently seen to traverse the lines of self-interest. It would rather appear to be a native and indefeasible bias in the race. That such should be the case is all the more reasonable in view of the fact that men have always lived in groups, that the existence of the race has been continued only in and by group life. That enterprising individuals now and again successfully trade on this sentiment of solidarity for their own advantage gives no degree of support to the notion that it is a derivative of self-interest; rather the contrary.

But however jealous and self-complacent this sense of solidarity may show itself to be, under circumstances which provoke its expression along lines of invidious comparison and emulation, the recognition of this temperamental bent does not of itself carry us beyond the conception of a community or commonwealth. There are still lacking the elements of personality and unfolding power, which are essential to the concept of the State as distinct from that of a community. This is the more evident if it be kept in mind that the State may — perhaps rather typically does — unfold its power and assert its initiative apart from, beyond, or even in contravention of, any consensus on the part of the community. The bias of solidarity is an essential element, no doubt, but it is a solidarity subservient to an extraneous initiative; an initiative not necessarily alien to the spontaneous consensus of the group, but also not necessarily coincident with or germane to the ends of life comprised in the consensus of the community. In the ideal case — and the Prussian case visibly approaches this ideal — the consensus of the community will, at least passably, coincide with the drift of the State's initiative; and that it does so is a fortunate circumstance and an element of power in the State, but it is a matter of coincidence rather than an organic necessity. Where the popular consensus so comes to coincide with the line of the State's initiative and unfolding power, as in the Prussian case, it will commonly happen that this happy consummation is reached through the community's accepting the State's ends as its own, and also commonly without such knowledge of the State's ends in the case as would enable the community to take stock of them and appreciate what has been accepted or assented to. In other words, the coalescence of the community's consensus of interest with the State's ambitions is a coalescence by submission or abnegation, whereby the community lends itself, willingly and even enthusiastically, as a means to the State's realisation of its own higher ends.

With great uniformity, wherever such a conception of a State as an over-ruling personal — or quasi-personal — entity prevails and takes effect as a working ideal, the State is conceived as a monarchical establishment, — it is what has here been spoken of as a "dynastic State." It is, as in the Prussian case, an autocratic monarchy that is had in mind as the only practical realisation or incorporation of this ideal of a State; an absolute dynastic monarchy, "constitutional" by concession perhaps, but paramount and peremptory at need. The State is personalised in the person of the sovereign. And this sovereign or dynasty is not on a tenure of sufferance or good will. He does not hold his authority by gift of the community. If he did he would be only the spokesman and administrative servant of the community, and the State would so disappear in a commonwealth woven together out of expedient compromises between the several interests living together in the community. It seems doubtful if this working conception of the State can be formulated in concrete terms as anything else than or short of a dynastic monarchy, absolute at least in theory.

To cast back again into European prehistory for such dim light as may so be had on the elements of human nature that come in evidence in this current conception of the State:

In the petty communities, perhaps kingdoms, managed on a basis of neighborhood solidarity and administered somewhat anarchistically by force of a neighborly consensus, — in these quasi-anarchistic groups of remote Baltic antiquity the common understanding that made group life practicable appears to have been in effect the rule of Live and let live. Apart from their anarchistic scheme of administration there is only one institutional fact that is confidently, or rather unavoidably, to be imputed to these communities of the Old Order on the evidence that has come down, viz., the ownership of property. But the evidence of ownership under that archaic régime goes back so near to the beginning of things in the north-European culture — as it commonly does elsewhere also — that there is not much to be surmised of an earlier antiquity. There may also have been kings in that early time, — the evidence is of course not conclusive — but there can scarcely have been a State; an anarchistic State will easily be conceded to be a misnomer.

As has appeared in other passages of this inquiry,[1] this state of culture, dimly shown in the archæological evidence, has the sanction of natural law, in that it was seen and approved as viable by a longer series of generations than have lived since it disappeared. Such slight institutional furniture as it gives evidence of should be near-hand expressions of a native bent in the peoples concerned, and may be taken as a naive indication of what is indefeasibly right and good in the sight of these men. Among these time-tried institutions is the right of ownership, the secure

---

[1]See Note III, p. 302.

usufruct of what the owner may have achieved or acquired, under the rules of the game as approved by common consent. From some far-off point in the cultural sequence, again apparently in remote antiquity, inheritance has been a legitimate method of coming into such usufruct. All this still approves itself to the common sense of the common man today.

In later time, when this people came to deal with aliens in the way of raiding and conquest, what a man might achieve or acquire and transmit by inheritance came to include such booty and such dominion over a subject people as his fortune and initiative put him in the way of — always subject to the rules of the game as seen and approved by the community on whose consensus he leaned. Out of these predatory beginnings, legitimised by convention and settled by use and wont, presently came the feudal régime; and out of this in turn, by further working of the anarchistic principle of usufruct applicable to whatever one might achieve or acquire within the rules of the game, came the dynastic State. The principle of usufruct by right of ownership, which once applied to a subject community (originally of aliens), is in the dynastic State extended to cover the usufruct of a community which has by use and wont grown to feel itself at one with its masters and has come into authentic acceptance of a comprehensive servile status.

The ancient principle of ownership has by historical permutation taken such a turn as to vest the usufruct of the community at large in its dynastic head. And so long as the situation at large continues to be transfused with dynastic ambitions and chicane, so that the alternative effectively offered any community would be subservience to its home-bred dynastic head or to an alien dynasty, so long the dynastic State continues in force, backed as it is by the sense of group solidarity and not violating the principle of Live and let live in any greater degree than the only visible alternative to its rule, — subjection to another and alien power of the same complexion.

In the Prussian environment the conditions of national life have favored the conservation of this dynastic rule; whereas in England, placed as that nation has been in modern time, the dynastic conception has disintegrated under the wasting impact of the common man's native animus to Live and let live. The truth and beauty of a régime of dynastic usufruct is not realised in the absence of a suitable background of war and rapine. And one finds that the encomiasts of this régime habitually protest against any proposal to remove or soften this background.

Now it happens, perhaps as an accident involved in the historical sequence, perhaps due to a recrudescence of the ancient anarchistic bent, that in modern times the drift of sentiment sets in the direction of Live and let live, and discountenances all institutional establishments of a visibly servile order. Such is peculiarly the case in those communities, — like the French, English-speaking, Dutch and Scandinavian countries, — that have been most intimately engaged in the latterday technological and scientific achievements. Now, whether by force of arrogation or by drift of sober common sense, this same group of industrial nations have at the same time come to be accounted the leaders among civilised peoples, in so far as bears on the scheme of civil and political institutions. There is in fact an apparently well-advised, or at all events well-accepted, preconception lodged in the body of current common sense to the effect that slavery, servitude and the like subjection to the dictates of an irresponsible personal master, is a moral and æsthetic impossibility among civilised mankind; that such personal subservience is a relic of feudalistic barbarism and disappears irretrievably from among the usages and the ideals of any people so soon as they emerge upon the levels of latterday civilised life.

While this modernism apparently owes its rise and its vogue to the growth of opinion among the advanced industrial peoples and to its congruity with the scheme of peaceable industry to which these peoples are addicted, it has also imposed itself by force of example on the later comers among the peoples of Christendom, at least to the extent of a shamefaced formal acceptance. So massive and so ubiquitous is this persuasion of the shamefulness of servitude, that even in those instances where the dynastic State still stands intact as a practical effect, and has not yet come to be felt as an irksome or insufferable grievance, it will no longer do to display its character openly as an organisation of servitude based on subjection to the person of the dynastic head. When conceived in these bald terms of usufruct and submission, the uses of a dynastic establishment are seen to be of the same nature as the uses of a tapeworm; and the tapeworm's relation to his host is something not easy to beautify in words, or even to authenticate in such convincing fashion as will insure his affectionate retention on grounds of decorous use and wont.

However, by taking thought one may conserve the facts and save appearances. The dynastic establishment may be sublimated into a personalised collectivity of "the people legally united as an independent power." There is no obnoxious trait of servile subjection to an irresponsible personal master in the community's so taking collective action. This is what would be understood by a "commonwealth." But a community so constituted is not a State; it is more like a joint-stock company. Its personality must become something more than a figure of speech. If such a community is to be a power — to exercise that "will to power" that one hears of — the usufruct of the collective strength must be vested in a personal agent with plenary discretion; and the requisite efficiency and stability of initiative and discretion can be had only if this personal head is possessed of paramount authority, and in so far as his jurisdiction rests on a tenure independent of the ebb and flow of vulgar sentiment. The State must find "a local habitation and a name" in the person of a dynastic prince, in whom must vest the unqualified usufruct of the community's powers. So will the dynastic State be reinstated, in effect, unimpaired and unmitigated.

It is some such theoretical construction of a personalised collectivity that is held up to view in the expositions offered by the spokesmen of the Prussian State and its high destiny. But it is at the same time difficult to make out that the patriotic sentiments of the Prussian subject effectually center on anything more shadowy than the personal dynasty of the Hohenzollern and the personal ambitions of its head. With this feudalistic loyalty goes an enthusiastic sense of national solidarity and a self-complacent conviction of the superior merits of the views and usages current in the Fatherland — the "Culture" of Germany; but all that is not integral to the conception of the State. The dynastic State, of course, is a large element in the "Culture" of this people; very much as its repudiation is an integral feature of the cultural scheme accepted among English-speaking peoples. Indeed, there is little, if substantially anything, else in the way of incurable difference between the German and the English scheme of things than the discrepancy between this ideal of the dynastic State on the one hand and the preconception of popular autonomy on the other hand. The visible differences of principle in other bearings will commonly be found to be derivatives or ramifications of these incompatible sentiments on the head of personal government.

The resulting difference between British and German in respect of personal freedom and subordination is less a matter of practical conduct than of "principle"; although it will not be seriously questioned, because it has been proven by experiment, that British, or English-speaking, popular sentiment will eventually submit to much less provocation before taking recourse to concerted insubordination. The margin of tolerance in this respect is visibly narrower in the British case. Yet the point of equilibrium reached by each of the two peoples in their everyday conduct of affairs and in their practical attitude toward the constituted authorities is by no means widely different; although the one may be held to reach this equilibrium of working arrangements by concessive abatement of the demands of insubordination, while much the same practical outcome is reached from the other side by expedient mitigation of the claims of absolute tutelage and fealty. The English-speaking peoples are democratic, indeed anarchistically democratic, in principle, but by reason of common-sense expediency fortified by a pervading respect of persons — what is sometimes disrespectfully called flunkeyism — the effective degree of freedom enjoyed by the individual, as restrained by law and custom, is only moderately greater than that which falls to the lot of the German subject whose point of departure in the regulation of conduct would appear to be this same flunkeyism, dignified with a metaphysical nimbus and mitigated by common-sense expediency.

"Flunkeyism" has an odious sound in modern ears, but unfortunately there is no equally precise term available to cover the same range of sentiment without invidious implications; it is a fault of the current vocabulary. Both German and English-speaking peoples make much of personal liberty, as is the fashion in modern Christendom, but it would seem that in the German conception this liberty is freedom to give orders and freely to follow orders, while in the English conception it is rather an exemption from orders — a somewhat anarchistic habit of thought.

It was this dynastic power of the Prussian State, resting on an authentic tradition of personal fealty, unlimited in the last resort, that was the largest single factor of a cultural kind entering into the Imperial era from the German side. It is at least conceivable that in the course of time the protracted disintegrating impact of the discipline exercised by modern industrial habits would have brought this dynastic

State and its coercive organisation to much the same state of decay as that which once overtook its smaller and feebler counterpart in Elizabethan England. But the course of time has not had a chance to run in this Prussian case. Elizabethan England, and its soaring imperialistic aspirations, was exposed to the slow corrosion of peace and isolation, with the common interest converging more and more on the industrial arts and the fortunes of trade; and it took a hundred years and more to displace dynastic statecraft and eliminate imperialist politics — in so far as these elements of the ancient régime can be said to have been lost — and it took another two hundred years to reach the farthest point along the line of liberal policy and peaceable ideals eventually attained by the English community.

CHAPTER VI

THE INDUSTRIAL REVOLUTION
IN GERMANY

ECONOMIC policy as pursued by German statesmen at the time when the new industrial era opens — say, in the second quarter of the nineteenth century — is still of the cameralistic kind. This is true of the German States throughout, including Prussia and Austria with the rest, even if minor and transient excursions out of the cameralist circle of traditions had been made here and there, *e.g.*, by various German followers of Adam Smith. It follows from the political constitution and traditions of the German principalities, absolute and militarist, that in effect none but a cameralistic policy could be entertained.[1] The economic sit-

---

[1] The patriotic economists of that generation (middle of the nineteenth century) in Germany, and the publicists who reflect their views, prefer the designation "National Economy," rather than Cameralism, in speaking of the policies which they propose. It may be worth remark, parenthetically, that the professed economists of the time were chiefly concerned with formulations of policy, rather than with theoretical inquiry in any detached sense; their protestations against the system of political economy offered by the English (Classical) school of theorists run chiefly on the ground that the practical guidance afforded by the Classical formulations is of no service, has in fact no particular bearing, towards the building up of a national power, and "national" in this connection connotes a dynastic State organised for defense and offense and jealously guarding its frontiers.

The difference between the typical Cameralists of the eighteenth cen-

uation entered on a new epoch in industry and trade, and the statesmen of the Fatherland therefore entered on a campaign of economic policy directed to making the most of what the new system in trade and industry had to offer. In this new campaign the ideals of statecraft remain the same as ever, but the new ways and means to be taken account of unavoidably alter the outline of the policy to be pursued, without deflecting it from the ancient cameralistic aim of making the most of the nation's resources for the dynastic purposes of the State.

The economic history of the new era might well be written as a history of the economic policy of the Prussian State and the Prussianised Empire. Such a history would not be the political history of Imperial Germany, although it would also at no point lose sight of the political use and bearing of the phenomena of trade and industry with which it would be occupied. It would be an account of the material

---

tury and the "Nationalist," or Historical, economists of the nineteenth century is a difference not of principle and purpose so much as of the wider range of ways and means necessary to be considered by the later theorists occupied with the economic foundations and *agenda* of the State. The state of trade and industry had visibly changed from the earlier time, and the economic policy most conducive to the material power of the State would necessarily be of wider scope than what had seemed adequate in that earlier time. Mere fiscal measures of exploitation were no longer adequate to the best utilisation of a community with extensive commercial relations and a capitalised industrial system. Yet it remains true that the material interests of the State continue to hold the first place in German economics of the nineteenth century, and that fiscal considerations are given a weight and prominence, in all their systematic exposition, such as they never had among the English. Financial Science has continued to be the strongest line of economic theory among the Germans, and it goes on the premise, uniformly, that the interests of the State are paramount; the reverse is true of the English, particularly of the Classical school.

fortunes of a great industrial and commercial nation, whose industrial and commercial concerns have been under the regulative control of an interest centering on other than industrial and commercial ends, on ends lying beyond the material welfare of the community, and indeed beyond the fortunes of the community in any respect. This need not, at least conceivably, imply the pursuit of an economic policy inimical to the community's material welfare, — indeed it is part of the convictions of these statesmen that the material interests of the community are best conserved by such a policy that looks to the success of the State as its ulterior end; but it will necessarily follow that these material interests will be conceived in such fashion, with such incidents and restrictions, as may best serve the State's usufruct. It is, of course, not the intention to attempt such a history here, but only to recall the special circumstances under which the history of this era has been enacted and to indicate how these peculiar circumstances have affected the outcome.

Whether in peace or in war, that is to say whether as a business proposition or as a proposition in international politics, modern technology does not tolerate a minuscular State after the fashion of the German principalities, even after the fashion of them as they stood subsequent to the Napoleonic disturbance. This technology and the business community in whose usufruct the modern state of the industrial arts lives and moves is of an impersonal and cosmopolitan character. Personal idiosyncrasies, local traits and national frontiers are disserviceable rather than otherwise in all that concerns the life of trade and industry in modern times. So patent is the inhibitory effect of circumscription, whether on grounds of personal or class prerogative or on grounds of national segregation, that even the statesmen of these German principalities, whose segregation appears to have been the sole end of their existence, were reluctantly brought to realise the futility of trying to live in and by the modern economic system as industrially and commercially segregated communities. Concessively, with much reserve and by tardy expedients, the States that got their material means of life from the industry of the German people drew together into the Customs Union, presently after into the North-German Confederation, and finally into the Empire. The good effects of this move, in the way of heightened efficiency and therefore of material prosperity, are well enough known, and they have been shown with sufficient publicity and commendation by many writers competent to speak of such matters. The most striking item in the reform so wrought is the removal of tariff frontiers and similar interstitial obstacles to trade and communication.

This furtherance of trade and industry by the statesmen was almost wholly of a negative or permissive sort, in that it consisted in the removal of restrictions previously enforced; and the like continues to be true of the Imperial policy in trade and industry down to a late date in Bismarck's administration. The good effects are traceable to the removal of obstacles. Which suggests that a farther pursuit of the same policy should have had similarly good effects in increasing the efficiency of German industry, such, *e.g.*, as the total abolition of the frontier, in respect of economic regulations of all kinds. The retention of the frontier and the return to more of a mercantilist policy of tariffs and the like that presently followed, was a political expedient, an expedient for the good of the State rather than of the industrial community. The furtherance of the community's material prosperity simply, regardless of the dynastic advantage of the German State, would doubtless have dictated the practical abolition of the frontier and of all discrimination between German and non-German business and industry; just as the same consideration dictated the abolition of frontiers and discriminations of the same kind within the Empire.

The advantage to the German people, simply in the material respect, would have been of the same kind as was derived from the removal of similar restrictions within the country, and the gain should presumably have been as much greater from such a conceivable abolition of the Imperial frontier as this frontier was a greater fact than the detail frontiers which it displaced. But the Imperial frontier, as a means of obstructing trade, was the chief means of making the Empire a self-sufficing economic community, and therefore a self-balanced whole to be employed in the strategy of international politics. It is true, the country would have been better off, simply in point of material prosperity and in the rate of its economic progress, if no such barrier as the Imperial frontier had been kept up; but the immediate result would have been such a specialisation of industry and such a web of trade relations as would have left the community dependent for a large and indispensable part of its current consumption on foreign countries; from which it would follow that the Empire would be relatively vulnerable in case of war, at the same time that the community, the people, would be much more reluctant to go to war. Such a policy would, in other words, nowise comport with the strategy of dynastic politics, at least not as seen by statesmen of the school of Frederick the Great. Therefore the policy that has actually been pursued in this matter has been a policy of reasonable restriction and pressure, whereby a compromise has been effected between a free development of industrial efficiency and the development of a self-contained industrial community, all of whose forces could be directed to a given political (warlike) end and which could with the least hesitation take a hostile attitude toward other countries. In the later phases of its development, as the warlike ideals have come more into the foreground, the policy has more consistently been directed to placing the country in a defensible position, by creating a self-contained industrial community.

The main line of interference with or regulation of industrial affairs has been by way of a protective tariff. Like other tariff regulation this has been almost wholly inhibitive, of course. Aside from this, the chief directive work of the statesmen in this field has been concerned with the building of railways, largely with a view to military strategy, and the subsidising and surveillance of ship-building, also in good part for warlike purposes. But the more substantial fact is always the tariff. What might have come of the new industrial era in the absence of the Imperial frontier and its customs is a speculative question, of course, and can not be answered with any degree of confidence, but an indication of the shortcomings which the tariff has sought to remedy may after all be interesting as going to show the nature of the outcome from which the State's policy has preserved the German industrial situation.

As is well known, the Fatherland is not at all specially fortunate in natural resources of the class that count toward modern industry. As regards mineral resources Germany has a decided advantage in the one item of potash alone. The iron and coal deposits are well enough, but can by no means be counted as better than second best, in point of quality, location or abundance. Beyond this Germany does not count even as second best in any of the natural resources on which the modern industry draws. Forests and fisheries are not exactly negligible, but they are also not of great consequence; the soil varies from good to bad, what there is of it, but there is not enough to support nearly the whole population without somewhat drastically forcing industry from other fields to an intensive cultivation — more intensive than would be an attractive business proposition under free trade in agricultural products. The shipping facilities, harbors and natural waterways, are also to be classed as inadequate by comparison with other commercial countries. The one large asset in the way of natural resources is an industrious, healthy and intelligent population; in this respect Germany was, on the whole, better off when the new era set in than any of the neighboring countries except France, together with the smaller nations of the class of Belgium.

In the conceivable case that the new era in trade and industry could have been left unregulated by State authority for State ends, it is fairly to be presumed that the outlines of the resulting situation would not even approximately have coincided with what has actually come to pass. In the first place, or rather as a preliminary admission, it may be remarked that the net aggregate efficiency of the industrial community, as well as its rate of gain in efficiency and consequent volume of output, would doubtless have been very appreciably larger — barring Providential intervention — and that the distribution of this gain among the population would presumably have been somewhat more equable. Agricultural production, and perhaps especially the production of meat and dairy produce, would have been relatively smaller, perhaps absolutely smaller; whereas the imports under this head would have notably increased. This would have been accompanied by a perceptibly lower cost of the necessaries and a better nourishment of the industrial classes, which might be counted on to bring a higher coefficient of increase in the population, together with a slightly longer average life and a higher efficiency per capita.

A further immediate consequence of the lessened home production in agriculture would be an increase in the oversea import of foodstuffs; resulting in an increase of the shipping industry, and presumably inducing some slight but continuous emigration in connection with this carrying trade and with the extension of agriculture in the countries from which these imports would be drawn. Something of this latter kind is already visible in connection with the oversea trade with both North and South America. With the added impetus given by such an enlarged over-sea trade as would result under a free-trade policy, the German emigration of this inconspicuous kind might fairly be expected to result in an effectual colonisation in more than one of these countries; one gets the impression that as things actually have run the German emigration has barely fallen short of the mass and consistency required to make effectual German colonies in Brazil, Argentine and the United States.[1]

Under a free-trade policy both the coal and the iron of Germany would have been worked, but to a less extent than has been the case. A larger proportion of these materials than at present would have been imported, and this should logically have amounted to a very appreciably larger absolute volume than the present imports. Consequently the industries that work up the raw and half-wrought materials into the fully wrought and merchantable goods should have correspondingly increased, involving in their growth an extension and further improvement of the transportation system, both internal and over-sea, required to take care of the increased volume of traffic. German industry would presumably have gone farther in the production of wrought goods, and would consequently have been bound

---

[1]Such German colonies would, of course, have but a slight dynastic value, if any; unless they might, conceivably, reach such a magnitude and retain so large a measure of loyalty to the crown as would lead to their secession from the national government under whose auspices they had grown up and to their voluntary affiliation as colonies of the Empire. Such an outcome would scarcely be presumed, since the pecuniary cost of loyalty to the Empire is notoriously high and its pecuniary advantage somewhat dubious. Nor does the alacrity with which German subjects who settle abroad seek shelter under some other — one might incline to say any other — flag than the German at all suggest that such a colony would willingly thrust itself in under the heavy hand of the Imperial State.

in more extensive and indispensable trade relations than at present; which, as an incidental result, would have made a breach of the peace by Germany or with Germany nearly impossible, since the dependence of the German people on foreign markets in such a case would involve as its counterfoil the like dependence of the other parties to the traffic on the German markets. The resulting situation in the general goods market would presumably have been something like what has recently come into view in the German-American trade in dye-stuffs on the one side and cotton on the other. Another secondary consequence of some magnitude would have been the absence of plausible grounds for an exorbitant military and naval establishment to keep a peace not intended to be broken. There are, however, a number of subsidiary considerations and secondary consequences of too speculative a character for detailed enumeration here, some of which will come in sight in the further discussion.

In the course actually taken by events in the new era the national frontier has always been a large factor, in many connections one of the chief determining factors. The most telling and most obvious way in which the question of the frontier comes into the case in the earlier phases of the Imperial era is the relative freedom within this enlarged national territory, — virtual free trade over a relatively large extent of country. Under the rule of Bismarck there was moreover a visible drift in the direction, not of absolute free trade in international relations, perhaps, but at least toward a greater freedom, somewhat after the British fashion. This policy, never very pronounced in practice, fell

quietly into abeyance following the retirement of that statesman; the new spirit of a larger and more militant *Welt-
politik* drew the economic policy of the Empire more and
more towards a position of self-dependence by exclusion,
incidentally heightening the alienation of sentiment, as
well as of interest, between the German people and their
neighbors. The trade policy pursued under the present
reign has had its substantial share in the growing antag-
onism between Germany and the other industrial nations,
perhaps a share no less considerable than that borne by the
increasingly ostentatious militarism of the same period. This
trade policy has been of a singularly mercantilistic kind,
aiming at the illusory ideal of a one-sided trade in exports.

A side issue of this trade policy, fortified also by visions
of imperialistic magnitude, has been the colonial policy of
the Empire since Bismarck's retirement. By the acquisition of colonies, it has been hoped the raw materials of industry could in great part, perhaps in the end exclusively,
be drawn from these dependencies; so making the Empire
independent of foreign nations for its supply of the materials of its industry, at the same time that the same colonies would afford a market for wrought goods. The aim
has been to achieve an industrially self-contained imperial
State. This traffic in colonial enterprise is one of the less
flattering and less profitable chapters of Imperial policy,
the dynastic statesmen of the Fatherland having been unable to assimilate the lesson learned by the English on this
head, — that a colony can not serve as a dynastic domain
and at the same time make its way as an industrial community and a participant in the world's commerce. The Ger-

man colonies have consequently been dependencies of the Empire instead of being, after the English fashion, ramifications of the German industrial community. So far as the German economic community has effectively put out such ramifications they have insinuated themselves, without too much concerted effort, along the ways of trade and industry in lands not subject to German rule.

What has been said above would seem to imply that the material success of the German people during the Imperial era has been achieved not by furtherance of the Imperial State but in spite of it. There is a modicum of truth in such a view, but there is doubtless much to be set down on the other side of the account. The more closely the dealings of the Imperial government with the country's economic concerns are scrutinised the more obvious becomes the obstructive character of its policy, and the more obscure and elusive will the benefits appear which it is currently claimed to have conferred in any of its endeavors to regulate, guide and foster the material interests of the country. Yet there is a substantial body of economic gains, subsidiary but none the less consequential, to be set down to the credit of this obscurer bearing of the Imperial policies on the country's material welfare, as it is hoped may presently appear.

In many accounts current of German economic achievement during the Imperial era much is made of the handicap under which the German people came into the concert of industrial communities in the nineteenth century. This handicap is doubtless substantial enough, and it has also been made sufficiently notorious by the various relations of these events, and there is therefore no need of recalling that side of the case here. This handicap is made up of the several difficulties that beset the newcomer who goes to work with scant means and slight experience.[1]

The chief difficulty so to be surmounted is commonly held to be the want of capital, understanding by that term funds available for investment. Such funds were not precisely wanting in the German case; nor were they, on the other hand, to be had in abundance on easy terms. The habit of investment in industrial enterprise was also wanting, though such a habit seems to have been readily acquired; at the same time the banking facilities needed appear also to have been readily found, so soon as the business situation called for a more extended recourse to the use of credit served by institutions of this class.[2]

---

[1]Even so competent an observer as Professor Sombart (*Die deutsche Volkswirtschaft im XIX. Jahrhundert*, bk. ii.) sees and expounds this side of the case somewhat to the neglect of the advantages given by the same state of things. It is altogether the common view and is fertile ground for admiration (doubtless deserved) of the German achievement, as well as for some self-complacency and "racial" esteem on the part of the spokesmen of Germanism. Cf., *e.g.*, W. H. Dawson, *Evolution of Modern Germany*, which has the distinction of having been somewhat extensively transcribed (without credit and therefore with unqualified approval) by a man eminent in the Imperial Diplomatic Service; so also, *e.g.*, E. D. Howard, *The Cause and Extent of the Recent Industrial Progress of Germany*. Of all studies on the modern economic era in Germany, Sombart's survey, cited above, is doubtless the most valuable to the student of this period.

[2]Any historical survey of a commercial or industrial epoch will suffice to show that the installation of adequate banking and similar financiering concerns is among the features of the case that may be taken for granted. They are much in the public eye and exercise a large discretion in detail, and so they commonly hold the attention, especially of persons readily impressed by statistics of trade, and come to be rated high as agencies of industrial growth.

A difficulty of a greater and more obstinate kind is the lack of experience or of knowledge in industrial matters, and the presence of such customs and legal rights as will hinder the free use of new-found ways and means. Difficulties of this class there were in the German case, and much of the retardation seen in the early half of the century is to be set down to the account of legal and customary obstacles which the German people were gradually getting rid of, between the Napoleonic era and the date of the formation of the Empire. During the same interval the necessary information was also being gathered, less by tedious experience than by imitative acquisition from British sources.

The necessary technological proficiency was of a kind to be readily acquired; much more so than the corresponding technological proficiency acquired by the English in Tudor times by borrowing from the Continent. In this earlier English case what had to be borrowed and assimilated was not only a theoretical knowledge and practical insight into the industrial arts to be so taken over, but a personal habituation and the acquisition of manual skill on the part of the workmen employed; a matter that requires not only insight but long continued training of large numbers of individuals, — apprenticeship, as is well known, used to run from five to seven years, and the training of the workman did not close with his apprenticeship. A favorite method of introducing new industrial arts under the handicraft system was to import the trained workmen, and one of the substantial services rendered the English commonwealth by the warring princes of the Continent was their driving skilled workmen into exile to England.

The machine technology which the Germans borrowed in the nineteenth century is a different affair in respect of the demands which it makes on the capacities and attention of the community into which it is introduced. It is primarily an affair of theoretical knowledge, backed by such practical insight into its working conditions as may be necessary to the installation of the mechanical equipment. In all this there is little of an obscure, abstruse or difficult kind, except for such detailed working out of technological applications of theory as call for the attention of expert specialists. The machine industry runs on certain broad propositions that are simple in themselves and have a very wide application in detail processes, so that it lends itself to oversight and control by a relatively few experts. The workmen employed need commonly not be specially trained, in any corresponding degree. The special training required for service as operative workmen in the common run of the machine industries is very greatly less than the corresponding training required to make an equally competent workman under the handicraft system. General information and manual dexterity, together with some, relatively slight, special habituation to the particular processes involved in the given mechanical occupation, is all that is needed in this way to make a very passable working force in the machine industry.[1]

---

[1]Much has been said, commonly in an acrimonious tone, of the extremely mechanistic, monotonous, and stupid nature of the part taken by the common workman in the machine industry. Not infrequently these invectives reflect a degree of ignorance on the part of the speakers, and the invective doubtless often runs near the limit of tolerance in overstatement, but after all due allowance for exaggeration there still remains

To appreciate the character and magnitude of the German achievement, and the rate of their progress, it is necessary to recognise the nature of what they borrowed in this modern state of the industrial arts. The premises and logic of this machine technology are not of such a nature as to offer any serious difficulty in themselves. Their acquirement, in essentials, is a sufficiently simple matter. It all, in its elements, calls for no profound or occult insight, no reach of shrewd wisdom and cunning, no exploit of faith or of poetic vision, no stretch of imagination or of ascetic contemplation. It is, indeed, the most commonplace achievement of the human race, and its premises and logic are patent to the meanest understanding at the first contact. Much of it, so much of it as makes the foundation and point of departure for the whole, is unavoidably and indispensably familiar to the common man in all his commonplace dealings with the commonest inanimate objects that surround him. Its point of departure and its scope and method are summed up in the phrase, "matter of fact."

The epoch-making intellectual achievement of the English technologists and their like, who prepared the Industrial Revolution and have afterward worked out its consequences in technology and the material sciences, is not so much that they gained a new manner of insight into the nature and working of material things, as that they were, by force of circumstances, enabled to forget much of what was known before their time; by atrophy of the habitual bent for imputing anthropomorphic qualities and characters

---

the fact of a very substantial difference in this respect between handicraft and the machine industry, such as is claimed above.

to the things they saw, they were enabled to interpret these things in terms of matter of fact. Circumstances, the chief of which appears to have been the decay of personal government consequent on the decay of dynastic enterprise, weakened the inveterate habit received from the past of construing material phenomena in occult, magical, quasi-personal, spiritual terms. This habitual imputation of spiritual potencies and correlations among material facts had fallen into abeyance in the Island sooner and farther than on the Continent, and the curious ones among its inhabitants therefore fell more readily than their Continental neighbors into the prosaic habit of taking these external things at their face value, as opaque matter of fact, and so construing them and their movements in terms of (relatively) unsophisticated sense perception, without metaphysical afterthought, or with a negligible residue of such afterthought.[1]

In their elements, therefore, the premises and logic of the machine technology are in every man's mind, although they may often be overlaid with a practically impermeable crust of habits of thought of a different and alien sort. This does not mean that everyone, or any community, is ready forthwith to evolve the working technology of the machine industry out of his inner consciousness, provided only that no one interferes with his cogitations. Even given the premises and the logical insight, there is a large field of empirical, matter-of-fact knowledge to be covered under the working-out of these premises; and this can be had only at the cost of large and long experience and experimentation;

---

[1]Cf. *The Instinct of Workmanship*, ch. ii. iii. vi. vii.

for the details of this knowledge are of the "opaque" nature of all empirical, particularly physical, information, and are to be had only by the narrow channel of sense perception. Even when and in so far as one is freed from superincumbent preconceptions of an alien sort, the necessity of acquiring this material content by slow degrees and by trial and error still remains; and it was this slow process of finding out the opaque matters of fact that make up the material of technological science that occupied several generations of the British before the Germans took over any appreciable portion of it. The first acquisition of this material knowledge is necessarily a slow work of trial and error, but it can be held and transmitted in definite and unequivocal shape, and the acquisition of it by such transfer is no laborious or uncertain matter.

It follows from this state of the case that no great difficulty need be experienced and no great interval of time need be consumed in assimilating the working elements of this technology when once they are presented. What is required to a sufficient understanding and an intelligent employment of the appliances and processes of the machine industry is nothing more recondite than a certain body of matter-of-fact information as to the physical behavior of certain material objects under given conditions. The details, all told, of course are sufficiently numerous and complex, and no man may hope to master the whole range of information that enters in the working of the system as a whole, but the system is after all the most matter-of-fact organisation of knowledge extant. It can therefore be taken over with extreme facility by any community whose cir-

cumstances otherwise are suitable to the employment of
those mechanical appliances and processes which it offers.

The German people, by native gift, were endowed with
the kind and degree of intelligence required, being in this
respect on identically the same footing with those British,
and other, communities which had worked out this modern
state of the industrial arts. They had at the same time, in
their educated classes, all the intellectual habituation necessary to its ready acquisition, and in their working classes a
sufficiently well-instructed force of operative workmen. So
that the rate at which they could attain proficiency in the
new industry was little else than a question of how fast and
far their circumstances would admit its use. The rate of its
introduction and expansion, therefore, became largely a
question of the enterprise of those who had the discretion
in matters of business and industry, which resolves itself
into a question of the pecuniary inducement and of their insight into the opportunities offered by this new industry.

In these matters the German community was peculiarly
well placed. The classes who were in a position to profit
from these new ventures were accustomed by tradition to a
relatively low return on similar industrial enterprises under
the earlier régime, and so a given rate of remuneration
would appeal more strongly to them than to a business community accustomed to larger returns; the natural resources
to be made use of, having been lying relatively idle, were
to be had at relatively slight cost; a supply of competent
workmen could be had at very reasonable wages; and last
but by no means least, the break with an earlier and tradi-

tional situation in trade and industry left German enterprise hampered with fewer conventional restrictions and less obsolescent equipment and organisation on its hands than the corresponding agencies of retardation in any of the contemporary English-speaking countries. This last count in the schedule of German advantages should be sufficiently evident as against the moss-grown situation of trade and industry in contemporary England, — as has already been indicated in an earlier passage. It may be less evident, perhaps less applicable, and may even be questioned, as concerns the American community, — which stands as the foremost of the outlying English-speaking countries. Americans whose vision is in any degree blurred with patriotic sentiment will, of course, repudiate such an aspersion on their vaunted spirit of business enterprise, but a dispassionate view of the relevant facts may be relied on to allow the claim as made.[1]

The German captains of industry who came to take the discretionary management in the new era were fortunate enough not to have matriculated from the training school of a country town based on a retail business in speculative real estate and political jobbery managed under the rule of "prehension, division and silence." They came under the selective test for fitness in the aggressive conduct of industrial enterprise, not under that of making good as prehensile conservatives in a distribution of pecuniary flotsam. The country being at the same time in the main — indeed, with only negligible local exceptions — not committed to anti-

---

[1] See Note IV, p. 332.

quated sites and routes for its industrial plant; the men who
exercised the discretion were free to choose, with an eye
single to the mechanical expediency of locations for the
pursuit of industry. Having no obsolescent equipment and
no out-of-date trade connections to cloud the issue, they
were also free to take over the processes of the new industry
at their best and highest efficiency, rather than content
themselves with compromises between the best equipment
known and what used to be the best a few years or a few
decades ago. So also in the financiering of the new ventures, since the aim was not so much to get something for
nothing by a financial shuffle as to find the pecuniary means
necessary for equipment and working capital for the production of merchantable goods and services, the road was
relatively plain, with virtually no necessary recourse to the
recondite and devious ways of the impecunious company-
promoter who aims to produce merchantable corporation
securities. Not that the company-promoter was out of sight
in the German community in the days when the French
milliards were in sight; but there remains after all relatively little waste or dissipation of means to be written off
the German account for astute financiering designed to divert funds from industry to the strategists of conservative
chicane.

These German adventurers in the field of business, being
captains of industry rather than of finance, were also free
to choose their associates and staff with a view to their industrial insight and capacity rather than their astuteness in
ambushing the community's loose change. And of suitable
men to choose from, men with a capacity for work, not

gone to seed in street-corner politics, and with sufficient educational qualifications and an interest in the new industrial perspective, — of such there was also no lack, for the German community was well supplied with educated men glad to find employment in some conventionally blameless occupation.

For want of means suitable to more drastic forms of dissipation, learning had long been a chief resort of young men with time and energy to spend; and since commonplace mercantile pursuits were conventionally somewhat beneath the dignity of a gentleman, as was also commonplace manual labor, and since the respectable callings of the civil service, clergy and university instruction were already crowded to the point of the subsistence minimum; this supply of scholarly young men flowed readily into the new channel so opened to them, in which a relatively lucrative, visibly serviceable, and not positively disreputable chance of work was offered. So soon as this drift of young men into the industrial field had once set in it directly served as its own legitimation; it gave a degree of pecuniary authentication to those who successfully followed the new pursuit, and its popularity served of itself to make it fashionable. The responsible staff and corps in these industries, being men who had come through the schools instead of through the country store and the pettifogger's law office, were not incapable of appreciating that range of theoretical and technical knowledge that is indispensable to the efficient conduct of modern industry; and so the German industrial community was as surely and unresistingly drawn in under the rule of the technological expert as the American at about the same period was drawn in under the rule of the financial strategist.

These subalterns, as well as the discretionary heads of the several industrial ventures, had been accustomed to a relatively frugal way of living and a relatively parsimonious income, for the whole German community was by tradition in consistently impecunious circumstances and in a parsimonious frame of mind. The deductions from gross earnings on account of salaries and current perquisites of management were consequently small, as compared with what was current practice in the older industrial communities, or even with what has gradually come to be the practice in the Fatherland in the course of prosperous years.

So also as regards the disposable labor supply, which was of abundant quantity and of good quality, both physically and intellectually, and which had moreover the merit of a ready pliability under authority and was well trained to an impecuniously frugal standard of living, — cheap, capable and abundant. This labor supply was also not in any appreciable degree made up of a "depauperate" population of that congenitally ineffectual kind — undersized, anæmic, shriveled and wry-grown — that bulks so large in the English industrial towns, as the outcome of that country's first hundred years of competitive business enterprise under the régime of the machine process.

This, too, has changed perceptibly in some respects since the beginning; the standard of living has advanced, though not to equal that of the English-speaking countries; and the workmen have at the same time grown difficult and discontented in some degree, but not after the refractory fashion in which they have tried the patience and narrowed the gains of their capitalist-employers in these other countries.

Working-class traditions, and indeed middle-class traditions, too, have rather favored the useful employment of women in manual occupations in the German past, and this tradition of usage stands over still in good preservation; though here again there are symptoms at least of a drift into the same general attitude of a conventionally reputable exemption or exclusion of women from manual employment, particularly from manual labor in the open. Not much loss has yet been sustained by the German community from this source of impairment; the German women, e.g., still continue to work in the fields and have not yet acquired much of a putatively inferior physical capacity, nor do they, apparently, suffer in a correspondingly increased degree from the diseases of idleness. It is perhaps unnecessary to remark that all this, of course, does not apply to the women of the well-to-do, who appear to be nearly as infirm (conventionally) as the best usage would dictate.

From the outset, and through much of the unsophisticated later course of this industrial era, both the men in charge and the body of workmen appear to have taken a lively interest in industrial, perhaps especially technological, concerns of all kinds; one consequence of this naive attitude toward their work being that they have had no crying need of systematic diversion, in the way of sports, cabals, sensational newspapers, drunkenness, political campaigns, religious dissension, and the like. Also, from the same cause, the relative absence of ennui, there was not the same need of vacations and occasional holidays as in those more mature industrial communities where industrial concerns and technological information have grown stale in men's taste from long familiarity and conventional irksomeness; and on the same ground working hours could profitably be longer, so long as the work had not entirely lost its appeal to men's curiosity and its attraction as an unfolding of workmanlike mastery. Diversions and dissipation extraneous to their workday interests are not greatly required to keep men in humor and out of nervous disorders so long as their workday occupation continues to hold their curiosity and consequently their interested attention; and the loss of appetite for information and of speculations on matter that appeals so directly to men's curiosity as the range of applied science called the machine technology is in good part due to fashion, and so requires to be propagated by imitation and borne up by the introduction of some satisfactory substitute interest; all of which takes time.

But in the nature of the case a substitute will eventually be found. Any community that lives by commercialised industry necessarily comes under the paramount jurisdiction of the price system, in all that touches its canons of propriety; a partial and transient exception may be made in favor of a religious or military hierarchical scheme of rank, but such exception is only partial and likely to be transient, at the same time that it does not traverse the award of the price system at the point here in question. And the price system quite unambiguously decides that no interest or habitual frame of mind of such an overtly serviceable and economical nature as this sentimental addiction to workmanship can long continue to be of good repute in a community given to pecuniary ideals, since it traverses the plain principle of conspicuous waste. It is only a question of how soon it will be found out, and how soon an adequate substitute, not obnoxious to that principle, can be found and worked into tenable shape. The common resort is some form of sport, some form of dissipation that is expensive and unprofitable at the same time that it will bear a plausible appearance of "something doing," such as will not leave the sense of workmanship instantly nauseated with its futility.

As has been remarked in an earlier passage, in England the addiction to sports, though in the main vicariously, is an inveterate habit and permeates the community in a degree fairly incredible to any German who may be unfamiliar with English everyday life. This addiction runs back to a date before the coming-in of the machine industry, although it is plainly more of a universal institution now than ever before. It has grown to its present pitch and ubiquity only gradually, although it has long been a serious abatement on British industrial efficiency, both in that it involves a futile expenditure of time and substance and in that it habitually occupies men's minds with matters that are worse than useless for the purposes of industry. It is fairly encrusted with reputability, however, being quite useless at the same time that it makes a sufficiently specious show of achievement and has also the countenance of the highest gentility. In the course of their brief experience under the paramount price system the Germans, too, have been elbowing their way into the circle of sportsmanlike observances, in a tentative and heavy-handed fashion, but in this as in their ingrained parsi-

mony they have much to overcome before they can hope
to take rank with the better sort among the peoples of the
pecuniary civilisation.

At least in its current phase, in the phase of it to which
the German people have fallen heir, the modern state of
the industrial arts is bound up with its administration by
business methods and by business men. This means that,
very presently, in any community that takes over this system of technology, the industrial system will be taken over
by the business interests and managed with an eye single
to the business men's pecuniary gain. Whereas, at the outset, the business management at least appears to be in the
service of industrial enterprise, the inevitable outcome is a
reversal of that relation; so that industry becomes a means
to business, and in the end comes to figure in practical management as an adventitious matter that waits on the exigencies of financial strategy.

This financial strategy is directed to getting the largest
net gain obtainable for the strategists, which may or may
not coincide with the line of management that would add
the largest net increase to the community's material wealth
or productive efficiency. In the early phases of the German
development the connection between the business men's gain
and the output of merchantable product was fairly simple
and direct — with such exception as may have to be allowed
for even here; but as time passes and the situation gets into
that maturer phase that prevails in the English-speaking
countries, where the business of financiering industrial corporations has become a distinct branch of traffic, this con-

nection grows less direct and consistent, until it becomes quite remote and wholly doubtful. In such a case a slackening off or stoppage of industry will easily arise out of the conservative management of the financial houses endeavoring to conserve their funded wealth — wealth as reckoned in money units — but with the effect of stopping or reducing the community's production of material wealth — wealth as reckoned by weight and tale — and so leaving the community poorer day by day as time goes on. Experiences of that class have, of course, been had in Imperial Germany; they are the necessary accompaniment of a businesslike management of industry; but, through the earlier phases especially, while Germany was in course of adopting the modern industrial system, experiences of that class were relatively less considerable, since the business men were occupied with meeting and directing the growing need of industrial equipment, and looked for their gains to come from the increasing merchantable output.

What was of particular effect in this direction was the wide margin on which industrial business in Germany was able to proceed, a margin between a fair price in a ready market on the one hand and a low cost and short supply on the other hand. Such was the situation in the earlier phases of the development, and such has continued to be the situation in an unremittingly decreasing degree as German industry has approached the conditions that prevail in respect of cost and markets among its commercial rivals. The margin has narrowed and grown precarious, become subject to doubts and fluctuations, partly because the ready markets have been invaded by competitors, partly because factory and selling costs have been increasing, and partly because the financiering costs have increased.

One of the elements in the decline of the market for industrial products has been the falling off in the home demand for increased equipment. This has quite evidently not been a falling off in the absolute magnitude of the requirements of new plant and facilities, including such concomitants as new habitations and apparatus of living for the industrial population, and the like; in absolute figures this demand shows no decrease, but relatively to the aggregate output of German industry at the earlier and later dates it would not be difficult to show that this division of the home market has suffered a shrinkage.

It is also a matter of course that the effective growth of the foreign market has not kept pace with the growing productive capacity. This is a matter of common notoriety and has had solicitous attention both from the German statesmen and from the various boards of trade. It is one of the motives alleged for the colonial policy adopted in the later half of Bismarck's administration and pushed with more determination under his successors. It may seem singular to anyone acquainted with the facts in the case that such a colonial project should have been seriously entertained for such a purpose, but it is also impossible to avoid giving some credence to the solemn allegations of these men that the quest of markets has been one of the leading incentives to this colonial policy. It is fairly to be presumed that no man would lay claim to such folly without believing himself entitled to the stultification, least of all men of such solemn self-complacency as the Prussian-Imperial statesmen.

A more substantial and at the same time a more stubborn difficulty that has grown with the growth of German industry has been a rising cost of production, which set in in a small way not long after the new era had got under way and has been gaining cumulatively ever since, — as indeed it will necessarily have to gain still further so long as the same factors continue active in the further unfolding of the situation. In some small part this increasing cost of production is of a factitious nature, in so far as it is an effect of capitalisation rather than of physical expenditure of resources or physical deterioration; but it is none the less effectual in that the capitalisation in question becomes an integral part of the conditions under which the financing of the industrial ventures is conducted. In Germany, as elsewhere, natural resources as well as differential advantages of location and differential benefits of legal exemption, subsidy, and tariff-made monopoly, have to some extent been capitalised on the basis of the prospective gains to be derived from these useful assets. And being so capitalised they have been made the basis of business ratings, and so of credit extensions, and have come to figure among the assets on which standard rates of earnings are due. Such is more particularly the case where assets of this class have been drawn into the capitalisation of corporations and have thereby become the basis of fixed charges due to be paid out of gross earnings. This process of capitalisation of differential advantages within the community, with the accompanying burden of fixed charges, has gone forward gradually and cumulatively. It is an unavoidable consequence, or rather a concomitant, of a businesslike management of industry, particularly where an extensive use is made of credit and corporate capitalisation, and it necessarily grows with the passage of time and the development of the capitalistic system.

At the same time, and unavoidably because it is intrinsic to the growth of the industrial system, these differential advantages of location and the like have in part begun to depreciate through obsolescence, so that they no longer have as high a value in point of earning-capacity as was imputed to them in the process of capitalisation; whereby an unfavorable discrepancy arises between the fixed charges which these items carry, or which the given business concern carries on the strength of its possessing these assets, and the earnings which come from their possession.

This obsolescence, as has been noted in an earlier passage, need not be of the nature of physical deterioration, or even of supersession by improved technological devices; but comes simply of the fact that the industrial system at large has in a degree outgrown their use, through a change of scale, a displacement of centers and routes of production, transportation and marketing, a shifting of other, correlated, industrial establishments, a change in standard requirements, or seasonal demands for labor, and the like, — matters which are in large part beyond control of the business concerns involved, and beyond remedy. These various causes of discrepancy between accepted capitalisation and effective earning-capacity have their effect, and they unavoidably come along as a concomitant of growth, change and readjustment in any industrial community governed by business considerations; and they increase in volume, on the whole, as time passes. So that while the German industrial community has had its modest share of these concomitants of modern industrial enterprise, there is plainly more of the same kind due and coming to them.

A further difficulty of a different kind but running to somewhat the same general effect arises out of the growth of the industry beyond the supply of raw materials that can be drawn from the nearer-lying, more available natural resources. Recourse must be had to increasingly distant or increasingly difficult sources of supply. This acts to increase costs, whether the recourse is to resources lying within the national boundaries or without. It will be said, and there need be no hesitation in assuming, that this increased cost per unit of raw material is likely to be at least fully offset by the increased economy of production given by the same larger scale of industry that so necessitates recourse to less available resources. Yet the fact remains that the higher efficiency of the larger scale and compass of the industrial system suffers this deduction, whatever it may be worth. Indeed, this was one of the foreseen difficulties which the statesmen of the Empire, by some curious twist of logic, argued themselves into believing that they could remedy by an acquisition of colonies!

More serious than either of these drawbacks inherent in the growth of the system, and equally indefeasible, is the rising cost of production due to a rising standard of living, —perhaps more correctly a rising standard of expenditure.

This involves the added mischief that in so far as it is a question of increased cost of maintenance of the working classes it carries a burden of discontent and irritation, with the obstruction and retardation of industry that is inseparable from "labor troubles." At this point, too, the German industrial era has had its handicap, beginning with negligible deductions from the margin of sale-price above costs in the early days, and growing by insensible degrees until in the course of some thirty or forty years it has come to be a somewhat formidable matter.

In Germany as elsewhere the discontent of the workmen growing out of the rising standard of expenditure has in part coalesced with the discontent of the subject classes as such with the exercise of irresponsible authority vested in the propertied and privileged classes, whether by virtue of customary and legalised privilege in the way of an aristocratic and autocratic government establishment or by force of the rights of ownership exercised by those possessed of property. This coalescence has never been complete, at the same time that it is not always possible to distinguish between the two in any concrete case. This difficulty, which besets industrial business in all the advanced commercial countries, has been very effectively dealt with by the authorities, both by concessions and remedies and by repressive measures; so that the German industrial community have suffered less than might seem their due share of disturbance, hindrance and irritation from this source. Yet it is evident that, in spite of all the shrewd management of the statesmen and the public bodies concerned, the demands of the working classes have latterly been rising to an inconvenient pitch, so as to have become something of a menace to German business by threatening the margin out of which "living profits" are to be paid on capitalisation. And it is at the same time also a perplexing issue for the State authorities, in that it brings into view a contingency that the disposable margin may by this means eventually grow too narrow to support the political and warlike establishment of the State on a suitable footing.

In this last connection the rising standard of living offers a singularly annoying problem of statecraft. There is, *e.g.*, no disloyalty felt or imputable to the workmen who ask for a larger share in the returns of industry, so that appeals to patriotic sentiment can not be made to them with the best grace or with reasonable hope of a successful issue; to hold the loyal affections of this class it is, rather, necessary to convince them that the State is with them in demands which they put forward in good faith and with conviction. On the other hand, appeals of a similar nature to the capitalist-employers are at least equally futile, since these are moved primarily by a view to the main chance — otherwise they would not be capitalist-employers — and are also tangled in a web of credit extensions, corporate obligations and fixed charges that leaves them little choice, beyond the alternative of eventually withdrawing from under the pressure and taking their business elsewhere. In neither of these bearings can the situation yet be said to have reached a climactic phase, although such an eventuality has latterly appeared to be not remote. But since all this has been dealt with by the Imperial and Prussian statesmen, and since it is in the last resort their concern more than that of anyone else, the inquiry will best return to this question at a later point, in reviewing the policy of the State bearing on these matters.

But the rising standard of living affects the rich and the well-to-do as well as those who work with their hands; and the conventional necessities of the former are no less pressing than those of the latter, even though they may run on a level more remote from the physical subsistence minimum. The standard of living is in all cases mainly a standard of reputable expenditure, also called "decent living," and the lesion suffered in falling short of such a standard of decent living is of a spiritual nature, — in so far as the spiritual needs of "decency" are not satisfied at the cost of physical comfort, so as to throw the impact of hardship over on the latter and make it appear that there is actual habitual privation touching the prime physical needs of subsistence. Such is commonly the case, however, and in so far as this takes place it is felt by the victims of privation as a *bona fide* physical privation, and is on that account all the less amenable to correction or amendment by appeal to reason or sentiment.

As among the indigent, so also among the wealthy and well-to-do, a standardised scale of decent expenditures will come to be mandatory; and, for reasons that can not be gone into at length here,[1] the scale of expenditure that so comes to be standardised and accepted as the staple of decency in any class or community is determined, roughly, by what the habitual income of the class or community

---

[1] Cf. *The Theory of the Leisure Class*, ch. ii.–vi.

will support in the way of wasteful consumption. It is another application of the principle of "what the traffic will
bear." The adjustment of such a conventional scale of conspicuous waste to the bearing-capacity of the habitual income is a work of habituation, however, and so requires
time and some attentive elaboration. But so soon, or rather
so far, as a staple run of decent expenditures has so been
worked into the texture of everyday habits, it takes its place
in the schedule of necessities and becomes good and indefeasible. In this matter the German community, with their
traditions of frugality handed down from the days of enforced parsimony, have hitherto made only moderate
progress. Not that the most expensive among them are not
sufficiently spendthrift, but the common run have scarcely
yet learned to consume large incomes with that unobtrusive
efficiency that marks the gentleman of inherited wealth who
has had the benefit of lifelong experience in a community
of wasters. It is probably still a safe proposition that an
English gentleman of the better sort will cost, all told,
several-fold the cost of a German gentleman of conventionally equal standing. Still, the Germans, wealthy and well-
to-do, are taking up the slack as well and as fast as might
fairly be expected. It should be called to mind that, as they
are racially identical with their English compeers, they will
also not be behindhand in this feature of the cultural advance, given only the opportunity and a reasonable allowance of time.

There is, of course, no inclination here to find fault with
this decent waste of time and substance. It is one of the
necessary concomitants of the price system. And it is one

of the points at which Imperial Germany has not yet caught up with the maturer industrial nations; but the German community is moving so effectually in this direction that, barring accidents — which is a large reservation just at the present conjuncture — the disposable margin between the industrial output and the current consumption might be expected shortly to disappear. What would hinder its disappearance by this channel would be the persistent shifting of fortunes from one line of business men to another, and the continued enhancement of industrial productiveness through the continued advance in the industrial arts.

CHAPTER VII

THE ECONOMIC POLICY OF THE IMPERIAL STATE

QUITE in accord with its cameralistic traditions and with the line of policy pursued with such eminent success by the long line of Prussian statesmen, the Hohenzollern rule in Imperial Germany has consistently made the requirements of the State, or the dynasty, the paramount object of its solicitude. It has guided the economic policy of the Empire with far-seeing wisdom and with uncompromising determination. But it has been dynastic wisdom, and consequently it has been substantially a mercantilist, or even cameralistic, policy. An aggressive dynastic policy necessarily means a policy directed to warlike success, and the Imperial policy has consistently made warlike power its first consideration.

The State, in the sense of a coercive war power, is held to be the first interest of the community, to which all other interests must bend just so far as may be expedient for the purposes of the State. Other interests than this politico-military interest are good and legitimate in so far as they subserve, or at most are in no degree disserviceable to, this abiding end of endeavor. The economic policy has accordingly been pursued with an eye single to the enhancement and husbanding of the resources of the State as a warlike power. It is true, this policy has been consistently coupled with professions of an undeviating determination to keep the peace at all costs. How far these professions have been of the nature of diplomatic platitude it is, of course, impossible, perhaps needless, to hazard a guess. They will perhaps best be interpreted, if there is need of interpretation, in the light of Prussian statecraft as it touches questions of war and peace, from its beginnings in the days of the Great Elector to the present.

This policy of militant statecraft is spoken of as "Prussian" by critics of the Empire. And such no doubt it is, in the sense that it runs in unbroken continuity from the earlier period of Prussian aggression down into the Imperial era. Such was also the view of it in the earlier days of the Empire, and in the times immediately preceding the formation of the Empire, as seen by men in the lesser, particularly the south-German, States. Such is perhaps still the view held by many peaceable citizens, surreptitiously, in these States that came under the Prussian hegemony tardily and reluctantly; but if such is the case now it is not confidently discernible by an outsider. The Prussian spirit, in this respect, has apparently been so well infused in the German people at large that there seems no arguable abatement to the claim of a "united Germany" today, and what Germany is united on is this Prussian ideal of a State.

But while the Imperial State and its policy are of Prussian pedigree, it is easy to over-rate that fact. It should be called to mind that while the subjects of the south-German States, particularly a large element among the educated classes, were disinclined to the Prussian rule and the Prussian aims, the population of these States have after all, and including the educated classes, passed under the Prussian hegemony and accepted the drift of Prussian political aims somewhat easily. In point of fact there was not much of anything available in the way of public sentiment and national aspirations in these non-Prussian states, else than a dilute form of the same thing. Their earlier experience had run along the same general lines, except for a certain lack of success attending their princely politics. They were, in fact, dynastic States of much the same complexion but drawn on an incompetently diminutive scale; and since there was no habitual bent of a different nature, no bias that would actively traverse the inculcation of the Prussian line of aspirations, the assimilation of the Prussian teaching has followed with great facility. There were no positive traditions of their own, and no inbred institutional bent, with which the south-Germans would have to break in making the Prussian outlook and discipline their own, so that the change meant little else to them, substantially, than more of the same kind as that in which they were already at home. It is not as if the Prussian system had been imposed on an English-speaking people, *e.g.*, with inbred notions of popular autonomy and private initiative.

The pursuit of this State policy has had many and wide-reaching consequences for the economic fortunes of the Fatherland and its people, some of which are sufficiently notorious through repeated publication by many and divers competent spokesmen. The exploits of Imperial policy in furthering the material progress of the country are among the most noted facts of current history. It is therefore need-less here to review these features of the case, particularly as it has already appeared in an earlier passage of this in-quiry that these exploits of furtherance have chiefly been of a negative character. Indeed, it seems quite probable that a united Germany without a superincumbent Imperial State —if such a thing were conceivable — should have prospered at least in as high a degree.

With a view to the fighting capacity of the State, and in-deed with no other view, the economic system of the coun-try has been controlled wherever control was conceived to be expedient for this purpose. The railway system was laid out under State surveillance on strategic lines, and some of the State-built roads were built with no expectation of their paying their cost in peaceful traffic. Shipping has been sub-sidised and adapted to naval use, in its building and equip-ment, and in its personnel, with the same object. Tariff legislation has been devised to so distribute and specialise the industry of the country as to make it a self-contained productive organisation, in so far as concerns the military and other needs of the community in times of war, with the incidental result of leaving the nation free and ready to go to war on short notice. The same tariff legislation has been made a means of favoring the agrarians, chiefly the so-called Junkers, whose support is necessary to the govern-ment in its warlike preparations, at the same time that it can be had only by concessions to their special pecuniary in-terests. So also the continued support of the same warlike element has been conciliated and substantially enhanced by studiously failing to carry out the constitutional provisions for a periodic redistribution of parliamentary districts. The resulting gerrymander is as scandalous a piece of corrupt party politics as the corresponding abuses that once supported the power of the landed interest in the British parliament at the high tide of parliamentary corruption in that country.

So, again, any growth of popular sentiment inimical to imperialism and coercion has been carefully pruned back and repressed by drastic exercise of the police power and a free recourse to juridical excesses. On the other hand the like suppression, or more properly subornation, of popular opinion has been sought by way of class legislation ostensibly favoring the working classes in the way of pensions and insurance for disability, old age, etc. Again, the educational equipment, schools of all grades and kinds, as well as the periodical press, has been censored, subsidised, coerced, comprehensively and effectually, to carry through an unremitting propaganda of "Germanism," that is to say of aggressive loyalty to the dynastic policies of the Empire. The whole reflects the highest credit on the Imperial statesmen and their agents for admirably thorough work and singleminded devotion to duty, — a singlemindedness obstructed by no consideration of law, equity or humanity, — in effect leaning on the principles of martial law.

All this characterisation of the Imperial system carries a note of reprehension, because many of the details necessarily involved in effectually carrying through such a systematic work of the "will to power" as the Imperial statesmen have had in hand are reprehensible in the eyes of modern men in whose scheme of right and honest living such details have no place. The working out of such a dynastic policy unavoidably involves hardship to one and another, and it is not always possible for the practical statesman nicely to observe the punctilios of usage and conventional taste in manhandling the human raw material that is to be shaped to his uses. The system has the faults of its qualities, and among its qualities are not amiability, toleration and ingenuousness. A dynastic State can not be set afloat in the milk of human kindness. Nor, indeed, does the equity or the æsthetic value of this adventure in imperialism concern the present inquiry, which is occupied with the conditions and limitations of its success.

Anyone entering on such an inquiry will necessarily face the question as to what is the end of endeavor in the case. In a striking figure of rhetoric this end sought has been spoken of as "a place in the sun" for Germany. This figure of speech seems intended to convey that what is wanted is a fair chance for the unfolding life of the people of the Fatherland. But this evidently does not mean simply a fair chance of material welfare for the German population, considered as an aggregate of individuals. Apart from the Imperial State, there is no special burden or obstacle resting on the individuals and hindering them each and several from personally following their natural bent and making the most of their opportunities and aptitudes. Indeed, there can be no question but that the common man has absolutely nothing to gain in the material respect from the success of the Imperial State.

There is also the plea, made in good faith and commonly allowed in good faith, that the increasing German population needs ground on which to house its increase, that the German population multiplies on the face of the earth and so needs its share of the earth's face on which to multiply. But the earth's face is, notoriously, as accessible for any such multiplication outside the German frontiers as it would be in case these frontiers were extended to include any outlying territory. In the material respect this is a question of transportation, and of the conditions of life offered in the new territories aimed at; and transportation would be in no degree facilitated by an extension of the German frontiers, while the conditions of life in the new settlements would be no easier under German rule than those now offered in the same localities. Indeed, experience would appear to teach, somewhat unequivocally, that German rule is a good deal of a material burden, and that, merely as a question of private economy, a man will commonly be more at ease under almost any other governmental establishment, within the civilised world. Taxation is relatively heavy, not to say exorbitant, under the Empire, and the degree of interference with private affairs commonly exercised by the State exceeds what prevails elsewhere, and is, indeed, endurable only by virtue of long and thorough habituation. There can in fact be no question but that in the material respect the (contemplated or prospective) excess population of the Fatherland would be happier in crossing the Imperial frontier than in carrying it with them.

It may be noted by the way that the German colonies have hitherto attracted substantially no German immigrants, settlers, apart from officials and business men engaged in enterprise of the nature of exploitation; nor indeed

have they attracted immigrants of any other nationality seeking a place in the sun under German auspices. Germans seeking to better their opportunities by emigration
have continued to escape from the Empire.

Considerations much to the same effect apply also in
sundry other respects, besides that of the material comfort
and opportunity afforded migrant individuals. Not that there
are no drawbacks to emigration across the national frontiers,
but as things commonly go today it is at least highly probable that the net aggregate of such drawbacks will, for the
present and the calculable future, continue to bear at least
as heavily on settlers going to German colonies as on those
going elsewhere. It is, of course, a hardship to find oneself
in a community speaking another language; but that contingency is no graver or more imminent in the case of German settlers in any of the larger British colonies, or in
similar countries open to immigration in which considerable German-speaking settlements are already established,
than for settlers in the colonies of the Empire. With the
passage of time it may be expected that the later generations of these German migrants will adopt the language
together with the other customs of the land of their adoption; but when that takes place it will not be felt as a hardship. Such migrants and their natural increase will be lost
to the German-speaking world, it is true; but that is another
matter and belongs in another connection. A graver and
more immediate difficulty encountered by such settlers in a
foreign country is their unfamiliarity with the laws of the
land. This is a grave matter for the first generation, scarcely
at all for the second. Beyond this it can scarcely be said that

such emigrants have anything to lose, as compared with migration to a German colony, beyond the sentimental loss involved in shifting their allegiance from one national establishment to another; and this step is optional, with little ground for choice other than personal inclination.

Any such recital of personal advantages or disadvantages attaching to emigration into a foreign country, as against migration to a colony of the Fatherland, is extremely unconvincing; as is any enumeration of individual benefits derivable from the Imperial establishment and its policies. It all fails to ring true and seems beside the point, very much like the grave protestations with which diplomatists are in the habit of masking the point at issue in their negotiations. In fact, it is as futile as the verbiage of a peace advocate. These matters are not of decisive consequence, even if they can be said to have any appreciable weight among the motives that hold men to an enthusiastic maintenance of such an establishment as the Empire, or that lead men to make material sacrifices for the Fatherland.

Patriotism, or loyalty, is a frame of mind and rests on a sentimental adhesion to certain idealistic aspirations. These aspirations, it is true, will commonly not bear analysis; but they are just as good and valuable assets for their particular use, for all that. The common man has no rational interest in the continued success of the governmental establishment under which he is living, except in so far as its failure would throw him under the rule of another government that would use him more harshly. But the Empire can make no defensible plea on such ground, since the fear of Turkish dominion in Europe has gone by. Yet the common man in the Fatherland is doubtless as loyal to his State establishment as any European subject, and probably very appreciably more patriotic than the subjects of most other European States, as is evidenced by the economic burdens and the coercive surveillance to which the German population has submitted without serious murmur during the Imperial era. It is not readily credible that any equally intelligent population would have lent itself with equal patience, not to say enthusiasm, to so costly and profitless an enterprise as the Imperial policy.

But it is not a question of profit and loss, whether in the pecuniary respect or as touches the conditions of life in any other bearing. For the people, the common man, it is a question of working together unselfishly for the realisation of an ideal accepted uncritically as the outcome of habituation; for the directorate, the dynastic establishment and their servants, it is a question of the use to be made of this unselfish spirit of devotion in the common man. But for all and several that stand together in support of this enterprise, it should be kept in mind, the enterprise on which they are bent is not an enterprise of a selfish kind — except perhaps for the Imperial establishment and the ruling class — and for neither the one nor the other is the ulterior purpose of the enterprise pecuniary or other material gain. It is something that can not be called sordid, unless a profitless self-aggrandisement of the dynasty should be so called.

While any censorious critic of the Imperial policies might readily, and defensibly, construe these policies as an enterprise of self-aggrandisement on the part of the dynastic establishment — superficially the appearances very strongly support such a view — yet it is to be noted that such a motive is not avowed by those who exercise the discretion in these matters, and that there is at the same time no call to believe that this is the chief and consciously accepted aim of the German people in supporting these policies. Such dynastic aggrandisement is doubtless present among the aspirations on which popular sentiment converges, but there is also much else. It can perhaps be of little use, but it should also do no harm, to attempt an analysis of what this "much else" consists in, that so is included in the burden of patriotic aspirations carried by the German people, and that so induces them to lend themselves to the policies of the Empire.

What one hears most commonly and convincingly avowed as an end of endeavor is the conservation and propagation of the German culture. Culture is an immaterial asset, of course, and it is an inclusive category, the content of which may not be altogether well defined in the mind of those who use it, but which is after all definite in such a degree as to be used quite intelligibly. An enumeration of the cultural features included under the term in its colloquial use in this connection could scarcely hope to be quite acceptable to all, or to do justice to the conception of culture at large, — which is a spiritual matter and does not lend itself to statistical formulation. Still, certain main features of the case will bear handling in objective and impersonal terms.

Culture, any given culture, is a balanced system of habits, essentially habits of thought. Among these habits prevalent at large in the Fatherland, e.g., the one that lies next to hand is the language. In certain other cultural, or national, communities the currently accepted religious cult might have to take the first place among the tangible characteristics that go to make up the community's distinctive civilisation. Such would be true, *e.g.*, in the Turkish case, or perhaps in the case of Spain, or possibly even in that of Russia; but such is not the case with Germany, where a distinctive religious cult is not avowed and could not be. In this matter of language it is not a question of retaining the current form of speech for the use of the current generation of German subjects, but of conserving it for later generations and extending its use to later generations of peoples who are not now in the habit of using it. This would seem to be a humanitarian question, bearing on the future welfare of mankind. It should, for one thing, apparently be a question of the serviceability of the German speech as contrasted with another — *e.g.*, English, — for use in the everyday affairs of life, including science and literature. On this head there appears in point of fact to be nothing much to say for or against the expediency of conserving or extending the use of this language. Its merits are not to be overlooked, but it is extremely doubtful whether such an endeavor to conserve or extend the use of it would be worth while as a matter of general utility.[1]

---

[1]While recognising that this is necessarily a question of sentimental predilection, in which arguments of expediency at large can have no more than a subsidiary bearing, an outsider, to whom English is not native and to whom at the same time German is not unfamiliar, may perhaps without arrogance confess a total inability to see any useful purpose to be served by a substitution of German for English in any of the uses which language serves.

As between German and English, *e.g.*, considered as a medium for science there is little to choose, German being perhaps rather the less facile on the whole. In point of the literary assets conserved in the one or the other of the two media, predilection will necessarily have much to say; English has had the advantage of being the medium employed by a longer line through the course of a more extended and more varied cultural experience. Any outsider, presumably, would scout the notion of a cultural gain at this point through the supersession of English by German. It is not improbable that the award of an impartial court would fall out to much the same effect if the comparison were to be made with French. And unless the question at issue is a question of supersession, there is no question.

The culture spoken for will, further, include such tangible elements as technology and the exact sciences. These are elements of the Western civilisation at large, not special features of German culture as contrasted with the other civilised nations, least of all, of course, as contrasted with the British. By historical accident, the British community has unequivocally led the advance in these matters down to a date within the memory of men still living, — in whom the lead vests today would be an unprofitable topic of discussion, since the lack of perspective will permit no dispassionate appraisal, and chauvinistic sentiment would admit no agreement. That the lead in technology and in the cognate field of the exact sciences has been with the British is an historical accident, as just remarked, and in itself it has no particular bearing on the question in hand. But this state of the case has a bearing in the sense that it throws the whole question out of court. In point of race, and therefore of capacity and native aptitude for this peculiar work of the Western civilisation, there is no ascertainable difference between the Germans and the British. Under modern conditions, again, national or linguistic frontiers are no bar to the diffusion of technological or scientific knowledge; and Christendom at large has none but a sportsmanlike interest in the national affiliation of its scientists or technologists, provided only that the governmental system of any given nation is not of a character to hinder the pursuit of knowledge along these lines.

Now, it happens that the governmental system differs notably in these two contrasted nations, so that the German, *e.g.*, is appreciably the more arbitrary and bureaucratic of the two. This difference should lead one to expect that the pursuit of scientific and technological knowledge under the auspices of the one will in some degree take a different scope and method, and yield an output different from what may be expected under the other. *A priori*, it should apparently follow that the current work, both in science and technology, should under the German discipline show more of "thoroughness," in the sense of a close application to detail and a diligent work of routine, with results more notable for elaboration and sobriety than for bold or large innovation in the range of general conceptions necessarily made use of in this work. Whereas, in a degree — and only in a degree, since the determining difference between the two cultural systems is only a matter of degree — the converse should hold true for the English-speaking nations, as it apparently also should in even a more pronounced fashion for the French.

Such, indeed, would also appear to be the run of the pertinent facts; although it is always conceivable that the antecedent probability of such an outcome may predispose one to see the pertinent facts in such a light as will bear out the antecedent probability. It may, of course, also be that the continued lead of the French and the English-speaking peoples in respect of the larger and theoretically creative conceptions in science and technology is of a transient nature, and that the German specialists may presently come into the lead, when that community shall have had time and opportunity for mature assimilation of that impersonal, matter-of-fact habit of mind that necessarily underlies all creative work in this field. Meantime the work of the two, in so far as they differ, should presumably continue to supplement one another very much as they have done in the recent past. It would appear, in fact, that the German culture has nothing characteristic to offer on this head; what the Germans have in hand being so recently borrowed from English (and French) sources that there could be no sensible gain looked for in any conceivable move to let it supplant its own source.

However, there is the further count of German achievement and accumulated assets in the field of philosophy, the free, or even the mandatory, diffusion of which it is felt would be of substantial cultural service to mankind. In so far as "philosophy" is not taken in the colloquial sense of a personal appraisal of the values to be attached to the various institutions and incidents of life, it must be taken in this connection to designate the moral and metaphysical outlook involved in this cultural complex. Here, as in the bearings already spoken of, the difference between the neighboring communities is necessarily a difference of habituation, not of racial or hereditary endowment, since there is no difference in the latter respect. And in point of habituation, and consequent habitual bent, such as would give a characteristic scope and method of philosophical thought, the peculiar features of the German case will therefore have to be conceived as a precipitate of the peculiar experience which their historical circumstances may have given them in the days before they began seriously to take over the modern technology and the logic of modern science. There is no later or other source or point of departure for a distinctively German philosophy; any philosophical system named "German" and not of such a derivation would be a misnomer, and any endeavor to conserve it as a landmark or cornerstone of German culture would accordingly be misspent effort.

The merits of this heritage of the German people, in point of its intrinsic truth and beauty, can of course not be made a subject of inquiry here; all that is, after all, a question of taste, about which there is no disputing. It is more to the point to recall that since this characteristic philosophical precipitate of the life-history of the German community, which makes its appearance in the eighteenth and comes to its mature climax in the nineteenth century, is a philosophical expression of the Romantic spirit, it is viable only within the spiritual frontiers of Romanticism; that is to say, since and in so far as the German people have made the transition from Romanticism to the matter-of-fact logic and insight characteristic of modern technology and applied science, the characteristic philosophy of Germany's past is also a phenomenon of the past age. It can live and continue to guide and inspire the life and thought of the community only on condition that the community return to the conditions of life that gave rise and force to this philosophy; that is to say, only on condition that the German nation retreat from its advance into the modern state of the industrial arts and discard such elements of the modern scheme of institutions as it has hitherto accepted. But with such a retirement in the direction of the mediæval and feudalistic scheme of life, if such a retreat were conceivable, the question in hand would also lapse; since such a retreat would involve a return to the small and incompetent conditions of Germany's pre-capitalistic and pre-Imperial age.

The peculiarly German philosophy is peculiarly ineffectual for the purposes of modern science, and peculiarly incapable of articulating with or illuminating any of the questions with which modern scientific inquiry is occupied. It is an idealistic philosophy; that is to say, at its nearest approach to the domain of fact it is a theoretical construction in terms of sufficient reason rather than of efficient cause, in terms of luminous personal valuation rather than of opaque matter-of-fact.

Its high qualities and great æsthetic value may not be questioned; it is a monument of what was best in German life in the days before the technological deluge; but it finds no application in the scheme of thought within which the modern science and technology live and move. Remnants of it are still afloat in the atmosphere of the German scholarly world, and it is even true that, under the shadow of the feudalising Prussian State, well-intended endeavors, whether well advised or not, have also latterly been made to rehabilitate it.[1] But this is to be taken as indicating the degree of reversion embodied in the Imperial policies and the degree of revulsion induced by the discipline of life under its institutional scheme, rather than as evidence of the viability of this philosophical scheme under modern conditions of life, properly speaking. Similar anachronistic remnants of the ancient régime are, of course, also to be met with in some degree of vigor elsewhere, and a correspondingly atavistic revulsion of taste in philosophical speculations is also to be found elsewhere; although, apart from the frankly mediæval aspirations of the theologically-

---

[1]Such will have to be the appraisal of the move toward vitalism and neo-Kantianism in latterday German speculations, as well as of the "return to Goethe" that has been spoken for with so much feeling. This endeavor to turn back may perhaps best be taken as a mere movement of revulsion, but it may also be taken as evidence of the efficacy of that discipline in personal valuation and of discrimination in degrees of occult virtues and potencies, which the coercive personal rule, and its government by personnel, constantly exerts. Cf., *e.g.*, Henri Lichtenberger, *Germany and Its Evolution in Modern Times*, bk. iii. ch. v.; Aliotta, *The Idealistic Reaction against Science*, perhaps especially part i. sec. i. ch. ii., sec. ii. ch. ii. and iii., and "Conclusion."

Any attentive observer will remark a characteristic divergence between the Anglo-American speculations in this connection and the German; where the former prevailingly resort to quasi-subjective conceptions, of the nature of Pragmatism, the latter are inclined to take refuge in mystical notions of a super-subjective or præternatural vitalism, a transcendent *Sollen* and an *Ueber-Ich*.

minded sons of the Church, such recidivism is greatly more in evidence in Imperial Germany, perhaps particularly in Prussian Germany, than among the scholars of Christendom at large.

The tedious caution may again be pardoned, that all this implies nothing in the way of praise or dispraise of the philosophical predilections so handed down from the pre-mechanistic past, and aimed to be rehabilitated in the mechanistic present by men schooled in the institutional methods carried over into this present under the ægis of the dynastic State. It is not even intended to imply that such endeavor to rehabilitate a logic and outlook that once articulated with the discipline of workday life in that institutional past need be a bootless endeavor. What is implied is that a competent rehabilitation of the Romantic philosophy is conditioned on the rehabilitation of the Romantic institutional and technological scheme, — perhaps somewhat after the fashion of things in the days when the Holy Roman Empire was in the hands of a receiver. It is at least extremely doubtful whether the dynastic system of the Empire and its institutional scheme will avail to effect a retention of or reversion to the Romantic philosophy, even as it stood in the immediately pre-Darwinistic days of German scholarship. One might go farther and say that unless the discipline of the Imperial system should have some such effect upon the prevalent intellectual attitude of its subjects, it will itself fall into decay under the impact of the same forces of habituation that go to make the Romantic philosophy futile in the eyes of modern men.

What remains to be spoken of under the head of German culture, distinctively so called, is the institutional scheme just referred to, substantially the administrative system of the Empire. In so far as the German scheme is distinctive and individual, so as to stand out in contrast with corresponding use and wont in other European countries and mark an aspect of German life, it is a distinctive form of the current compromise between the irresponsible autocracy of the mediæval State and the autonomy of popular self-government. By and large, the German system differs from that of other modern countries in being of a somewhat more coercive character, comprising a larger measure of authority and a smaller measure of popular self-direction.

In the British case, e.g., — that is in the case of the English-speaking peoples — the compromise embodied in the accepted, and more or less popularly acceptable, scheme of institutions, goes relatively far in the direction of a reversion to that anarchistic neighborhood autonomy that has appeared in earlier passages of this inquiry to have been the prehistoric constitution of society among the north-European peoples. Not that the boasted "self-government" of the "Anglo-Saxons" is a precariously near approach to neolithic anarchism, or even to the quasi-anarchistic rule of the petty kingdoms of late Scandinavian paganism. But it is nearer than the German compromise, by nearly all the difference between them; and to the spokesmen of the German scheme of mitigated repression it looks much like a dubious playing fast and loose with anarchy, a harboring of "license" under the sign of "liberty." The reversion toward the archaic quasi-anarchistic rule has gone but a relatively little way in the German scheme, answering to the relatively brief and relatively scant exposure of the German population to the disintegrating impact of the mechanistic state of the industrial arts, — disintegrating in respect of those habits of subjection and subservience to personal rule that characterise the dynastic State and constitute the spirit of personal loyalty.

Here again, it is bootless to argue the intrinsic merits of the two contrasted institutional schemes. It seems plain that the quasi-autonomy to which the English-speaking peoples turn their affections is more nearly the institutional counterfoil of the modern state of the industrial arts; but that amounts only to saying that it is more nearly the unguarded outcome of the habits of thought fostered by modern science and technology, not that it is therefore a more suitable scheme of life for civilised men, even when this life is carried on by means of this science and technology.

It seems likewise plain that, with a more protracted experience of modern industry, the popular predilection among the German-speaking peoples should, by force of habituation, also come to incline more and more to the like popular autonomy in their institutional scheme. But even if such a change of spiritual base may be in prospect, it remains true that to the German people of today such a change would seem untoward, not to say disastrous. The current Imperial system of mitigated repression and bureaucratic guidance is apparently acceptable to the German people and apparently works to good effect among them, although it would presumably not be workable if imposed on a population with a different recent historical past. That it works so well in the Fatherland would appear to be due in part to the fact that the population has so recently emerged from a state of unconditional fealty and subjection, that even the slight and dubious mitigation of irresponsible personal rule embodied in the Prussian bureaucratic system is felt as a relief and a privilege; it is "freedom" by contrast with conditions that still live in tradition, and to some extent in the continued habitual attitude of the subjects, although it might seem "bondage" to another population with a different traditional experience and a different habitual bent.

This bureaucratic system of guidance and control has the merit of great efficiency and of being visibly serviceable for the purposes which it is designed to serve; and its purpose is one that meets, on the whole, the cordial approval of the subjects of the Empire. That it is so eminently efficient and successful is not unusually ascribed by its spokesmen to the peculiarly high degree of honesty, sobriety, intelligence, and energy that is held to be native to the German character, — that is to say its successful operation is ascribed to the presence of certain hereditary traits in the German people. But since there is no racial, that is hereditary, difference between the people of the Fatherland and their neighbors, either east or west, that explanation fails, and one's curiosity returns to the question: Why is the Prussian-Imperial system of bureaucratic guidance and control more efficient and freer from abuses than, *e.g.*, the somewhat stale bureaucracy of Austria, or the massive web of official corruption that has until recently carried on the administrative government of Russia, or, again, the Turkish system, structurally of the same class, that is colloquially referred to as "unspeakable"?

Since an explanation in terms of hereditary race characteristics will not serve, except for homiletical edification, the only recourse for analysis of the case is to peculiarities of habituation. In this respect the Prussian-Imperial scheme occupies a peculiar place, on several accounts, the leading ones of which may be called to mind. Chief among these peculiar features of the case that make for efficiency and integrity would appear to be its recency; it has not yet had time to grow old and mature into a competent routine of perquisites and sinecure. There is said to be evidence that such a growth is not altogether lacking, but it is at least commonly accepted that what modern colloquialism calls "graft" is relatively absent; whereas in the more mature establishments of the class, *e.g.*, the Turkish or the Persian, "graft" appears to be the structural core of the system and the prime mover in its functioning. The traditions of the German people, including the personnel of the civil service, are traditions of frugality and parsimony, quite necessarily so, and these are fortified in this connection by a traditional loyalty of service to a master, to whom the civil servant stands in a relation of personal stewardship. The improvement in the material circumstances of the civil servants effected by the liberal emoluments of the service, as contrasted with past penury, has not yet grown into a commonplace insufficiency and become a point of departure for discontent and larger pecuniary aspirations. At the same time the immaterial emoluments in the way of rank, decorations, and royal condescension, mean more in a community that has long been fed on distinctions of rank and that has not yet achieved an adequate appreciation of commercial standards. These and the like incidents of immaturity may be outgrown.

The like reflection will apply as regards the current efficiency of this bureaucratic system. It is apparently unavoidable that such a system should gradually achieve a certain consistency of procedure, a binding texture of routine and precedent. So long as the routine is still in process of adaptation to the exigencies to meet which it is being elaborated, it will have but a slight if any retarding or hindering effect in the work to be done. It is flexible so long as it is engaged in establishing precedents; but so soon or so far as the precedents have once been established, and in the measure in which the exigencies gradually change their character, so as to be less well served by routine embodying precedents already established, in the same measure the bureaucratic system working under such routine will grow inflexible and inhibitive, the amount of lost motion and wasted energy will increase, and the margin of perquisites and sinecures will widen. What may be the rate of growth and the final degree of such senescence to be looked for in the Prussian-Imperial bureaucracy is of course only a matter for conjecture, at the best; but its extreme volume, comprehensiveness and elaboration would suggest that something very appreciable in that way is fairly within the probabilities, since this state of things leaves relatively little of German life outside the sweep of the bureaucratic system, and so affords little purchase for any combination of forces that might conceivably hinder its perfect decrepitude.[1]

At this point, therefore, the aspiration of patriotic Germans to extend the benefits of the Imperial system to mankind at large in its further generations, is at the best a dubious speculation. On the one hand, if the system of bureaucratic direction maintains its ascendancy it is in all human probability bound to change its character somewhat pronouncedly in the direction which other bureaucratic administrations of an autocratic character have followed; while if, on the other hand, the modern habits of thought as shown in latterday science and technology take effect in a popular disavowal of autocratic and dynastic institutions, as has happened in the countries that have preceded Germany on the road of industrial advance, and bring on a consequent disintegration of the foundations of this bureaucracy, the blessings conferred by its extension would at the best be of a wholly evanescent kind.

Apart from a feudalistic ambition, patriotic in the bald and naive sense, to further the dynastic dominion of the Imperial State as a regnant power, it does not appear that there should be much in an aggressive Imperial policy to engage the serious affections of the German people. There is no substantial ground for an aspiration to propagate or to conserve the distinctive German culture; and assuming

---

[1] It is true, the present (April 1915) conjuncture may so turn that speculations as to the future of the Imperial bureaucratic system will have little more than a speculative interest.

that something could be done towards its diffusion abroad, the chance of such diffusion producing a substantial or enduring effect would seem to be small.

As a cultural community the Fatherland is at present in an eminently unstable, transitional phase. Its population is in the singularly untoward position — untoward, that is, in the present immediate bearing — that they have come out of an obsolescent cultural situation so recently as in effect not to have forgotten what is necessary to forget, at the same time that they have not been in contact with the things of the modern world long enough or intimately enough to have fully assimilated the characteristically modern elements of the Western civilisation.

This is not saying that they may not, for the transient time being, be all the better off in any and every respect that may conceivably be worth while; but it does say that they are not in a position to take up a relation of tutelage to any other community, with the slightest chance of a successful issue, for good or ill. They are physically, technologically, politically, socially, comprised within the frontiers of modern Christendom; but they are, in certain indefeasible respects, notably the industrial respect, newcomers whose scheme of life has not yet been made over in the image of that culture into which they are moving by force of unavoidable habituation, — unavoidable except by a precipitate retreat into that more archaic phase of Western civilisation out of which they have latterly been escaping.

It is not yet too late, perhaps. They may yet be able to effect such a retreat by recourse to so drastic a reaction in their civil and political institutions as will offset, presently neutralise, and eventually dispel the effects wrought by habituation to the ways and means of modern industry and the exact sciences. There is the object-lesson of Turkey, of course, which teaches that there is always another way, and that one should not underrate the cultural efficiency of a tenacious adherence to archaic institutions in the face of any eventuality.

CHAPTER VIII

THE NET GAIN

IN the course of the last preceding chapter it has appeared
that any project for transfusing the characteristic elements
of the current German culture abroad among the other
nations of Christendom would be nugatory, owing to the
fact that, however intrinsically desirable it may be, what
the Fatherland has to offer in this way is, in its elements,
out of date and therefore out of touch with the habits of
thought in such communities of a maturer culture as, *e.g.*,
the French or the English; the chief distinctive characteristic of the German culture being a retarded adherence to
certain mediæval or submediæval habits of thought, the
equivalents of which belong farther back than the historical
present in the experience of these others. It is further argued, on similar ground, that any endeavor to hold fast the
main body of this peculiarly German culture *in statu quo*
within the confines of the Fatherland would similarly be
nugatory, because as a cultural scheme it is out of date and
touch with itself, in that it is in part archaic and in part quite
new. All this, of course, does not bear on the intrinsic merits
of this body of culture or on the question of its desirability.
It is also, of course, intended only to describe the facts in the
case and the effective practicability of such conceivable en-

deavor, and it is by no means intended to set forth the run of convictions current on this head among loyal German subjects.

So seen in its historical setting and in the light of the circumstances that have shaped it and that will continue to determine its further life-history — that is to say, considered genetically — this variant of the Western civilisation is evidently an exceptionally unstable, transitory, and in a sense unripe phase. Comprising, rather than combining, certain archaic elements — as, *e.g.*, its traditional penchant for Romantic metaphysics and feudalistic loyalty — together with some of the latest ramifications of mechanistic science and an untempered application of the machine industry, it necessarily lacks that degree of homogeneity in its logic and orientation that would characterise a maturer cultural complex. The resulting want of poise is not to be accounted an infirmity, perhaps; it makes for versatility and acceleration of change; but it is also a clear warrant that the existing congeries of cultural elements does not constitute a stable compound.

Such is, of course, not the appraisal of the spokesmen of this culture, in whose apprehension it necessarily stands as a finality, since it is all their own. And doubtless, sound and kindly men as they are, they are sincerely concerned to benefit mankind at large by its extension over the civilised world. Indeed, in their appraisal, as it abundantly comes into view, much is made of the stability, poise, deliberation and "profundity" of the national character in which this culture is conceived to be embedded. Doubtless, a penchant for profundity and deliberation bulks large among the habits of those who cultivate this culture. But nothing can be more profoundly and meticulously deliberate than the measured footsteps of the man who no longer knows where he is going, though he is on his way.

Now, to carry out this benevolent design of extending the dominion of the culture of the Fatherland it is indispensable that the Prussian-Imperial State should extend its dominion; inasmuch as the prime postulate of the faith that moves these its spokesmen runs to the effect that the State is the first need of any cultured community; and as the Prussian-Imperial State is central and intrinsic to the German cultural scheme, it follows that this State will necessarily be the indispensable prime mover and chief end in the regeneration of humanity that so is to be effectuated. Whoever wills the end must make his peace with the means. So it has come about that the higher fortunes of humanity are conceived to be bound up indissolubly with the paramount dominion of the Prussian-Imperial State; which in its turn, in concrete fact, is identified with the suzerainty of the Hohenzollern dynasty. All of which greatly simplifies the plan of cultural salvation, at the same time that it brings the clear call of human duty to accord with the sportsmanlike impulsion of patriotic sentiment.

It is true, the run of the reasoning by which such a patriotic conclusion is reached may in fact be the reverse of that here given. The initiative and point of departure may in effect lodge in the patriotic sentiment, from which the analysis may then be run back into these profounder grounds of human duty and high intent, which so come to authenticate and sanctify the sportsmanlike zeal of the patriotic devotee. But the policy to be pursued is more commonly justified on some such moral grounds as indicated, rather than as an impulsive onset of sportsmanlike patriotism. And the outcome is the same in either case; it is an admirably singleminded devotion to the ascendancy of the Imperial State.

Something has already been said of the economic policy pursued by the Imperial government. This policy has been much commended for the benefits it has conferred on the German people. No doubt, much of this commendation is an uncritical laudation of success; and earlier passages of this inquiry have shown reasons for believing that this industrial success has in part been due to circumstances not connected with the State or its policy. But after all due allowance for adventitious circumstances there doubtless remains much to be credited to the government's policy. A critical scrutiny will probably bring into relief the meritorious deeds of omission and riddance that should be credited to the Empire, but the Imperial policy is by no means without merit on the side of its deeds of commission also.

The economic policy of the Empire has not run the same throughout its course, although it has consistently aimed at warlike power throughout. In its earlier period, the administration of Bismarck, the aim seems to have been warlike security rather than Imperial expansion; since the present reign it has, with fair consistency, been the latter. But throughout the Imperial era the material fortunes of the nation have consistently been furthered and conserved for the ulterior end of warlike power. To this end it has been sought to make the Fatherland, as near as practicably may be, a self-contained industrial community, — a policy which conduces to no other end, and which, incidentally but unavoidably, lowers the industrial efficiency of the nation.

A policy directed to making a nation industrially self-contained or self-sufficient necessarily depends on measures of inhibition. It is only by obstructing the free ramification of the industrial system across the national frontiers that such self-sufficiency can be achieved. A self-contained industrial community is one whose industry draws for its raw materials only on the natural resources comprised within the national frontiers, whose population draws its subsistence from the soil of the country, and which imports only superfluities, or at the most, articles of consumption that can readily be dispensed with. On the other hand the modern state of the industrial arts is drawn on an international scale, in that it works to the best, that is to say the most productive, effect by the free use of materials drawn from many sources, far and near, and by such free local specialisation of industry as will permit the supply of any given line of goods, finished or half wrought, to be turned out wherever the facilities for their production are at their best. This is the chief service of the modern means of transport and communication.

Illustrations of this point should seem needless, yet an illustrative instance or two drawn from the German situation may not be out of place. So, it is evident that German industry would better depend on outside sources for its necessary supply of copper and petroleum, as well as for the precious metals, and it is only a degree less evident that the industrial community at large, as distinct from special interests, would profit by free access to outside supplies of iron, coal and lumber. With modern means of transportation, the economy of such free access is sufficiently evident. So, again, it is evident that the German population can find their needed supply of fruits, grain, meat and fish at less cost by drawing a large proportion of it from outside, in exchange for their wrought goods, rather than from the soil of the Fatherland.

It is only by putting obstacles in the way, or — what comes to the same thing —.by offering special inducements to special interests, that the ramifications of the industrial system can be prevented from extending across the national frontiers; which comes to saying that that end can be achieved only by hindering the industrial community from taking full advantage of the modern state of the industrial arts, and so lowering its industrial efficiency below what it would be in the absence of such hindrance. This, of course, is commonplace. In the German case as in others elsewhere, the chief instrument of this obstructive nationalist policy has been the national tariff. The results achieved have, of course, fallen far short of the desired self-sufficiency on the part of the German nation. To set aside the effects of modern technology to that extent has not been feasible.

Doubtless the Imperial endeavors to create such a self-contained war power in the Fatherland have materially abated the net industrial efficiency of the German community; but the effects of the control and inhibition exercised with this end in view have after all not been so serious, nor has the net waste involved in armament and warlike preparation been nearly so grave a matter, as the mere *prima facie* statistical computations in the case would tend to show. The effects of this governmental management are not exhausted in the first incidence of the measures taken; in effect there is involved something like that "repercussion" of which the theories of taxation take account. Most obvious among such secondary effects, after the analogy of "repercussion," would be the effect intended by the Imperial tariff system. It has diverted industry to less productive channels, but it has also had much of its intended effect in making the nation self-dependent in the material respect, and has bred an enhanced attitude of national animosity toward foreign nationalities. These are valuable assets for the Imperial purpose. It has also had the further intended effect of holding the loyal affections of the agrarians and maintaining them in their position of preponderance. These are obvious matters, and notorious.

Less obvious are certain secondary consequences and circumstances due to this Imperial war policy. In earlier passages of this inquiry attention has been directed to the cumulative growth of wasteful expenditures, euphemistically spoken of as a rising standard of living, in the British community in modern times. Enforced by a sense of conventional propriety, this wasteful consumption has been institutionalized and so has taken on a character of moral necessity. As has also been noted, the German population brought relatively little of this line of conventions with them when they came into the modern industrial world, half a century ago, having been trained in a school of penurious frugality under the earlier régime of small means and princely rapacity. Now, the Imperial draught on current resources,

while it has not fallen directly and formally on such wasteful expenditures, has after all acted to reduce the margin of
surplus available for such wasteful consumption; so that it
has in part, to that extent, merely diverted to warlike waste
what would otherwise have gone into conspicuously wasteful living at the hands of its recipients. In the measure in
which the resulting draught on the nation's income for warlike expenditure has so constituted a deduction from expenditures on conspicuous waste, it may on a large view
fairly be said to have cost the country nothing. It may perhaps safely be taken as a matter of course that the cost of
the warlike establishment is not all to be checked off in this
way against bootless private waste foregone; but it is
equally a matter of course that under the peculiar circumstances affecting the life of the German population during
this period a very appreciable compensatory effect of this
kind will have been had.

Yet, while warlike expenditures have in the aggregate
undoubtedly exceeded what any reasonable allowance for
conspicuous waste in the service of gentility might amount
to; and while the drain of military and Imperial needs
has doubtless reduced and retarded the growth of wasteful
standards of living, still such a growth has by no means
been altogether wanting. The decencies — mostly pecuniary and emulative — can not be denied their equitable
claim, and the German people have after all done something appreciable toward bringing their standards of decent
expenditure into line with those of their neighbors. The
disposable margin of output above (conventionally) necessary consumption has doubtless been narrowed appreciably

by this means. And still, to the extent to which this policy of warlike expenditure has reduced the conventionally necessary waste, it has not only not impoverished the community (directly, at least) but has left the country by so much the more capable to bear any sudden strain put on it by warlike enterprise in the event of actual hostilities.

There is another count of the same general bearing that similarly comes into view on contrasting the German case with the English. Distinguishable from, but inextricably woven into the broad web of wastefully respectable living in the United Kingdom, is the addiction to sports. Taken merely as a matter of wasteful consumption — which means in statistical terms approximately one hundred per cent — this cultivation of sports will count up simply as a wasteful dissipation of time and substance, of course; but it has its value also as a staple means of diverting the energies and attention, and therefore the acquired proficiencies and the further habituation, of a large section of the community into this, economically speaking, arid channel of dissipation; whereby the time, use and effect of this fraction of the population are diverted from useful ends to the production of a moderate output of mischief.

When the modern era set in in Germany that country was not possessed of anything like a full complement of these genteel and manly dissipations, and what there was to carry over of a home-bred equivalent was largely jettisoned in the transhipment, so as to leave something of a margin of energy, intelligence and manly conceit free to be taken up by any reputable interest that might offer. Such an outlet, reputable, sensational and conspicuous, was found for the Fatherland's sporting blood in drafting this susceptible element of the idle classes into the service; with no loss to the community in any visible respect and with great gain to the warlike preparations of the State. All this has in some measure hindered the free development of sportsmanship in Germany, and has also doubtless contributed materially to the growth of an aggressive war spirit.

The comprehensive and exacting demands of universal military service as it applies to the population at large have had a somewhat similar effect on the common man, by diverting interest from the make-believe of sports to that of war; and it is not at all certain that the loss to industry from this cause, considerable as it has unquestionably been, has not been fully offset by the greater docility of the working classes resulting from their experience of surveillance and subjection in the army. A military organisation is necessarily a servile organisation, and the discipline of servile obedience will always have its effect.[1]

Running to the same general effect, and working in harmonious concert with the servile discipline of the army, is the government policy of tutelage for the working class, in

---

[1]So, universal military service has proved the most effectual corrective yet brought to bear on the socialistic propaganda and similar movements of discontent and insubordination; and the discipline of servility, or of servitude, enforced in the service is probably to be accounted the chief agency in bringing about the definitive collapse of socialism in Germany, — definitive, that is, for the present and the calculable future, and in all respects but the name, the ritual and the offices. The concomitant warlike propaganda and unstinted dynastic magniloquence have contributed their share to this consummation, but except for the positive training in subjection to personal authority given by universal military service it is at least very doubtful if the German socialist movement could by this date have fallen into its present state of "innocuous desuetude."

the way'of hospital service, insurance and pension arrangements, and the like. In this, again, there is no visible economic loss, perhaps even a visible economic gain, in that
it offsets some of the untoward effects of a businesslike
quest of profits on the part of capitalist-employers gifted
with a scant regard for the long-term welfare of the community. What will be the ulterior consequences of such a
policy of tutelage can not well be surmised, but among these
consequences should come a more passive dependence of
the common man on the directive authority of the government and its bureaucratic machinery, together with a slackening of initiative and of the spirit of autonomy, and the
growth of a certain partisan loyalty to the reigning house.
Past experience and discipline, it should be remarked, predispose the German workmen for this tutelage and its effects. As is well known, though not always avowed, under
the circumstances of the large-scale industry as managed
for business ends, the indigent workmen are helpless while
acting in severalty, and no effectual remedy for this individual helplessness has yet been found in any form of self-
directed collective action. The economic value, and the
political expediency, of the crown's tutelage are all the more
evident, and the ulterior consequences of this tutelage may
accordingly be expected to be all the more far-reaching.
But such ulterior consequences are chiefly to be looked for
among the effects of habit, and in the main they are yet in
the future.

It will be seen, then, that both in its cultural antecedents
and in the current circumstances there are several factors

of considerable scope peculiar to this German case and converging to an outcome different from what has resulted, so
far, among the English-speaking peoples as a consequence
of their taking over the modern industrial arts, — different,
indeed, in a very appreciable degree from what can by any
dispassionate line of reasoning be looked for among the
English-speaking peoples within the calculable future.

Germany carried over from a recent and retarded past
a State, of the dynastic order, with a scheme of detail institutions and a popular habit of mind suitable to a coercive,
centralised, and irresponsible control and to the pursuit of
dynastic dominion. Quite unavoidably, the united Fatherland came under the hegemony of the most aggressive and
most irresponsible — substantially the most archaic — of
the several states that coalesced in its formation; and quite
as a matter of course the dynastic spirit of the Prussian State
has permeated the rest of the federated people, until the
whole is now very appreciably nearer the spiritual bent of
the militant Prussian State of a hundred years ago than it
has been at any time since the movement for German union
began in the nineteenth century.

This united German community, at the same time, took
over from their (industrially) more advanced neighbors
the latest and highly efficient state of the industrial arts, —
wholly out of consonance with their institutional scheme,
but highly productive, and so affording a large margin disposable for the uses of the dynastic State. Being taken over
ready-made and in the shortest practicable time, this new
technology brought with it virtually none of its inherent
drawbacks, in the way of conventional waste, obsolescent

usage and equipment, or class animosities; and as it has been brought into full bearing within an unexampled short time, none of these drawbacks or handicaps have yet had time to grow to formidable dimensions.

Owing in part to the same unprecedentedly short period of its acquirement and installation, and in part to the nearly unbroken mediævalism of the institutional scheme into which the new technology has been intruded, it has hitherto had but a slight effect in the way of inducing new habits of thought on institutional matters among the German population, such as have formed the institutional counterpart of its gradual development among the English-speaking peoples. Such institutional consequences of a workday habituation to any given state of the industrial arts will necessarily come on by slow degrees and be worked out only in the course of generations.

In the English case, as has been indicated in earlier passages, such growth of popular institutions and ideals of autonomy and initiative as may be observed in modern times has not placed popular autonomy in anything like a position of unqualified domination in any of the collective concerns of life. There is much standing over from the earlier, feudalistic and dynastic, régime, as, *e.g.*, the crown, the nobility with its house of lords, and the established church; although these remains so left over are in a visibly infirm state and have something of an air of incongruity and anachronism in their modern setting. "Dead letter" and "legal fiction" have a large place in English conceptions, and these archaic strands in the institutional fabric are in great part to be viewed in that light. At the same time, while the modern institutional notions of popular autonomy have been encroaching on the domain once held by feudalism and the State, there has, along with this growth, also grown into the scheme a new range of customary conceptions and usages that greatly circumscribe the *de facto* supremacy of popular institutions in the British commonwealth.

Any English-speaking community is a commonwealth rather than a State; but none of these communities, for all that, is a commonwealth of free, equal, and ungraded men; their citizens are not "masterless men," except in the cognizance of the law. Discrepancies of wealth have grown great and found secure lodgment in the institutional scheme at the same time that these modern communities have been falling back on those ancient ideals of personal insubordination that makes the substance of their free institutions. And serious discrepancies of wealth are a matter not provided for in that ancient hereditary bent that once made the petty anarchistic groups of the Baltic culture a practicable engine of social control, and that is now reasserting itself in democratic discontent. While property rights work no *de jure* disturbance of the democratic scheme, their *de facto* consequences are sufficiently grave, so that it is doubtful if a free but indigent workman in a modern industrial community is at all better off in point of material circumstances than the workman on a servile tenure under feudalism. Indeed, so grave and perplexing has the situation in the English-speaking countries become, in respect of the *de facto* control of the community's material fortunes by the owners of large property, that none but a graceless "pessimist" is conceived to be capable of calling attention to so sore a difficulty for which no remedy can be discovered. Yet, while the current administration of affairs may be carried on by bailiffs of the wealthy and well-to-do, and primarily in their interest, it remains true that in point of popular sentiment the sovereignty vests collectively in the common man; and it will scarcely be questioned that if brought to a sufficiently sharp test, this popular sentiment would stubbornly assert its paramount dominion.

Partial and incomplete as this shift to popular autonomy proves to have been in the English-speaking nations, it has taken some centuries of experience to carry the community from a position comparable to that occupied by the Germans at the formation of the Empire to the compromise in force among these peoples today. This growth of free institutions and insubordination, such as it is, has apparently come partly of the positive discipline in mechanistic habits of thought given by the modern industrial arts, but partly also as a reassertion of the hereditary anarchistic bent of this population in the absence of duly rigorous circumstances going to enforce a scheme of coercion and loyalty. The net outcome may be rated as a gain or a loss, according as one is inclined to see it. But it is an outcome of the working of the modern industrial system, and if it is to be rated as an infirmity it is also to be accepted as one of the concomitants of that system, inseparable from it in the long run because it is made of the same substance as this technological system.

It is this "long run" that is still wanting in the German case, and it must necessarily be all the longer a run for the care taken by the Imperial State to prevent such an outcome. Meantime the Imperial State has come into the usufruct of this state of the industrial arts without being hampered with its long-term institutional consequences. Carrying over a traditional bias of Romantic loyalty, infused anew with a militant patriotism by several successful wars, and irritably conscious of national power in their new-found economic efficiency, the feudalistic spirit of the population has yet suffered little if any abatement from their brief experience as a modern industrial community. And borne up by its ancient tradition of prowess and dynastic aggression, the Prussian-Imperial State has faithfully fostered this militant spirit and cultivated in the people the animus of a solidarity of prowess. Hence a pronounced retardation in the movement toward popular autonomy, due to follow from habituation to the mechanistic logic of the modern technology and industrial organisation.

In this work of retarding the new and conserving the old the Imperial State has been greatly furthered by finding ready to hand a large and serviceable body of men, useless for industrial purposes by force of conventional and temperamental disabilities, who have eagerly entered the career of prowess opened to them by the warlike enterprise of the Empire and have zealously fallen in with the spirit of that policy, — such being the run of traditions out of which they have come in the recent past. Indeed, so large, so strongly biassed, and so well entrenched in the use and wont of the Fatherland, have this contingent of specialists in prowess been, that even with a very moderate degree of moral support from the constituted authorities, perhaps even on a footing of tolerance — if such a footing were conceivable under the Imperial auspices — their organisation into a specialised corps of war-leaders should have followed as a matter of course; and the presence of such a body of professional military men, pervaded with a headlong enthusiasm for warlike enterprise, would of itself have had the effect of heightening the war spirit abroad in the community at large and inducing a steady drift of sentiment leading to a warlike climax.

It has been the usual fortune of military establishments and warlike class organisations presently to fall into a certain state of moral decay, whereby rank, routine, perquisites and intemperate dissipation come to engage the best attention of the specialists in war. Like other works of use and wont this maturing of the warlike establishment takes time, and the corps of war specialists under the Imperial auspices has not yet had time to work out the manifest destiny of warlike establishments in this respect; although it may be admitted that "irregularities" of the kind alluded to have by no means been altogether wanting. The corrosion of military use and wont, in the way of routine, subordination, arrogance, indolence and dissipation, has perhaps gone so far as would unfit this picked body of men for the duties of citizenship under any but an autocratic government, but they have probably suffered no appreciable impairment in respect of their serviceability for war and its advocacy.

In the same connection, it is also credibly reported, though not officially confirmed, that the highly efficient school system of the Empire, perhaps especially of Prussia, is, under Imperial auspices, made a vehicle for propaganda of the same patriotism of prowess that pervades the body of officers. Something of the kind is known to be true of the Prussian universities. Much can of course be done toward giving a bent of this kind to the incoming generation by well-directed inculcation during the impressionable period of schoolboy life.

One further item should be included in any recital of the special circumstances that go to make Imperial Germany and shape its destiny. Among the gains that have come to the Imperial State, and by no means least among these gains if one is to judge by the solicitous attention given it, is the use of the modern technology for warlike equipment and strategy. It has already been noted that the railway system, as also the merchant marine and its harbor equipment, has been developed under surveillance, with a view to its serviceability in war; in part this transportation system has been projected and built avowedly for strategic use, in part under specifications and with subventions designed to make it an auxiliary arm. The importance of such a competently organised transportation system in modern strategy needs no argument; its bearing on the animus of the statesmen at whose disposal so efficient a factor of warlike equipment is held, as well as on that of the people at large, should also not be overlooked.[1]

---

[1]"There is something in the possession of superior strength most dangerous, in a moral view, to its possessor. Brought in contact with semi-civilised man, the European, with his endowments and effective force so immeasurably superior, holds him as little higher than the brute, and as born equally for his service. He feels that he has a natural right, as it were, to his obedience, and that this obedience is to be measured, not by the powers of the barbarian, but by the will of his conqueror. Resistance becomes a crime to be washed out only in the blood of the victim. The tale of such atrocities is not confined to the Spaniard." — Prescott, *Conquest of Peru*, bk. iv.

But beyond this, and doubtless of graver import, is the direct service rendered by the modern technology and applied science to the art of war. Since the modern technology fell into the hands of the Germans they have taken the lead in the application of this technological knowledge to what may be called the industrial arts of war, with at least no less zeal and no less effect than in its utilisation in the arts of peace. In the "armed peace" of Europe, Imperial Germany has consistently aimed to be the most heavily armed and the readiest for any eventual breach of the peace. These preparations, it has been usual to declare, have been made with a view to keeping the peace. Some weight may perhaps attach to these declarations. They have been made by statesmen of the school of Frederick the Great. The run of the facts in the case is that throughout the forty-four years of its life-history hitherto, and more particularly through the later quarter of a century, preparation for war on a large scale has been going forward unremittingly, and at a constantly accelerating rate, whether as measured in terms of absolute magnitude or as measured in terms of expenditure per capita of the population, or of percentages of current in-

---

Such loss of moral perspective through an overweening sense of power appears to follow equally whether the stronger is or is not superior in any other respect, — perhaps even more pronouncedly in the latter case. The Huns and Turks show it in their dealings with the Romanised Europeans, just as the Children of Israel show it on contact with Canaanites and Philistines, and as it appears again in the animus of Gauls, Goths, Visigoths and Vandals, in their time. So also the swaggering Elizabethan "gentleman adventurer" in his degree, as well as the Spanish conquistador or the Prussian-Imperial statesman. It is the moral attitude of the pot-hunter towards the fur-bearing animals. One does not keep faith with the fur-bearing animals.

come or of accumulated wealth, or as compared with the corresponding efforts of neighboring states.

This drift toward a warlike fatality has been facilitated by subsidiary consequences that should, in their immediate incidence, seem to have no bearing of the kind. So, *e.g.*, their great success in business and industry has inspired the commonplace German subjects with a degree of confidence and self-complacency that impresses their neighbors as conceit and braggadocio. Human nature being what it is, it is unavoidable that German subjects should take the German successes to heart in this way and that they should fall into something of an overbearing attitude toward other nationalities; and on similarly sufficient grounds it follows that those who are brought in contact with this very natural magisterial swagger find it insufferable. All of which engenders a resentful animosity, such as will place all international relations on a precarious footing. So, by force of circumstances over which no control could be had, and which it must be admitted have not been sought to be controlled, it has come about that their economic success has brought the German people an abundance of ill-will; not unmixed with envy, but good and competent ill-will for all that.

It may be worth noting that something of the same sense of estrangement is visible in the attitude of the Continental peoples toward the English of the swaggering Elizabethan times, and after. But the resulting animosity in that case appears not to have reached so high a pitch, and the insular position of the English served in any case to prevent any such animosity from becoming a menace to the public peace.

The consciousness of this pervading ill-will has doubtless contributed appreciably to that patriotic solidarity of prowess in the German people on which the warlike policy of the Imperial government leans, and so has served to accelerate the shifting of the Empire's forces, material and spiritual, into a strategical position incompatible with any but a warlike outcome.

Latterday events have so turned as to cut off speculation as to the chances of war and peace contained in this posture of German affairs. And efforts to place or shift or distribute the blame for the state of war into which Europe has fallen would be little if any more profitable.[1] Yet it may not be altogether beside the point to look farther into the circumstances, as distinct from the diplomatic reasons, which have brought events to this climax. It may safely be said that the outbreak came as a shock to everyone; but it was a surprise to none but the diplomatists, and to them it was only a diplomatic surprise. Along with the shock there was a perceptible sense of relief as from long suspense. It may also safely be said that it was not necessary formally to

---

[1]Much has been said and little has been accomplished in the diplomatic recrimination by which the blame has been sought to be apportioned. All parties to this exchange of blame deny any intention to bring on the war; the German denial being on the whole the more voluble. The reason for this denial is the need of it. There can be no harm in recognising the entire disingenuousness of all parties to the controversy. That the German volume of prevarication is the larger is something of a fortuitous circumstance, due to their more urgent diplomatic need. With the same opportunities and provocation it is doubtful if British diplomacy would not have done just as well, and it is not doubtful that the Russians would have done better.

desire the war in order to bring it to a head, if only care was taken to make the preparations so complete as to make war unavoidable.

The Imperial government is said not to have desired the war, but the proposition is not formulated to the effect that the Imperial government expected to avoid this war in the long run. It has been tacitly assumed — the overt affirmation is officially disavowed — that the conjuncture of circumstances has made recourse to war unavoidable, and it is for Germany specifically that the war has so been recognized as unavoidable. Had there been no Imperial Germany included in the concert of nations the outcome might not have been substantially different in the long run, so far as regards Europe's eventual fortunes in respect of peace and war; but with Germany included there has been no room to doubt that, whenever this prospective war should break out, Germany would be the seat of the disturbance, whether on the offensive or defensive. On this account the case of Germany is of especial interest in its bearing on the conjunction of circumstances.

The decisive circumstance in this German case is what has been strikingly summed up in a phrase as Germany's need of "a place in the sun." The meaning of the phrase is sufficiently plain, and it is currently accepted as sufficiently cogent, and there need be no quarrel with it. But it is well to call to mind the commonplace and obvious fact that this need is a need on the part of the Imperial State, and that the population of Germany — the inhabitants, individually or collectively — have no material interest in this quest of a place in the sun, except the sentimental interest due to that solidarity of prowess that has been alluded to before. It is a need of sportsmanlike patriotism; and the material fortunes of the common man could not conceivably be benefited in the slightest degree by a successful pursuit of this quest.

It lies in the nature of a dynastic State to seek dominion, that being the whole of its nature. This Imperial State has had a certain situation to take care of and to make use of, as has been outlined above. The industrial community at its disposal has been gaining in efficiency, and therefore in point of serviceability as a material basis for the Imperial policy; but this gain or at least the rate of acceleration of this gain, has slightly slackened off in the later years. The rate of gain in population has also declined, indicating among other things an unprofitable rise in the under-class standard of living, — itself a deduction of increasing consequence to be made from the net output of industry available for Imperial (political) use. The like wasteful consumption among the wealthy and well-to-do classes has meantime been taking the same untoward upward turn, — untoward in that it acts to narrow the margin of disposable surplus for Imperial use. In spite of the partial repression and domestication of the socialist partisans, under-class discontent has also increased of late years, particularly, it is said, in the immediately recent past. These are elements not of present weakness, perhaps, but of eventually threatening weakness. While the coefficient of movement in these several lines is still a coefficient of gain, it is in each and several of these lines a gradually and cumulatively declining coefficient.

Of themselves these untoward, or rather prospectively untoward, changes have, at least hitherto, brought no positive or absolute weakening of the material foundations of the Imperial State. But war and dynastic politics are emulative enterprise, competitive; and in competitive enterprise strength is a relative, not an absolute, magnitude. While the Fatherland has been gaining in material powers, its competitors in world politics have also been gaining; and latterly these competitors have on the whole been gaining at a cumulatively accelerating rate.

Other European countries, as, *e.g.*, France, Italy, Russia, and the minor and outlying nations, have also increasingly come in for the usufruct of the same British machine technology to which Imperial Germany owes its dominant place in the industrial world; and while none of them may have made, or even prospectively will be expected to make, gains of the same absolute importance as those recently made by Germany, they still have already begun to narrow the lead of Germany in the industrial field. Their larger resources, more commodious emplacement, and greater aggregate mass will make their competition sufficiently serious even without the same efficiency per capita. So, *e.g.*, even on a smaller coefficient, Russia, with its large mass and unlimited resources, might be counted on presently to overtake Germany in point of aggregate industrial strength, and therefore presumably in point of warlike capacity; and Russia has of late been making disquieting advances in modern industry.

Relatively to the situation at large, therefore, Germany has latterly been gaining, if at all, only at a lessened rate.

It is perhaps safe to say that in this relative sense the Empire has latterly begun to lose. It is even possible that the statesmen of the Empire have come to perceive the fact, or have at any rate begun to be apprehensive of some such untoward eventuality. The best guess of a shrewd outsider not unduly influenced by clamorous laudation of the German achievements would probably be that the date at which Germany ceased to gain in industry and commerce, relatively to the situation at large, came some half a dozen years ago. At the same time, this date marks no abrupt shift in the course of events and has nothing of a catastrophic meaning.

So far, therefore, as regards the material conditions underlying the Imperial policies of dominion, it would appear that these were in their most propitious conjuncture for Imperial utilisation some time, say, within the past half-decade. On the other hand, as regards the factors making directly for a present recourse to arms, the military and naval preparations of the Imperial government were going forward all this while at an accelerated pace. In absolute terms, it is not to be doubted, the equipment and personnel have grown very appreciably larger, and at the same time more efficient per capita, year by year. But here again it is doubtful if this absolute increase in warlike capacity is safely to be counted as a sustained gain in relative warlike force, relatively to the European situation at large. The other European nations have also been making gains, also at an accelerated pace, especially during the past few years; and it should seem that even if the coefficient of increase has been slighter, yet the resulting massive aggregate of increase in warlike capacity among the nations with whom Imperial Germany has had to make up its account has been such as would, during the last few years, throw the net balance of the differential gain slightly against the Empire's score.

This posture of affairs, consequently, has placed the Empire on the defensive. Such, at all events, is the avowed apprehension of the matter on the part of the Imperial statesmen. The German theory of a defensive offense is sufficiently well known. It has been the burden of voluminous diplomatic explanations bearing on certain late occurrences. Placed as the Imperial State has been, with large schemes of dominion, partly avowed and partly matter of common notoriety, and with grievances of obstruction to its legitimate movements waiting to be redressed, the strategy of the defensive offense should demand an unfolding of all available force at the point in this precession of differentials when the cumulative Imperial strength was at its best, relatively to the cumulative strength to be counted with in its environment.

Doubtless these matters have had the solicitous attention of the statesmen. But the statesmen have been patriotic subjects (and sovereign), and being nearer to their own work of preparation than to that of their prospective enemies, in spite of any conceivable efficiency of espionage, they appear to have unduly discounted the gains latterly made by the latter, or perhaps rather they have somewhat overrated their own elements of strength; with the result that the defensive offense has apparently been delayed beyond the most propitious date.

Certain concrete items in this large scheme of Imperial dominion and strategy may be cited as conducing to this untoward delay. So it would appear that the latterday rate both of recuperation and of new growth on the part of Russia has been unaccountably undervalued by the Imperial statesmen, both in the economic field and as regards military equipment and organisation. The like can, of course, scarcely be said for the case of France, nor for the United Kingdom; although in the case of the latter there appears to have been some appreciable, and for the Imperial cause unfortunate, discrepancy between the effective support contributed by the British colonies and the German statesmen's estimates of it. Minor states involved in the present conflict appear also to have been disappointingly strong and ready. On the other hand the colonial possessions of the Empire have during these years not been in a securely defensible condition, and it has apparently not been found practicable to give them the necessary security by surrounding them with the requisite diplomatic defenses. There would rightly be some reluctance about risking the loss of these colonies when a respite might add materially to the chances of holding them intact, whether by diplomatic guaranties or by warlike defences. Specifically, the continued occupation of Kiao Chao, e.g., could be rendered reasonably secure with a suitable allowance of time to complete its defences. In like manner there was the sanguine, perhaps over-sanguine, project for taking over Turkey in Asia, or more specifically the Mesopotamian-Chaldæan tract and the right of way to the Persian gulf, coupled with the rehabilitation of the Ottoman power as a dependent state under the

Imperial suzerainty. This latter may well have been the most seductive provocation to procrastinate unduly in the execution of that defensive offense to which the State has been committed by its policy of dominion. There was much to have been gained here, both as an outlet for the Empire's commerce and disposable population and as a direct accession of military force, if only the necessary work could have been accomplished within the time limit imposed by the menacing growth of these other nations. On any circumspect calculation of the convergence of events it should have been reasonably plain that the time required for this project would unduly postpone the day of accounts. The miscalculation at this point appears to have lain chiefly in an overrating of what could be done with the Turkish establishment to bring it up to an adequate level of serviceability within a scant allowance of time. In any case it would appear that the defensive offense had been delayed beyond the date at which the warlike force of the Empire was at its best, relatively to the situation at large.

Again it is bootless, of course, to speculate on what might have been. It may be more to the point to inquire into the effectual value and consequence of this Prussian-Imperial diversion, in its bearing on the civilisation of Christendom. The pursuit of the Imperial policy has led Christendom into an unexampled war, — an outcome which all men deprecate, whether sincerely or otherwise. At the best rating that can be had, the current war will necessarily be accounted an untoward episode. In the perspective of history it may also some day be so rated. Meantime the fact should not be lost sight of that it was entered on in a sense deliberately and advisedly, and with the best intentions on both sides. This is particularly true for the Prussian-Imperial statesmen and their strategy of defensive offense, though the *bona fides* of the party of the second part are perhaps more perspicuously evident on the face of the returns. Interest, therefore, can not center on the question of praise and blame. Neither can the purpose of the contest, as seen from either side, claim sustained attention, since on the one hand the aim on either side appears to have been sufficiently creditable in the eyes of those in whom discretion vested, while on the other hand the contest will run its course to much the same outcome, and carry substantially the same consequences, whatever the aim may have been.

It is a plain and easy generalisation that the more consequential and enduring effects of the conflict will be of an immaterial nature, in the way of bias and sentiment, affecting the spiritual and intellectual outlook of the peoples, and so coming to an ulterior effect in more or less of a revision of the current institutional scheme. Hitherto the distinctive gains made by this civilisation have been made by way of peace and industry, — by "gains" being understood whatever has conduced to an advance in the direction of the latterday cultural situation among the distinctively Occidental peoples, as contrasted with the cultural scheme of their own barbarian past, in the Dark and Middle Ages. By the generality of civilised men this advance will be rated as, on the whole, an improvement over what it has displaced. Such an appraisal, however, is a matter of taste and opinion, in which the habituation embodied in this modern cultural scheme is itself taken as a base-line of appraisal; and it could, therefore, not be accepted as definitive in any argument on the intrinsic merits of this culture, in contrast with any other. But it is useful as showing that the current consensus, such as there is, runs to the effect that the change from mediævalism to the modern régime is, on the whole, to be rated as an advance, and that consequently this meaning of the term is the only one that is at home in current usage in these premises.

This modern régime, like any other cultural scheme, late or early, is possessed of a certain systematic solidarity, due to the fact that it is pervaded by a certain characteristic logic and perspective, a certain line of habitual conceptions having a degree of congruity among themselves, a "philosophy," as it would once have been called. The exceptions, digressions, excursions and discordant incumbrances carried over by tradition from earlier usage or drawn in from side lines of interest or of constraint, — all this is scarcely to be rated as adventitious or negligible, and it will bulk large in any given cultural scheme, particularly in such a one where the range is wide and the changes are rapid and diverse. Yet, owing to the fact that the community which carries this scheme and is exposed to its discipline is made up of individuals each and several of which is a single agent and is therefore bent as a whole by any habituation to which he is exposed, it follows that just in so far as it is possible to conceive any given cultural complex as a distinctive scheme, it will be characterised by one generally pervading habit of mind, — by no means universally prevalent, but prevalent so extensively and pronouncedly as to be effectual as a common run. Where and in so far as this solidarity of habit does not prevail, the cultural situation is currently recognised as lacking homogeneity, as being a hybrid civilisation, an unstable or transitional phase, etc.

As regards the civilisation of modern Christendom in this bearing, what marks it off pervasively and dynamically from its own earlier phases as well as from other cultures with which it is contrasted, is a certain character of matter-of-fact; showing itself on the institutional side, *e.g.*, in a nearly universal avowed repudiation — often futile enough in practice — of all personal discrimination and prerogative; and showing itself more unequivocally on the side of knowledge, in an impersonal, mechanical conception of objective things and events. So, the most characteristic habit of thought that pervades this modern civilisation, in high or low degree, is what has, in the simplest terms hitherto given it, been called the mechanistic conception.[1] Its practical working-out is the machine technology, of which the intellectual precipitate and counterpart is the exact sciences. Associated with these in such a way as to argue a correlation, of the nature of cause and effect, is the modern drift toward free or popular institutions.[2]

---

[1]Cf. Jacques Loeb, *The Mechanistic Conception of Life.*

[2]This pervasion of modern communities by such a mechanistic conception and by a bias inimical to prerogative and personal government is, of course, to be taken as a matter of habituation and acquired bent, not a derangement or deflection of the underlying instinctive proclivities of human nature. Yet, the habituation leading to this mechanistic, matter-of-fact drift in Western civilisation may presumably be better conceived as a disciplined obsolescence of habitual elements derived from the recent past and no longer enforced by current circumstances, instead of newly acquired habits of thought coercively enforced upon a human nature to

Coercion, personal dominion, self-abasement, subjection, loyalty, suspicion, duplicity, ill-will, — these things do not articulate with the mechanistic conception. Whatever human experience conduces to this range of habits of thought will, by so much, act to retard and defeat the cultural drift toward matter-of-fact; and any scheme or order of control that runs on these grounds will not enduringly contain that range of conceits and convictions that make up the modern body of theoretical knowledge and the principles of the common law. Personal dominion is essentially incongruous with the logic and perspective of this modern culture, and is therefore systematically incompatible with its ascendancy. Warlike experience is experience in personal rule, spoliation, loyalty, hate, subordination and duplicity. Therefore, whatever may be the nominal balance of profit and loss in the way of what is called the "fortunes of war," the net consequences will be much the same; and these consequences can not but be of the nature of retardation to Western civilisation in those respects that mark it as Western and modern.

This warlike-dynastic diversion in which the Imperial State has been the protagonist is presumably of a transient

---

which they are essentially alien. It would appear to be a work of divestment or riddance, quite as much as of investiture or inculcation of a new proficiency. In the absence of, or under reduced pressure from, discipline conducive to personal subjection and abasement, or to the interpretation of objective things and relations in the personalised terms of magical or occult forces, it may be conceived that human faculty will, in a sense atavistically, assert its native bent of matter-of-fact in both of these cognate directions. With the obsolescence of putative occult powers and qualities in the conception of objective reality, such as is required by the machine technology, the like obsolescence of a similar habitual imputation of occult grounds of privilege, authority, and subservience will take effect in the institutional scheme.

nature, even though it can by no means be expected to be ephemeral. The Prussian-Imperial system may be taken as the type-form and embodiment of this reaction against the current of modern civilisation; although that State is not thereby to be accounted the sole advocate of mediævalism among the nations, nor is it a whole-hearted advocate. In the long run, in point of the long-term habituation enforced by its discipline, the system is necessarily inimical to modern science and technology, as well as to the modern scheme of free or popular institutions, inasmuch as it is incompatible with the mechanistic animus that underlies these habits of thought; not necessarily hostile in respect of the sentiments that animate its statesmen and spokesmen in their attitude towards these landmarks of the Western civilisation, but inimical in respect of the set and fashion of the habit of mind which it inculcates.

Yet the Imperial system of dominion, statecraft and warlike enterprise necessarily rests on the modern mechanistic science and technology, for its economic foundations and its material equipment as well as for its administrative machinery and the strategy necessary to its carrying on. In this, of course, it is in the same case with other modern states. Nothing short of the fullest usufruct of this technology will serve the material needs of the modern warlike State; yet the discipline incident to a sufficiently unreserved addiction to this mechanistic technology will unavoidably disintegrate the institutional foundations of such a system of personal dominion as goes to make up and carry on a dynastic State.

The Imperial State, therefore, may be said to be unable

to get along without the machine industry, and also, in the long run, unable to get along with it; since this industrial system in the long run undermines the foundations of the State. So that what the Prussian-Imperial State is, in effect, contending for in its offensive defense of German dominion, is something in the nature of a reprieve for personal government; but the situation has this singular feature that whether the Imperial State wins or loses in the contest for the hegemony, the movement of cultural reversion for which in substance it is contending stands to gain at least to the extent of a substantial, though presumably temporary, impairment and arrest of Western civilisation at large.

While these and the like immaterial consequences of warlike enterprise — its cultural consequences in the conventional sense of the term — are doubtless its most substantial and far-reaching effects, the material cost and the economic sequelæ of the conflict in which this concert of dynastic enterprise has culminated are also no slight matter.

It is usual, especially among the peace advocates, to speak eloquently of the waste of property and life involved in warfare, and to make much of the consequent impoverishment of the countries at war; and no doubt rightly so. So much as the common peace advocate takes note of in these premises being taken for granted, then, there remains to add and deduct what further items a dispassionate scrutiny necessarily would bring into the account.

As to the destruction of property, it has been noted as worthy of remark by many careful writers that countries overrun and devastated by armed force in modern times recover their material prosperity in a surprisingly short time, — surprising, that is, to the historians who record the facts without much reflection on the concatenation of circumstances that bring about this prompt recuperation. Their capacity for surprise in this connection is in some degree helped out by standard economic theory, which makes much of "production goods" as a productive agency.

The material equipment in such a case of devastation will have been greatly damaged, and that is always a handicap; but the immaterial equipment of technological proficiency — the state of the industrial arts considered as a system of habits of thought — will have suffered relatively slight damage, provided the season of hostilities is not protracted beyond reasonable expectation; and what damage it may have suffered in the way of a loss of specially trained personnel is relatively easy to remedy under the current technological system. This immaterial equipment is, far and away, the more important productive agency in the case; although, it is true, economists have not been in the habit of making much of it, since it is in the main not capable of being stated in terms of price, and so does not appear in the statistical schedules of accumulated wealth.

On the other hand, under settled conditions of peace and commonplace prosperity a large share — commonly somewhat over fifty per cent — of the customary, and conventionally necessary, consumption of the population will, as has already been remarked before, consist of articles whose use is only conventionally necessary, and the consumption of which may be discontinued without physical hardship and without lowering the productive capacity of the popula-

tion. In time of stress, as in a season following warlike
devastation, the conventions governing the necessary consumption of decent superfluities are likely to be seriously
demoralised, so that this "unproductive" consumption will
be greatly reduced for the time being. At the same time,
and on similar grounds, the conventionally decent avoidance
of productive work, whether on the strength of sacred or of
secular tabu, will also fall somewhat into abeyance. Of
minor importance, but of the same general bearing, is the
slighter need of and the slighter attention given to sports
and similar dissipations at such seasons of general stress,
when everyone has something more interesting to occupy
the attention. The "secret" of this phenomenon of recuperation would accordingly be that under these circumstances
the net production of the community rises nearly to the
level of its gross productive capacity, or at least comes much
nearer that level than in piping time of peace. While there
need be no intention, therefore, to minimise the devastation
of war, it appears also that the gravity of the material destruction involved may readily be overrated.

The economic effects of war finance should also not be
overlooked. Modern wars, as, *e.g.*, the one now current,
are largely conducted on a credit basis. Taxes and similar
imposts, mandatory and voluntary, of course, play their
part, and these might also afford interesting topics of inquiry; but war taxes are after all of much the same character
and incidence as taxes for governmental consumption in
time of peace, and a pursuit of their idiosyncrasies in this
place would lead too far afield. War loans, and all the class
of credit extensions in which they belong are, on the other

hand, so large and consequential a feature of the case as to merit some special attention.

The aggregate of war taxes, plus loans and similar obligations floated on occasion of the war, may be taken as roughly indicating the aggregate wealth consumed in prosecuting the enterprise, not including the incidental waste due to devastation of one kind and another. This is of itself a sufficiently notable matter; but it is also sufficiently notorious, and it is matter for the eloquence of the peace advocates. An ulterior effect of these fiscal transactions has not had the same degree of attention. War loans, and floating obligations that will presently be funded, effect a redistribution of wealth, which may not be of large proportions as counted in percentages on the face of the securities issued, but which will bulk large in the aggregate and in the long run because of the large volume of these obligations and because of their presumably perpetual character. The demand for war loans invariably advances the date of interest on securities of its class, which leads immediately to a re-rating of outstanding securities with a fixed income, at a lower capitalisation. Apart from disturbances of trade and markets incident to the war, property is in effect recapitalised on the basis of a higher rate of interest.[1] The volume of obligations is also increased, probably by a figure not far short of the total war obligations issued.[2] At the same time

---

[1]See Note V, p. 341.

[2]It has been estimated, with apparent care and good faith, that the current cost of the war now in progress, to the United Kingdom alone, aggregates some seven and a half million dollars a day. This sum may without exaggeration be tripled to represent the current aggregate cost of the war to the belligerents. This does not include the costs incurred

neither the aggregate property in hand among the nations of Christendom, nor their aggregate productive efficiency, is increasing at any comparable rate, if there is not rather a decrease than an increase in these items. The new claims on the aggregate income so established by this issue of securities, and the covert lien on the aggregate wealth in hand conveyed by these instruments, constitute in effect a transfer of ownership to the holders of these securities, of an undivided interest in the community's wealth amounting approximately to the aggregate face value of the securities issued. By that much, the usufruct of the productive capacity of these countries passes to the holders of the securities. And since no wealth and no productive capacity is created by this enterprise, it should follow that the ownership of the existing aggregate of wealth, including the capitalisable productive resources of all kinds, personal and impersonal, will in effect be redistributed in the measure which these considerations may indicate. How far the newly credited claims may, in the end, fall short of the total wealth in hand or of the aggregate usufruct of the productive capacity of the Western nations it would be hazardous to estimate just yet. Incidentally, this extensive transfer of ownership raises an interesting question also as to whose discretion is to guide the affairs of these nations on this new pecuniary footing, and in whose behalf.

The loss of life incident to the enterprise is doubtless a

---

in this behalf by neutrals, or the obligations issued by them. It will perhaps not be excessively wide of the mark to assume that the volume of loans outstanding increases at the rate so indicated; since the loans to neutrals on account of war costs will probably offset whatever costs incurred by the belligerents are not defrayed out of loans.

more serious matter than the loss of wealth, and a more interesting one even apart from any humanitarian reflections on the hardships and obscenities of the campaign. But there are certain (economically) mitigating circumstances that should not be overlooked, also in this connection. Probably the most consequential loss as touches the personnel engaged in the warlike operations is the loss of morale, loss of the frame of mind serviceable for peaceful occupations, due to the discipline of the service, to incidental dissipation and "irregularities," to exposure to the vicissitudes of a vocation made up of those things that would in private life be called arson, treason, murder, larceny, and the rest of what the decalogue forbids. These are infirmities that unavoidably beset the personnel and unavoidably lower their industrial serviceability.[1] The like is true for the physical infirmities due to disease and exposure.

But at this point, as at so many others, there is a margin between gross and net; although the margin at this point may not be so wide as in the matter of the industrial equipment spoken of above. As regards the actual mortality

---

[1] Such experience of irresponsible outrage and irremediable calamity as is brought on by war has also the effect of driving the men (and women) exposed to it into recourse to magical and supernatural aid, — the futility of which is only known, not proven. With ill-concealed glee the clergy are already calling attention to a recrudescence of religious superstition among the troops engaged on both sides in the current campaign, and the like evidence that common sense is being superseded by spasmodic sentiment is to be seen also among the unfortunate ones left at home, whose addiction to devout observances is said to have greatly increased. Of much the same bearing, by some sort of inversion or repercussion, is also the notably increased volume of profanity in which, it is credibly reported, the ostensible unbelievers are seeking refuge from their sense of helplessness and incurable wrong.

caused by such a war, the loss of economically valuable personnel is by no means precisely the same as the aggregate loss of life. Even under a system of conscription and universal service there is a degree of self-selection takes effect in the formation of a military or naval force. Those individuals whose temperamental bent fits them for a military rather than an industrial occupation are after all drawn into the service somewhat more inclusively, and to the (slight) extent to which such a selective process is operative in drawing men into the service it will also be effective as touches the mortality in the service. As regards the rank and file the mortality will probably have little of this selective effect, particularly under a system of universal conscription. But the case is not the same as regards the officers, especially where they are drawn by self-selection chiefly from the well-to-do classes, as happens, e.g., in the case of the Germans and British. These will presumably be men peculiarly fit for warlike enterprise, and so presumably unfit for the arts of peace. Also, whatever may be the case in respect of their congenital fitness for war, it should be noted that officers commonly are gentlemen, in the several senses which that word conveys; and gentlemen commonly have no industrial value. Indeed, as bears on the net industrial efficiency of the community they have appreciably less than no value, being typically unproductive consumers. The mortality among the officers may therefore be set down as net gain, in the economic respect; and since they will at an average be highly efficient consumers, their demise should count as an economic relief to the community at large, and count at something more than a mere per capita rating.

Among persons who are solicitous to credit warfare with many evil consequences it is not unusual to hold that the mortality of war works a permanent detriment to the population by destroying "the best" of the male population and selectively leaving the dependents, delinquents and defectives to continue the breed. The modicum of truth in this sensational allegation is not to be denied, but the necessary qualifications are nearly sufficient to set it aside. "The best," as contemplated by this proposition, are the best for the warlike purpose, not necessarily for any other. And under the Mendelian rule of heredity, breeding from what may be called the "depauperate" representatives of this hybrid stock should in the course of some two or three generations give the same results as breeding from the best exemplars. Some slight and transient lowering of the average is doubtless to be looked for from this cause; but the current state of the European populations in respect of physical vigor and of the other qualities of manhood should be sufficiently reassuring on this head, in so far as touches the long-term effect of mortality in war. These populations have been subjected to a selective weeding-out of the men fit for warlike consumption, ever since the barbarian invasions began, and there is not the slightest evidence of a lower average fitness in their manhood today than at any previous period.

SUPPLEMENTARY NOTES

SUPPLEMENTARY NOTES

I

(Note to Chapter I, page 7)

Confining attention to the tract of country immediately in question, and accepting the scheme of European races offered by Mr. Ripley[1] and by the wide consensus of anthropologists for whom Mr. Ripley speaks, it appears that the European populations are made up of three main racial stocks — the Mediterranean (dolicho-brunet), the Alpine (brachycephalic-brunet), and the Northern (dolicho-blond) — neglecting minor factors, some of which may be of appreciable consequence locally.[2]

In rough outline, and so far as bears on the German population, these three main racial stocks are found to be distributed in three broad, overlapping bands which tend loosely to conform to parallels of latitude, in such a way that the area of greatest frequency for the Mediterranean race falls along the Mediterranean seaboard, while that of the Alpine runs across the middle of Europe, and the dolicho-blond is found chiefly in the north, and

---

[1] W. Z. Ripley, *The Races of Europe.*

[2] Much the same result will be had, so far as bears on the question in hand, if the scheme offered by Deniker (*The Races of Man*) is adhered to, but with the difference that the argument would then have to do with five or six main racial stocks composing the European population at large. (Cf. C.O.E. Arbo, "Den blonde Brachycephal og dens sandsynlige Udbredningsfelt," *Christiania Vid. Selsk. Forh.* 1906.) Neither do the special considerations offered by Sergi's scheme (*The Mediterranean Race*) affect the present question in such way as to disturb the line of argument based on Ripley's presentation of the racial traits of the contemporary European peoples.

more particularly in the seaboard region of the Baltic and North Sea. But in this geographic distribution of races no one of the three occupies any one of these three zones to the exclusion of either of the other two; this being particularly true of the tract of country occupied by the German people and their immediate neighbors. While each race is at its strongest within the zone so indicated as its area of greatest frequency, each is also seen to be diffused through the other two zones, but more sparingly the farther outward from what may be called its home area. Of these three stocks it is safe to say that the dolicho-blond is the more closely confined to the region of its own latitude, at the same time that it also visibly tends to be confined, somewhat loosely, to the seaboard country — taking "seaboard" in a large and liberal sense.

It follows that the German population is made up in the main of the two races that center upon the middle and northern latitudes of Europe — the Alpine and Northern races — but by no means to the exclusion of the third — the Mediterranean race — which comes into this resulting hybrid mixture in such considerable force that it can not fairly be rated as a negligible or minor factor, even if it is present in a less obtrusive way and in smaller volume than either of the other two. Each of these three stocks, then, is diffused as a constituent in a hybrid population throughout the German area, as also through the territories occupied by those other peoples with whom the Germans are most frequently compared or contrasted; and there is no class or condition of men, and no locality, either in Germany or in these neighboring countries, that does not contain a mixture of these races; but this racial mixture varies from place to place in respect of its average composition in such a way that, e.g., the dolicho-blond is found in a decreasing proportion at each farther remove from the seaboard region of the Baltic and North Sea, while it virtually disappears on the Mediterranean seaboard. The brunets, therefore, preponderate in the south, while the blond stock is at its strongest in the north, where, as, e.g., on the Baltic seaboard, it may in given localities account for as much as one-half of the population.

It may be remarked by way of parenthesis that there is quite commonly something of an inclination to overstate the prevalence of the blond stock in the north-German and Scandinavian region.

As has been indicated above, while these several racial stocks are diffused at large through the length and breadth of Europe, the diffusion of each tends at the same time to follow parallels of latitude, loosely, it is true, but still somewhat consistently. This applies more decisively to the dolicho-blond than to either of the other two, at the same time that this stock does not readily or permanently spread very far from the seaboard, or out of the climatic reach of the seaboard. It follows that the geographical distribution of the racial mixture that characterises the German people takes the shape of a roughly oblong or rectangular region, confined on the west by the Atlantic and on the east, with a much less definite frontier, by the limits of the eastward reach of the climatic area of the North Sea. This region lies approximately within the meridians of 10° west and 30° east of Greenwich. Its northern and southern frontiers are much less easy to define, depending greatly on the configuration of the land surface and on the reach of the Baltic-North Sea climatic area. In the most general way it is confined toward the south and southeast by the height of land that makes the watershed between the North Sea and the Mediterranean. On the north the (highly irregular) frontier may fairly be said to be determined by the same climatic dependence. It will be seen that the delimitation is essentially a climatic one and that the central and dominant factor in this climatic area is the Baltic-North Sea littoral, with a cool, humid and equable meteorological character. The region in question lies (roughly) between, though its limits do not in any way coincide with, the parallels of 48° and 60° north latitude.

So consequential a part does the seaboard climate play in determining the limits of this anthropological region that it might, again, be indicated in rough outline as the area covered by the sweep of a vector measuring some 12° to 15° latitude and pivoted in the neighborhood of Christiania or Stockholm; its sweep would then include the British Isles on the west and Petrograd on the east. Within this extensive tract the racial complexion of the population will be found to vary less through its length on any parallel so determined than across its width at any cross-section. An exception to this general statement would perhaps be found in Russian territory, where such a cross-section would probably show relatively little systematic variation; while the general proposition is, on the other hand, well illustrated in German territory, where the difference in racial composition is greatly larger between north and south than it is between east and west.

Some slight chance there will always be, of course, that through long continued natural selection among this hybrid population, under local conditions that have strongly favored a given one of these racial types as against its co-rivals, a so-called "pure line" may have been established, — effectually pure-bred in point of heredity though not of pedigree.[1] Such an episodic outcome of selective breeding might not unreasonably be looked for, *e.g.*, among the blonds of Finland, or among the brachycephalic-brunets of the Alps or the Tyrol, or again among the dolicho-brunets of Sicily or Sardinia. The irrelevancy of any such conceivable episodic "pure line," as bearing on the question of race purity in any of the European nations, is sufficiently evident.

For reasons evident to all students of race distribution in Europe, the chance of such a selective working-out of a pure line is also much smaller as regards the blond stock than as regards the other two main races. The climatic tolerance of this type of man is much more restricted than that of either of the two brunets, and very greatly more restricted than that of the brachy-cephalic-brunet. While the blond does not survive, even in a dilute hybrid form, for many generations in the special habitat

---

[1]"Pure line" is borrowed from the usage of Professor W. Johannsen (cf. *Elemente der exakten Erblichkeitslehre*, IX. Vorlesung, esp. p. 133), but it will be noticed that the term is not here used in precisely the sense which he assigns it.

of the Alpine, the latter has apparently very little if any handicap as against the blond in that North Sea habitat in which alone the latter type can permanently maintain itself. From this viability under varying climatic and topographic conditions on the part of the Alpine type, it follows that while the blond tends incontinently to disappear from among the brunet populations lying to the south, the brunet shows no tendency to disappear from among the blonds in the north. So it has come about that there is presumably no community, assuredly not within the limits of the German Empire or of the British Isles, that can safely be rated as more than half blond. What can be said in these premises is that, by and large, this hybrid population of Germany, or of the British Isles, is more blond towards the north and more brunet towards the south, but that taken in the aggregate the brunet elements will doubtless greatly outweigh the blond in both countries.

Before leaving this matter of European races and their hybrid offspring a further consideration may be in place, bearing on questions of the stability of national types. The theories of heredity currently held by the general body of biologists conceive the type of any given species to be invariable throughout the life-history of the species. So that under this rule of the stability of specific types no effectual change, no change transmissible by inheritance, can come in so long as the race (species) endures. Transient changes of adaptation — "ecological" variations — are not excluded; but these changes are ephemeral only; they are only such changes as will not permanently alter the complement of hereditary traits that mark the type.

Hitherto anthropologists and ethnologists have not made up their account with this biological tenet; although they have long been in the habit of tacitly assuming such a stability of types for the races of mankind, in so far as their researches have turned on race identity over intervals of time or space, but with the (tacit and matter-of-course) infraction of this rule in all inquiries into the rise and derivation of any given race. Historians have, quite naturally, not been troubled with biological conceptions of this recondite order. That such has been the state of things on this head is doubtless due to the fact that the biologists themselves have come to a realisation of the scope and bearing of this concept of invariable types only within the last fifteen years, since Mendel's experiments on hybrids have been known and their bearing on heredity and variation is coming to be appreciated.

Whatever laws of heredity may prove to hold for animals at large will necessarily hold for mankind. And, accepting what is commonly accepted among biologists on this head, it follows that the several racial stocks that go into the make-up of the European populations today are what they were in the beginning. Ever since these types of man extant in Europe today took their rise — in quaternary, or tertiary time perhaps — the complement of hereditary traits with which they are capable of endowing their offspring have not varied, for better or worse. So that no heritable amelioration or deterioration (with the exception of ephemeral fluctuations as spoken of above) has taken place in any of the races of Europe since these races made their first settlement, presumably in the neolithic age. In point of native gifts, therefore, the population of Christendom today is a faithful reproduction of its ancestry in the stone age.

Some slight special attention may here be given to the case of the dolicho-blond stock and its origin and heredity, chiefly as a convenient illustrative instance of the position which this biological tenet of stability assigns any given race of men as regards their hereditary traits. This race is not known to have lived (except by transient excursions) outside of Europe, nor indeed in any permanent way outside the climatic reach of the Baltic-North Sea region; nor is it known ever to have lived in isolation from other races, the archæological evidence running uniformly to the effect that the communities in which blonds have been found have had a mixed population. It is also not known, with any approach to certainty, to have lived in Europe earlier than late quaternary time, — perhaps not until at or near the close of the last period of glaciation. In archæological chronology this would mean neolithic time.

This state of the archæological evidence, taken in conjunction with the biological rule that specific types are stable and can therefore arise only by abrupt mutation from previously existing types, gives at least presumptive force to the view that this type of man arose in Europe, presumably in late quaternary (neolithic) time, by mutation from some (neolithic) stock of men then inhabiting that country.[1]

Little — some say nothing — is known by direct observation of the rise of a new specific type or stock by mutation from another parent stock. The theory is held on grounds of unavoidable inference from evidence mainly supplied by observations of reversion to type among hybrids, which takes such a direction as to involve the necessary assumption of the stability of specific types. But even with the rejection of the mutation theory as a method of explaining the presence of the dolicho-blond in Europe, the acceptance of the dictum that specific types are stable — and that position appears to be unassailable — leaves the force of the argument at this point much the same as if the mutation theory were accepted. This argument, then, leads to the conclusion (a) that since this type of man makes its appearance in Europe in early neolithic time and survives as an element of enduring and growing importance in the neolithic population, it, or rather its hybrid offspring produced by crossing back on its parent or associate stock, must have been well suited by native gift to the conditions of life offered at the time. Its later, and permanent, restriction to the peculiar habitat offered by the Baltic seaboard argues further that this type (or its hybrids) was well adapted to the conditions of life, climatic and other, offered by that region. What these conditions were, as well as the manner in which this neolithic population met and took advantage

---

[1] Cf. "The Mutation Theory and the Blond Race," *The Journal of Race Development*, April 1913.

of these conditions, is coming to be passably well known from the archæological evidence of life in .he neolithic on the Baltic littoral. The eminently successful way in which that blond (hybrid) population made good its survival and multiplied under the given conditions argues further also, though less conclusively, that the type and its ordinary range of hybrid offspring were peculiarly suited to the manner of life adopted in so making good the survival of the type, and therefore presumably less well adapted to any other, widely different, manner of life. The run of evidence from other species of animals appears on the whole to go pretty consistently to the effect that each species is less well suited to survive under conditions widely different from those to which it may be said to be native. Most species suffer with any radical change of environment, many to the point of extinction. Specifically applied to this type of man this proposition would be formulated to the effect that the European blond-hybrid is native to the neolithic culture and will thrive under the (widely different) conditions of civilised life only by tolerance and by force of assiduous training. The parallel offered by the domestic animals, particularly by trained animals, as contrasted with the same species in the wild state, is suggestive on this head. The European blond's (hybrid) state of nature, or wild state, would be the neolithic culture of Europe, rather than anything more primitive or anything more recent.

(b) Placed as the blond stock has been in early European time, in a tract of country occupied by a mixed population, this stock can from the outset have survived only by way of cross-breeding with the other race or races with which it has been associated. This proposition takes on an added degree of force and definition if the blond is recognised as a mutant type, arisen in Europe as suggested above. In such a case the stock that so arises by mutation is born into a community made up of its parent stock, and it will have no chance of breeding except by crossing back on the parent stock. A degree of reflection on the known distribution of races, far and near, will leave little doubt that what is here said of the special case of the dolicho-blond applies with more or less cogency to the case of any other race, whether in Europe or elsewhere; and in every case the acceptance of the mutation theory, with the consequent definite recognition of the stability of racial types, will further enforce this proposition and give a sharper definition to the conception of "race" as distinct from "people."

(c) What has taken place in the domestication of animals and their adaptation by selective breeding to their special uses and the special conditions of life under domestication suggests a line of argument that might seem applicable to the several nationalities of Europe, and here specifically applicable to the German population. The domestic animals are commonly held to be, in the main, of hybrid derivation. Selective breeding extending over long intervals of time has been directed to certain fairly definite ends, and therefore to the production in each case of a certain fairly definite range of hereditary traits; with the result that certain artificial races have been established, showing in each case a certain, passably well-defined, racial character. These artificial races of hybrid derivation are passably stable — breed true approximately — so long as they enjoy the selective surveillance and degree of isolation that has given them their characteristic type. Latterly, by strict and intelligent selection, it has proved possible to establish new racial types of this artificial kind within a relatively short series of generations. But these types so established by selective breeding are stable only in a provisional sense. When these artificial races escape from domestication they will commonly either revert in the direction of one or another of their ancestral types (as, *e.g.*, in the case of the mustang — broncho, cayuse — of Spanish-Arab derivation, which appears when run wild to have made appreciable progress in the direction of the type of *Equus przevalskii*) or they presently disappear (as, *e.g.*, commonly happens with the domestic fowl escaped from domestication), with or without concomitant loss of their characteristic marks.

Pursuing the analogy so afforded by the domestic animals it might be argued that any given cultural scheme or system, as, *e.g.*, the latterday German, acting with a consistently selective effect on a hybrid population, should in the course of time give rise to an hereditary national type, after the analogy of the several breeds or races of domestic animals. Such a national race would then be of a provisionally stable type, in a manner and degree comparable with the stability of type characters found in the artificial races of animals, as, *e.g.*, in the various breeds of hens or geese. The several nations or peoples of Europe would then, on this view, be fairly regarded as hybrid races which have been selectively bred into a passably, but effectually, uniform type — uniform in respect of the characters required by this cultural scheme — which will stand so long as the selective conditions out of which it has arisen may continue in force.

Several considerations come in to disable this line of argument as applies to any European nation, and specifically as regards the population of Germany. Man is a slow-breeding animal, some thirty years being conventionally given to one generation; the length of time required to effect the definition of such a hybrid type as is contemplated would therefore be very considerable, even if the selective breeding for type were carried out under the strictest conceivable control and with the most intelligent and unwavering aim. But the selective action in the case is nothing more exacting than a relatively lax and shifty differential advantage in favor of such individuals as conform with exceptional facility to a given traditional manner of life and system of opinions and ideals. At the same time the system of institutions that is supposed to work this selective adaptation is engaged in an incontinent process of change, such as to change the conditions of life unremittingly, and therefore progressively to vary the ground of selective breeding by that much. These changes in the cultural situation have been going forward at a visibly rapid rate in modern times, particularly as regards those technological factors that directly affect the material conditions of life; and it is necessarily these material conditions that will have the strictest and most immediate selective effect on the population.

It would be only under the (presumably) stable or slow-changing conditions of prehistoric times that this population could conceivably have been exposed to sufficiently active selective forces through a sufficient series of generations to give rise to a selectively established hybrid type of the kind in question; and assuming that such a national type had been achieved in prehistoric times, it must in any case have gone to pieces in the succeeding turmoil of the barbarian invasions and the troublous times that have made up the later history of the peoples about the Baltic and North Sea.

So also it is a matter of common notoriety that immigrants of pure-bred German, Slavic, or British extraction who settle in America, or in any of the other north-European colonies, lose their distinctive national character in two or three generations; that is to say, just so soon as they have outlived the traditional views, prejudices, habits and ideals brought from home; which goes to show that none of these nationalities, or others that might be named, have worked out a national type of hybrids. Whether the matter is taken from the side of current everyday observation or from that of European race-history, the outcome appears to be the same: there is no hereditary difference between, *e.g.,* the British, the German and the Slavic population — say of Great Russia — when these are considered as aggregates. Each varies by wider differences within itself than the average difference between one and another.

II

(Note to Chapter II, page 17)

In any such survey recourse will necessarily be had chiefly to Scandinavian sources, and primarily to the Danish evidence and the work of Danish archæologists. Not that the civilisation in question is in any consequential sense to be accounted Danish, as contrasted with other nationalities of northern Europe. This whole early phase, or sequence of phases, of civilisation lies so far in the past, beyond the beginnings of a Danish nationality, that any such territorial delimitation would be meaningless, as would also any attempt to discriminate between Danish origins and the origins of the other Baltic peoples in that early time. The precedence necessarily given to Danish antiquities and archæologists, even as related to those of the other Scandinavian countries, is in a way a matter of accident.

Geographical circumstances decided that what are now Danish coast lands came to be the central area of this cultural region; though it would perhaps be equally true and more perspicuous to say that this Baltic culture centered upon the narrow waters of these Scandinavian shores, of which, however, a great share falls within what are now Danish lands. The remains of the early Baltic culture occur more abundantly in Denmark; but southwestern Sweden is nearly as important a field; and the work of Swedish scholars in this field is scarcely to be rated second to that of the Danes, assuredly second to none else.

There is a second reason for turning by preference to the work of the Danes, and of their friends in Sweden and Norway. They were the first in this archæological field and have cultivated it the most diligently — as they also have had the largest and most immediate access to the materials. At the same time, doubtless in part because they have been occupied with this study so long and intimately, they are also fortunate in having reached a more sober and matter-of-course appreciation and insight than many of their neighbors who have spent valuable work in the same field. The bias of chauvinism has perhaps not yet been wholly lost by these Scandinavian scholars, but it has at least ceased to dominate their inquiries, to infuse their premises, and color their conclusions in the degree that it once did long ago when the early generation of them began the work; one can not truthfully say the like, or at least not with the same assurance, for their nearest neighbors, whose work in any case is of a slighter character and is more pervasively marked with the blemishes that come of youthful haste.

There were several material circumstances that threw these Scandinavian lands, or waters, into their central position in the early Baltic cultural region: these narrow waters afforded an abundant food supply as well as, presently, an easy means of movement and communication; the Danish lands, particularly, afforded an abundant and accessible supply of flint of the best quality, — the indispensable primary material for tools in the neolithic technology; and the forests yielded an excellent and plentiful supply of timber, while the soil — prevailingly sandy with sufficient marl — was fertile and easily tilled; all of which quickly and easily brought the population to such a density as would most efficiently make use of the resources at hand with the state of the industrial arts at their disposal. Presently, in the course of the stone age, there was added to this combination of advantages the discovery of the amber supply on the beaches of Jutland, and of its commercial value, which further acted to maintain the Danish lands in the central position they had already taken.

With such security as material of this kind can afford, the available evidence goes to show that the culture which so grew up about the Scandinavian waters ran a fairly even course, with a moderate and not notably fluctuating rate of advance, over a long interval of time; long even as counted in generations, and coming near enough to an unvarying character to exercise a somewhat consistent and presumably decisive selective action on the mixed population that so got their living under its rule. The Baltic stone age shows a sequence of changes, both in technological and in other matters, but they are, after all, such changes as circumstances will permit within the relatively narrow compass of a neolithic technology; and such changes as occur are distributed over a period which doubtless exceeds by many fold the interval that has elapsed since its close.[1]

The age of bronze is of shorter duration, its close being considered by Scandinavian students to fall between 800 and 300 b.c. Montelius speaks for 500 b.c. At the same time changes or disturbances are more visible in the evidence from the bronze age. Yet its one thousand years or more will scarcely be rated as comparable with a like interval elapsed since these Baltic peoples came into history, in point of wide-reaching innovations and shifting fortunes for these populations. The prehistoric iron age shows a still less settled state of things, whether in the state of the industrial arts or in the conditions of life more at large. In the amplitude and frequency of the changes that passed over the Baltic population, indeed, the iron age is rather suggestive of the restless state of western Europe since the barbarian invasions set in.

The age of stone, and less convincingly that of bronze, therefore, are the only period in their life-history that offers a technological situation of sufficient stability and duration to have exercised a decisively selective action on this north-European hybrid population, and so to have tested their hereditary fitness to live and enduringly to prosper under its dominion. Congenitally, therefore, this population should be preëminently fit

---

[1]On the chronological basis offered by Montelius, who is to be rated as conservative in the matter, the Danish stone age should have run from the close of quaternary time — the last recession of the north-European ice-sheet — to about 1700 b.c. What this interval may amount to in centuries is a question for the geologists, but there is apparently no consensus among the adepts at present that would rate it at less than 10,000 years for the Scandinavian stone age as a whole, and allowing at least 3,000 years for its period of full development. Cf. O. Montelius, *Les temps préhistoriques en Suède;* Sophus Müller, *Vor Oldtid;* A. Penck and Ed. Brückner, *Die Alpen im Eiszeitalter,* vol. iii. Schluss, ch. ii. "Chronologie des Eiszeitalters in den Alpen"; also Sophus Müller, *Aarböger for nordisk Oldkyndighed,* 1909, "Bronzealderens Begyndelse og äldre Udvikling i Danmark, efter de nyeste Fund."

to conduct their affairs by the ways and means which the stone age placed at their disposal and according to the scheme of life which resulted from the use of those means in this peculiar environment.

The available direct evidence from the stone age necessarily is altogether of a material kind, and it therefore bears witness directly to nothing else than the material conditions and the state of the industrial arts; indirectly, by way of circumstantial evidence, something, but not much, is also shown as to the state of institutions. So, it is known that this Scandinavian (Danish-Swedish) region through the best part of this prehistoric period was furnished with abundant forests, productive fisheries, including shell-fish, a good supply of game, and with an equable climate.[1] In addition, as already noted above, it offered a fertile soil and a ready supply of excellent flint, the material of the primary tools in the stone age.[2]

The country is drawn on a small scale, in that it is so cut into strips and patches of land and water as to interpose an insuperable obstacle to the coercive control of extensive territories by any industrial organisation or by any authority of a governmental kind which has command of only such ways and means as the neolithic technology will afford. Yet it is a tract of country that includes relatively little waste land, and what waste

---

[1] In all this there is a suggestive resemblance to the Northwest Coast region of America.

[2] Owing to its peculiar geological formation Denmark, and southwestern Sweden in a less pronounced way, was fortunate above all other European countries in its large, excellent and readily accessible flint supply. The Danish islands and much of the peninsula are superficially of the nature of a moraine on a large scale, thrown up across the south end of the Baltic trough by glacial action which scooped out that trough and left a moraine-like bar carrying non-chalky boulders, boulder clay, sand, marly soil, and particularly the refractory flint nodules derived from the chalk. The underlying formations are also mainly cretaceous. The flint consequently occurs in extraordinarily large proportion, as compared with places where it is found only in place in the chalk beds, as, *e.g.*, on the English downs.

land there is is not sufficiently rough to interpose serious barriers to communication; and the like may be said for the waters of the region, which cut it into parcels, but at the same time afford a convenient means of intercourse. The parcelment and diversification goes far enough effectually to hinder extensive control without hindering extensive intercourse, with the material means at the disposal of the Baltic peoples; in that state of the industrial arts it may be said that the character of the country facilitated escape from any undue or irksome coercion, while it hindered effectual pursuit as well as an effectual reach of economic pressure, such as will support a large political power or a wealthy idle class.[1]

From the diversified character of the country and its resources follows the peculiar character of its industrial system. During the greater part of the stone age, but more pronouncedly through the period of its full development, it appears to have

---

[1]There is in this respect a good deal of a parallel between the Baltic and the Aegean regions; but the parcelment is harsher in the Aegean, the barriers of waste land are more mountainous and more discouraging to travel and traffic, and the stretches of water are more open and more difficult for a primitive navigation; neither does any one spot in the Aegean region hold a place of such differential advantage in resources and location as is to be found on the Danish waters (with the partial and doubtful exception of Melos and its obsidian deposits). The outcome, in early times, also shows a parallel in that the population of both regions are scattered in small communities, independent but in close communication and showing a community of the arts of life. But with it all, the Aegean region, offering sharper and more stubborn natural lines of delimitation, shows also a closer and more coercive organisation of its early peoples, into sharply defined and differentiated communities that choose defensible positions and take precautions against coercion from without.

On the other hand this Baltic situation comes in contrast with the large-scale continental regions of the East, as, e.g., the Asiatic steppes or the Mesopotamian-Chaldæan lowlands; where large bodies of serviceable land have lent themselves to the early organisation of a pastoral, or in places also an agricultural, industry on a large scale, with consequent large groupings of population, wide discrepancies in the distribution of wealth, and a close and often coercive governmental control.

been a country of mixed farming, with a good deal of fishery and hunting as accessory means of living. Except for an indefinite, though perhaps very considerable, interval at the outset, it can not be claimed that hunting and fishing were the main dependence; and there is room for serious doubt as to whether these pursuits were more important than tillage even from very near the beginning of the Danish stone age.

This mixed farming makes use of the crop plants — chiefly grains as far as known — that have since continued to feed Europe; the earliest being barley, with other grains presently added. Its complement of domestic animals is likewise the usual range of European live-stock; the number of species used gradually increasing with the passage of time. As a characteristic trait of its industrial system, it is eminently a wood-working people; stone work being relatively absent — except in the matter of stone tools, — and even pottery being less in evidence, either for quantity or quality, than might be looked for by students unfamiliar with the local conditions of climate and the local supply of raw materials. Far and away the most characteristic and frequent article among stone-age antiquities is the woodworker's axe, — a polished flint blade of a size and shape to suggest the steel blade of the modern woodsman. Next to this axe, in numbers and in workmanlike quality, are the woodworking chisels, of various forms for different uses. Weapons, whether for hunting or for warfare, make a notably scantier showing, although the care and workmanship bestowed on them are often of the very best that the stone-age craftsman has put in evidence. It may be remarked parenthetically that there is evidence that some form of machinery, possibly of an automatic kind, was in use for the manufacture of flint tools in the best days of the polished-flint industry; as also that there appears to have been something in the way of production for a market.

In characterisation of this stone-age mixed farming it should be noted that all crop plants and domestic animals made use of are of introduced species, from outside of Europe, so far as the evidence shows. It is always possible, though it is not in evidence, that some form of cabbage or turnip, or some domestic derivative of the kale, may have been in use; so that that much in the way of original plant domestication might (problematically) be credited to the Baltic culture. Apart from this possibility, the Baltic peoples plainly borrowed all that complement of crop plants which their tillage made use of. Likewise as to their live-stock; it is a borrowed outfit, introduced presumably from Asia, with the problematic exception that a strain of the wild cattle of northern Europe may have been introduced by cross-breeding into the stock of introduced cattle. And in the same connection it is perhaps worth remark that no other element of their technology can at all confidently be asserted to be of home growth; the initial move in every technological device and expedient employed in this culture appears to have come from abroad. So far as touches the state of its industrial arts, this people drew all the elements they made use of from outside, and the like statement will apply with great generality also to other than technological elements. The explanation of this state of things may of course be that all the great inventions and exploits of technological initiative serviceable in the premises had been made before their time; but it is after all a feature of the case. It is to be supplemented with the further statement that while these Baltic peoples borrowed with facility they made effective use of what they borrowed, and that they worked out the borrowed elements into their full efficiency, so as to meet their own needs in their own way.

So also — although this is only negative evidence, and indeed negative evidence of a particularly neutral value — there is nothing going to show a system of cadastration, such as is to be expected where anything like a "landed interest" controls the agricultural industry, more particularly where husbandry is carried on by some form of servile tenure or slave labor. But the negative suggestion is not to be overlooked when taken in connection with the like absence of symmetrical parcelment in the distribution of the cultivated land even at a very late date in this central area of the Baltic civilisation; it stands out by contrast with what occurs throughout those outlying territories of the Fatherland that came in the course of time to be occupied by force and organised on a system of servile tenure, as, *e.g.*, the lands lying beyond the border of Holstein and Friesland.[1] This meticulous cadastration of the cultivated lands takes different forms in different localities, but wherever it occurs it is presumed to be a mark of servile tenure and to have been worked out on behalf of a coercive control of the agricultural industry for the benefit of some form of a "landed interest." It occurs in those parts of the German territory at large that are believed to have been acquired by invasion and held by right of prowess. It is virtually unknown, as a survival from antiquity, in the lands about the narrow Scandinavian waters.

In what has been said it is not intended to imply that there were no class differences of wealth or of social consequence in this Danish stone-age community; still less is there any ground to believe that any form of a communistic organisation prevailed. Neither the state of social organisation in later and better-known times, nor the circumstantial evidence of the stone-age antiquities, will afford ground for such a belief. So, *e.g.*, the chief, almost the sole, structures standing over from this period are certain sepulchres (grave-mounds, dolmens, chamber tombs), numerous, widely distributed, and elaborate, but far too few after all to have served as the ordinary burial places of the common people, at the same time that they will have been too costly to come within the reach of all. They are an item of such wasteful mortuary consumption as the common man could not compass. Plentiful as these sepulchres are in this region, their number and capacity shrinks to very moderate proportions when contrasted with the

---

[1]Cf. Meitzen, *Siedelung und Agrarwesen*, vol. ii. part xi., and the corresponding pages of the Atlas. Meitzen is here referred to for the facts only; his own inferences by no means coincide with the present line of argument.

mass of tools and appliances that served the needs of the living population.

On the immaterial side of the arts of life this culture, then, appears to offer nothing of appreciable magnitude, in the way of empire or statecraft. There is no ground for assuming any large or powerful political or civil units, nor any elaborate governmental machinery. The most that suggests itself in the way of public control would be a loose neighborhood organisation, perhaps on lines resembling the organisation of local self-government in the earlier period (900–1100 a.d.) of the Icelandic republic. And the conclusion is fairly unavoidable that warlike (predatory) enterprise of any kind is no integral part of the scheme.

Of the religious life, or perhaps of superstitious conceits and practices, in the stone age there is less evidence than might be looked for; or if the evidence is at hand it must be of such an improbable character as to have escaped attention. There do occur some few articles that are interpreted as "cult objects," — figurines, amulets, and the like; but the whole is so slight in volume and so apparently trivial in character as to be extremely disappointing to persons interested in religious antiq ities. The sepulchres and the articles buried with the dead afford the most substantial, and most circumstantial, evidence available of a belief in the supernatural; but even these yield little. So also in objects of art these antiquities are poor. There is a little something in the way of decorated pottery, but it is crude both in design and in execution, and there are some few other articles that show a tentative movement of the æsthetic impulse; but it remains true here as in the domain of religion that the available evidence is surprisingly scant, and such as it is it is barely sufficient to argue an extreme poverty in both respects. Yet there is a certain large reservation to be made in any argument on the materials at hand in this domain of the æsthetic arts — a reservation that applies perhaps equally to the question of religious observances.

As has already been indicated above, the Baltic population were

eminently a wood-working people; from which it should follow
that their decorative art, and their cult objects, will presumably
have been worked in wood, and so will have disappeared with
the disappearance of the perishable material in which the work
was done. This caution, indeed, gathers very considerable force
from what is known of cult objects and decorative art in the
Scandinavian countries at a later period, in late pagan and early
historical times. This latter period, too, is eminently an age of
woodwork, and by far the more characteristic and the most
abundant examples of Scandinavian decorative art from this
period are in wood and in colors; the next in importance being
the work done in woollen textiles, which suffer in the same way
from the perishability of the material. The evidence of the material at hand is accordingly not to be taken without allowance
as bearing on the state of the æsthetic arts in antiquity, nor does
it necessarily indicate in any adequate way what may have been
the range and character of contrivances employed in the service
of religion or of superstitious beliefs. Of course, a caution of the
same kind is to be observed in judging of industrial appliances
and articles of daily use, and therefore in any appraisal of the
state of the industrial arts, in this prehistoric culture; the chief
materials were wood, skins and wool. Yet the flint tools, which
have been preserved, being the primary tools — the tools of the
tool-makers — they yield a competent, even if inadequate, cri-
terion of the character and efficiency of the technology of the
stone age.

With the passage of time, as bronze comes in to supplant or
supplement the flint in the Baltic technology, the apparent poverty of this culture in the domain of art is relieved in an appreciable degree; and in a less degree the like will apply to appliances
designed for religious or magical uses. The best of the decorative
work in bronze has scarcely been surpassed by any people living
on nearly the same level of civilisation, either for its consummate
æsthetic sensibility or for the perfection of its workmanship. This
characterisation will apply without reserve to the decorative art

of the Baltic bronze age at its best, and it should be noted that this best output of bronze work comes from the early half of the bronze age. The slight attempts at representative art from the same general section of prehistory can not be spoken of with the same respect. This latter is puny and futile in a degree scarcely credible when taken in juxtaposition with the purely decorative work from the same period; it runs about on a level with the contemporary Etruscan commercial art work at its worst, which it visibly resembles and from which it appears to have drawn much of its inspiration. Intercourse with the Adriatic seaboard at the time makes such an affiliation of the Baltic art work probable, and the borrowed forms, style and mannerisms may serve to show how the affiliation took effect.

But these considerations of intercourse with the commercial centers of northern Italy and the head of the Adriatic yield no plausible explanation of the highly characteristic decorative work in bronze, particularly of the early bronze age, which is distinctive in style and is artistically superior to the best work imported from the Mediterranean. There remains the alternative suggestion that this earlier decorative work in bronze is a derivative of the like decorative art in wood and colors carried over from the stone age; so that the art-life of the age of flint may perhaps best be appreciated in the reflected light of the output of the succeeding period, which for the first time afforded the Baltic artists a material in which their work could endure.

III

(Note to Chapter II, page 45)

What was said above (page 44) of the extreme paucity, not to say total want, of contemporary documentary evidence on the state of society in north-European prehistory does not overlook the existence or the value of the contemporary classical writers on Germanic antiquities. These old writers have been so fully utilised and so exhaustively canvassed by many able scholars that what they have to say has already gone into the common stock of information on this head, and may therefore fairly be taken for granted as the stable background against which any representation of Germanic antiquities will unavoidably be seen. Such doubt as may bear on the value of these classical sources is not a doubt as to their veracity and substantial consequence, but rather a question of their inherent limitations. What they have to offer is at its best of the nature of fragmentary outline, and the best of them — Tacitus — is a *Tendenzschrift*, an account rationalised in the sense of the views then prevalent among Latin scholars as to primitive social conditions, and drawn with an eye to the discipline and edification of his Roman audience. But it is more to the point, since for the purpose in hand it is a more substantial infirmity, that his account, like the rest, is drawn from observation and informants of Germanic communities that had, notoriously, wandered long and far from their ancestral seats, that were still engaged in a mass movement — a "barbarian migration" — with a view partly to booty, partly to the seizure of profitable territory, or that were (at least provisionally) settled as a master class on an underlying population already settled on the land. The peoples whom these accounts describe are the later generations, in a more or less mature state of reorganisation, of bodies of adventurers who had gone out from their initial habitat on an errand of predation, and they afford at the best about as true an image of the state of society out of which they came as did the viking raiders of the tenth century. Of course, the fact remains that they carried out from home the preconceptions which they had acquired at home; but it is equally evident that the circumstances under which they had lived since leaving home had done much to shape their habits of thought and current use and wont among them at the time they came under observation; as also that the longer and farther they wandered the greater would be the resulting changes in their habits of life and of thought as affected by their experience under alien skies. In other words, they faithfully reflect the Baltic culture of their forebears in somewhat the degree in which the Mongols or the Manchus in China, or the Moguls in India, reproduced the culture of the steppes out of which they came; or as the resident administration of the East India Company reproduced British institutions and gave an object lesson of British culture; or, again, at the best, as near as the Forty-niners in California gave a faithful exhibition of American society.

Therefore, since it may be assumed that these classical sources are sufficiently known by common notoriety, and since they are scant at the best and afford ground only for remote inference as to the state of society out of which the Germanic peoples to which they relate had once come, — for these reasons no further use will be made of these standard documents in this place, beyond a general regard to their suggestions, and particularly an avoidance of what they forbid. A second range of documentary material, of which the several codes of the "Barbarian Laws" are typical, falls under the same limitations.[1] In a less, but after all in the least degree, the literary remains of the barbarian peoples themselves are liable to the same line of objections; and as being the best evidence available, both in point of the immediacy of its testimony and in point of its relative abundance, it is to this class of material that recourse must chiefly be had by anyone who wishes to find a working conception of what society was like in Baltic prehistory, — in its industrial system, its social organisation, its political life, its principles of equity, its prescriptive conventions, beliefs and ideals. By what may be called historical accident it happens that the most considerable of this material relates to the Scandinavian peoples, most considerable both for its volume and for the character of its testimony; and it happens, again, that within this Scandinavian domain the most valuable in all its bearings is the material afforded by the Icelandic literature. In so far as bears on the

---

[1] More to the point are the several collections of Scandinavian laws, *Grágás* more so than any other perhaps, although even here the late and Christian influences are in evidence. In what follows, regard is had to these texts, with such allowance as seems due.

present inquiry the Icelandic material relates primarily to Norwegian prehistory, though at a slightly further remove it reflects
also the condition of society in the other Scandinavian countries,
and more remotely on the run of events and institutions in the
Baltic-North Sea region more at large. The strongest plea that
can be made for such recourse to this material is that it is the best
there is to be had, not that it is all that could be desired. It is plain
to students familiar with the pertinent facts that all other documentary material is fully intelligible only in the light afforded by
the Icelandic accounts, and that these other sources are useful
rather as appendices and minor correctives than as prime sources
of information and independent grounds of secure inference.

These Scandinavian countries have for the present purpose the
differential advantage as against the rest of the Germanic world
that history overtook them in their prehistoric state. These communities were the last survivors of the Germanic pagan world,
standing over intact in a degree far beyond what can be alleged
of the rest at their entrance into European history. They have also
the second and no less consequential advantage that they comprise virtually the only area within the Baltic-North Sea cultural
region that had, at its entrance into history, not been disturbed by
invasion from alien cultures, or acquired by seizure and reorgan-
ised by predation from this Baltic central area. All the barbarian
raids—*Völkerwanderungen* — that were of a Germanic complexion ran outward from this broad center, while nothing of the
kind penetrated into this hyperborean "cradle of the nations."
They comprise, in other words, the initial home area of the Baltic
culture and of the north-European racial mixture, and they stand
over as the last working model of Baltic paganism.

These preferential claims of the Scandinavian material are,
of course, not to be allowed without abatement. There is, first,
the objection that the documents relate primarily to Norway, —
doubtless the least significant of the three Scandinavian countries
as bearing on the Baltic prehistoric culture. Yet taking things
as they come it will be admitted that the records of Norwegian

paganism, with their excursions and reflections on the state of society in neighboring lands, are after all the most significant body of material extant. Norwegian conditions at the close of the pagan era are not a faithful reproduction of Baltic prehistory at large, for Norway was comparatively slight, poor, and lay outside of the center, but with due allowance they yield information not otherwise to be had. Further, the Icelandic records are not contemporary; they come from the hands of Christian scholars who lived some couple of centuries after the formal close of the pagan era, and under conditions differing notably from those that prevailed in Norway in late pagan times. In extenuation it is to be said that while paganism conventionally closes with the end of the tenth century, it is easy to overrate the magnitude and the abruptness of this shift to the new faith in this outlying corner of Christendom; so that the laying of the spirit of paganism among the Scandinavian population by no means coincides with the conventional date of its obsequies. Also, the literature in question is voluminous enough in great measure to correct its own shortcomings in detail, by recourse to the consensus of its testimony as a whole; all the more so since there is in these earlier narratives no sensible bias of criticism or apology with respect to the events and conditions described; the animus of the whole being, with remarkable singleness, that of the story-teller's art. The sagas are in this respect, as in many others, in the same class with the histories of Herodotus. A more serious difficulty with the Icelandic material is that it relates, directly, not to the state of things current even in Norway in the midst and high tide of pagan prehistory, but rather to the condition of things during the last period of prehistory, when the pagan system was engaged in all that movement of change that presently brought its era to a close. It yields an account of how the pagan system came to its end, rather than how it stood through the long reaches of its life-history.

This period of prehistory that leads down to the close of the pagan era in the eleventh century is spoken of as the viking age, as being characterised by the growth of an organised piratical enterprise; it is conventionally said to begin with the closing years of the eighth century, though such piratical enterprise is known to date farther back in the Scandinavian countries, and it is, indeed, evidently a long established fact and in a flourishing condition by that time. Indeed, the roots of this growth reach very far back.[1] So much so that the more the matter is looked into the less occasion does there seem to be to draw a line of any hard and fast kind between the pirate raids and those overland raids of marauders that are known by the politer name of the "migrations of the peoples." And to follow up these latter to their origins would lead very far back into prehistory.[2]

Yet the viking enterprise will after all have to be recognised as specifically characteristic of the closing phases of the pagan era, whether the conventional duration assigned it, of some two hundred and fifty years, be accepted as a sufficient allowance, or it

---

[1]Cf. *e.g.*, Alexander Bugge, *Norges Historie*, vol. i. part ii., especially sec. ix.

[2]While the causes that led to the migrations of the peoples, the barbarian invasions overland, may have been substantially of the same kind as those that occasioned the rise of the viking raids, the reaction of each on the habits and workday conceptions of the home population should be somewhat widely different. The free-booters who set out overland did not return, brought nothing home, and had nothing further to say in the run of affairs; whereas the pirates habitually returned home over winter — for the most part and especially during the earlier part of the period — and they also brought home both slaves and superfluous articles of decorative consumption, and they retained their place as citizens in good standing and eventually settled down as farmers and heads of families. The contrast is, of course, not quite so broad as this would make it. Many of the pirates stayed away, settled abroad, in the various centers of piracy or as settlers in some foreign country; and on the other hand there is sufficient evidence that communication was free and continuous between the Baltic seaboard and the countries of southern and central Europe through the period of the migrations, so that many of the migrants, or their descendants, will have found their way back from time to time, and the home community will have kept more or less adequately in touch with these wandering hosts for some time after their departure. Yet, on the whole, the contrast between the two fashions of excursion into foreign parts is too substantial to be overlooked.

be allowed something like twice that length of time, as inclusive both of its rise and its maturer development. It comes on as a characteristic factor in the later pagan scheme of life, and its presence requires explanation both as to its antecedent causes and as to its effects on the state of society at the time.

In outline, the immediate economic and social consequences of incorporating such an institution as piracy in the scheme of use and wont should be fairly plain: there should result a heightening of the warlike animus; a lessening of the security of property and industry, and of life and limb;[1] an increase in the number of slaves, and, presumably, an increase of their hardships, along with a decline in their price, — the slave trade being one of the main supports of the viking traffic; a consequent sharper conception of and insistence on class distinctions. Among the causes of its growth there is only one that can be cited with full confidence; viz., an improvement in the technology of boat-building and navigation such as to make extensive sea voyages practicable in sufficient force and with sufficiently reduced risk of accidents by sea. Less plainly is it required, as a condition precedent to such a development, that there must have been something of a surplus population, and that the country's industry must have been sufficiently productive to afford the very considerable investment in equipment and supplies necessary for such enterprise, — an expenditure for which no substantial equivalent was gained from the traffic, apart from the slave labor imported. Apart from the slaves, what was brought home from these raids appears to have consisted almost wholly of superfluities, trinkets, and the precious metals; and even on the most liberal valuation of these "imports" there is no chance of their having, at an average, equalled the cost of their acquisition.

Regard being had to the very appreciable prevalence of mutual raiding, both as between different pirate bands and as between

---

[1] It may be noted as a side light on this particular point that the practice of the *hólmgang* most commonly comes into the sagas in connection with the vikings and their traffic.

different communities, within the Scandinavian countries, it is doubtless well within the mark to say that on an average all that went into this viking traffic, in equipment, supplies and personnel, is to be counted as a total loss. So that, economically speaking, it is a sheer drain on the resources and productive capacity of the communities concerned; which argues, among other things, that they must have been in such a position, in respect of productive efficiency, as to be able to afford this systematic waste without serious weakening through the centuries of its duration. That there was no serious decline of the country's industrial capacity during this era is evidenced, *e.g.*, by the fact that the viking enterprise itself went on uninterruptedly advancing, in the volume and character of its equipment, down to the period of its collapse in the early eleventh century.

Now, it is Scandinavian life in the viking age, so called, that is immediately reflected in the Icelandic material, and what is reflected in the way of use and wont and institutional preconceptions will be not the untroubled prehistoric situation of remoter antiquity, but this prehistoric culture as it stands after the archaic state of society has suffered whatever measure of change this growth of piracy may indicate, or that may have been induced by it or by the causes that brought it about.

Some slight account of the place which the viking traffic held in the interest of the community, therefore, and of the manner in which it fitted into their workday life, may serve to show roughly what measure of weighting or allowance is necessary on this score in making use of the available material. As it typically comes in sight in its simpler and apparently earlier phases the viking traffic is an enterprise of adventurous young men, commonly the sons of substantial farmers, who have the means at their disposal for the equipment of such an expedition; though it should be noted that something like an extension of credit may sometimes be involved in the outfitting of a viking crew. The crew may be made up of volunteers who combine their means, or of these young country gentlemen of means spoken of, together with unpropertied farm hands and disengaged young men of the neighborhood. The organisation of the crew is (commonly) of a democratic character, the officers for the cruise being chosen by the members of the crew; though the choice, which seems to have been theoretically quite free, will commonly fall on the gentlemen of means or of experience among them. As one might say, they "sign articles" for the cruise — the articles being of a somewhat exacting character and apparently well settled by convention in a traditional form. As has already been remarked above, the purpose is piracy, in the most liberal construction of the term. The expedition may consist of a single boat or of several such boats, and it may last (most usually) for a single season, or for two or more. When the cruise is done the pirates return home, commonly with the beginning of winter, house their boats and other equipment, and disband and fall into their several places and occupations in the neighborhood as before, but usually with some accession of standing and weight in the community due to the glamour of great deeds and to whatever pecuniary gain they may have made. Such is the simplest and perhaps the more archaic type, in case of a successful issue. It was also rather expected that young men who so went out on adventure and made good would follow up this piratical work for several seasons, before they finally settled down among their neighbors. However, this is only the simplest type. There were also vikings who followed this calling as a permanent business and sole occupation, and who grew old in the trade. So also there were businesslike undertakers who organised piratical concerns of a larger and more enduring character, with hired crews and with considerable investment in equipment, — suggestively resembling the traditional whaling business of the New Englanders. In the course of time, particularly at a period well along in the tenth century, a more permanent and businesslike organisation came into effect, and coalitions of piratical bands were formed, resembling, but by all accounts far outnumbering, the similar coalitions of the buccaneers along the Spanish main.

Yet, while the permanent establishments and businesslike coalitions of the later viking age were undeniably a factor of grave import in the social situation, even rising to the rank of a political power,[1] it remains true that it is after all the homelier, one might almost say the domestic, ventures in piracy that continue to lend their color to the state of society and of the arts of life as reflected in the sagas.

The economic foundations of this early society were husbandry (mixed farming) and household industry of the order of handicraft, with fishery as a subsidiary and hunting as an incidental source of livelihood. There also goes everywhere an itinerant trade, mostly in such necessaries as iron and salt, together with luxuries like wheat, honey and spices, and decorative superfluities; and there is in the later period the viking enterprise. As regards exports through this itinerant trade, the chief article in late pagan times appears to have been furs and pelts, at an earlier date mainly amber, with wool or woollens and possibly dried fish. The trade is not of first-rate importance to the community, which is self-supporting in all essential respects. The economic unit is the farmstead, with its population, commonly of a loosely defined number, but running all the way from a single moderate-sized family to an aggregation of perhaps a couple of hundreds. Typically the farm is of a relatively large size and with a large equipment, sufficient to take care of its own needs in nearly all necessary lines of industry; but there seems to have been a considerable number of half-dependent, outlying farms, partly freehold, partly worked on some form of customary tenure which varied very appreciably from one case to another. All classes and conditions of men took part in the work, there being apparently no leisure class exempt from manual labor — unless a (partial and doubtful) exception is to be made in favor of royalty and the more prominent and wealthy among the landed

---

[1] As shown, *e.g.*, in the *Jómsvíkinga Saga*.

gentry. Both men and women took part in the field work, and skill in some form of industry was expected of all reputable persons.

The community falls into a system of social classes, based on wealth and birth; either of which gives standing in the community and neither of which will long suffice by itself. At the bottom are the slaves, which according to tradition appear to have formed a class in the community from remote antiquity, although it may be difficult to understand how there should have been an appreciable number of slaves present before the rise of piracy. Their numbers appear to have been considerable, though it is fairly clear that they were not the largest class among the inhabitants. These slaves were the chattels of their masters, in full ownership, though the system of slavery appears, on the whole, not to have taken an extremely harsh form; owing probably to the relative difficulty of controlling a slave population which differed neither in physical appearance nor in speech from their masters, in a country where waste lands and scattered settlements offered favorable means of escape. Above the slave class is the (probably) larger class of the half-free tenants, cottiers or dependent working class. And above these again what may be called the commonalty made up of the freehold farm population (*bœndr*), great and small; these would appear to have been appreciably the more numerous of the several social classes, and they are unquestionably the main body of the community considered as a civil society. Distinct from the freehold farm population in popular apprehension, though not so clearly distinct in either economic or civil consequence and rank, are the people of noble or gentle birth (*jarl* and *hersir*). The place and consequence of these in the social fabric are not clear, but their presence is undoubted and appears to be a typical feature of the fabric. They appear in effect to have, typically, been substantial farmers and men of local influence; they may also, by conventional tolerance, have enjoyed certain ill-defined prerogatives and immunities. Somewhat the same is to be said of the kings, who make up a distinct class in this social scheme. Royalty is probably (though not beyond a doubt) the smallest of these classes, as it is unequivocally the first in rank.[1]

It will be noticed that nothing is here said of a tribal or clan organisation; the reason being that there is no trace of such a system in the original documents, and there is no word in the old language that can by any reasonable use of violence be construed to cover the concept of a tribe or a clan. The imputation of a tribal system, as a matter of course, to the German peoples is a work of rationalisation by the scholars who have dealt with these matters under the guidance of those Latin scholars of antiquity, who spoke in these terms because the concept of a tribal organisation was familiar matter of course with them from home. On the other hand the "kin" is a substantial fact in the case. The individual is responsible to and for his kindred; but this kindred is a vague category; there are no definite limits to the degrees of consanguinity which it covers, on the male or female side, by ties of birth or of marriage; though in a general way, other things being equal, the dues of kindred reach (perhaps) farther and bind closer on the paternal than on the maternal side, and on the whole the ties of blood have greater force than those of marriage. Except for their greater extension and greater constraining force, the bonds of kinship work out to surprisingly near the same effect in Scandinavian paganism as among the modern

---

[1]The earliest known exposition of class distinctions in Scandinavian paganism — the "Rigsthula" — makes four social classes: slaves, commoners, earl folk, and royalty, and appears to hold that these class distinctions rest on racial differences, all but the last two, — royalty, it appears, being derived from the race of earls. At the same time it seems also to be the meaning of the ancient theorist that these follow one another in seniority in the order named, the race, or class, of slaves being the earliest and the kings the latest comers. A second point on which the poem dwells — not usually brought into the foreground by the commentaries — is the gift of occult and magical lore intrinsically belonging to the king, and which alone apparently serves as a distinctive trait to set off the breed of kings from that of earls.

Scandinavian or English-speaking peoples. The rights and duties of the "next friend" are doubtless more exacting and by legal definition more specific in Scandinavian paganism, particularly in cases of death by violence, than in modern Britain or Scandinavia, but even at this point the difference is one of degree rather than of principle. There is so much of a patriarchal régime as may be implied in the use of patronymics as the sole legally competent designation of persons, and in an uncertain tutelage of women, — this latter is legally rigorous, apparently, but is not thoroughly effective, being often disputed by the women and not infrequently falling into abeyance. One might easily be persuaded, on slight direct evidence, that the tutelage of women was a relatively late innovation, perhaps an item of civil rights borrowed from the feudalised countries to the south or from the Romanised countries to the east. But the use of patronymics shows none of the marks of an upstart institution. Except as nicknames, metronyms are not used, and surnames, in the feudalistic or modern sense, of course are unknown.

While a tribal system or anything like a well-matured patriarchal régime is not included among the civil institutions or the legal antiquities of this culture, the kingship on the other hand appears to be intrinsic to the scheme. The kingship is a matter of course; but the king's place and value in the community's life is not easy to define. In the process of consolidation into larger units that went on through the viking age the kings, on whose initiative and by whose intrigues the coalescence into larger kingdoms was effected, arrogated to themselves many and extensive powers, an imitation of the prerogatives and perquisites enjoyed by the feudal rulers of the larger countries of south and middle Europe; and the royal office so took on much of the dignity and militant air that belongs with feudalism. But the kingship as it comes down in use and wont from earlier prehistoric ages is evidently an institution of slighter material consequence, though it is apparently an indispensable factor in the social fabric. This royalty of the ancient line, as seen in hazy outlines against the prehistoric background, is suggestive of the King of Yvetot. The king is the first gentleman of the realm; that much may safely be asserted and may stand without further phrase or qualification. But beyond this the case of royalty is in an obscure state. The crown has apparently little if any legislative authority and no police power, beyond what the king's personal force and private means may enable him transiently to arrogate, and it is not clear that he has any stated revenues except from his private estate in farmlands, which he apparently holds on the same tenure and with the same incidents of ownership as any common freeholder. Perhaps the only semblance of political or civil power that can confidently be imputed to him — apart from exceptional cases of forceful personality — is his presumptive leadership in times of war, defensive or offensive.

However, there is at least one further item of what may be called the royal prerogative. The king appears to stand in something like a priestly or quasi-priestly relation to the national solemnities of paganism, on such occasions, *e.g.*, as the convoking of the popular assembly and the attendant peace-hallowing of its precincts. He comes in evidence on these occasions in some sort as the assembly's chaplain, and perhaps its chairman. And through the various references to the king and his work there runs some suggestion of such a semi-sacred or quasi-priestly nature in other connections as well. This connection between the kingly office and the pagan cult is a sufficiently obscure matter, which has not had the benefit of due attention from the students of Scandinavian antiquities. And no light on this question is to be looked for from outside Scandinavian paganism, since the wandering hosts of predatory migrants engaged in the barbarian invasions had no kings, except self-made ones, war-lords installed for purposes of war and predation and not endued with the sacred character vested by birth in the royal line. The kingly office, it may be added, appears to have been loosely elective, by popular choice, which may of course have often amounted to nothing more than a tolerant consent; but by exacting use and wont the choice is confined to persons of royal descent, with a presumption in favor of the next of kin, and of the male line, and with a loosely held presumption in favor of the eldest son.

In this dimmer past, out of which the traditions of the pagan kingship have come down to color the legends of a later time, little is seen of the kingly power but more of the kingly presence. Direct evidence bearing on the size, as well as on the constitution, of these prehistoric kingdoms comes almost entirely from Norway, that being the only one of these Baltic countries in which the process of consolidation and royal aggression had not taken serious effect before the beginnings of recorded history. Even as regards Norway it is almost wholly a matter of conjecture how many and how large these kingdoms were before the prehistoric situation was disturbed; but it is quite safe to place their number as high as several dozen. Their boundaries appear to have been drawn on topographical lines; so that wherever a relatively large tract of country would fall readily into a single system of neighborhood relations the resulting realm would have some appreciable extent; under the reverse circumstances the realm might comprise a very moderate area indeed. One gets the impression that the normal kingdom may have ranged in extent from that of a parish to that of a county, or thereabout. Tradition says, *e.g.*, that once upon a time there used to be a total of five kingdoms in the valley of Valdres, counting from the head of the valley to Næs at the head of Lake Spirilen. On the other hand, Ringerike seems by tradition to have been a single kingdom; and so it also appears that, *e.g.*, in the ninth century Hördaland, Rogaland, Agdir, Sognefiord, made one kingdom each; whereas Harald Fairhair is said to have dealt with some six or eight kings in what is now Trondhjem.[1]

---

[1] The tradition of this pagan kingship has survived in a singular state of preservation in the folk tales of this region, being best preserved among the Norwegians and Swedes, as would be expected, but also giving its color to the folk tales farther afield, wherever the Germanic legends come in evidence. The king and his domestic circumstances and establish-

As regards what may be called the domestic range of institutions under this prehistoric régime, they appear to have been neither so rudimentary nor so out of scale with modern conditions as the civil and political system. Of these institutions the tenure of property and the incidents of ownership are precise

---

ment come in for frequent attention in these tales, as they do in the similar — or in many cases the same — tales told in divers and various places through the length and breadth of the Asiatic-European continent. But traditional royalty wears a different character in this western world from what it does elsewhere, so that even in the same story, as told, *e.g.*, in the Punjab or on the Euphrates and in Scandinavia, the same kingly stage-figure will play his part in the East as an august monarch ruling with despotic power over large dominions, while on the Baltic seaboard he is reduced to a somewhat genial but headstrong gentleman-farmer whose dominions are of such extent that the wedding bells, which ring in the conclusion of the story, can be heard "across seven kingdoms."

In practical fact within the historical period, the folk who tell and who listen to these tales in the West have had no experience of kingdoms or kingly rule of anything like this diminutive scale and homely style. They have in fact revised the ancient tradition in the light of their historical experience on such matters as the church-bells and the clergy, which have come into the frame-work of the tales at a later date than the disappearance of the last of the petty kingdoms; so also fire-arms and other technological innovations of a later date, as, *e.g.*, chimneys, have found easy lodgment in this reminiscent folklore. These things have become matters of course to such a degree that they neither help nor hinder in the furtherance of the tale, whereas the petty kingship and the homely scale of life in which it belongs are so indefeasibly embedded in the popular sentiment touching what is right, good and normal, that it all stands over unquestioned as the ideal type of things in spite of its having all disappeared from popular experience at a still remoter date. The folk tales carry the suggestion, to be taken for what it may be worth, that this small-scale, half-anarchistic, neighborhood plan of society is the only one that will stand the long-term test of popular sentiment among these peoples — the one plan, in effect, to which they will drift by natural bent and in which they instinctively see the land of the heart's desire and the empire of content for their kind.

What further there may be reflected, in the way of long-term ideals or reminiscence, in these tales, where they speak in a complacent matter-of-course way of the transmission of the royal office by the spindle side to the lucky young man who marries the princess, — that line of surmise

and of fundamental consequence beyond any other, — unless one should be inclined to give precedence to the somewhat less well-defined but indefeasible claims of kindred. Property is held in severalty, with a conventionally effective but ill-specified reversionary interest on the part of the kindred. This applies, apparently without qualification, to realty and personalty alike. A distinction of principle between realty and personalty does not seem to have been contemplated; although it is evident that the law (of the nature of common law) was elaborately worked out in all its bearings on property rights.[1] Property passed by in-

---

need perhaps not be attended to. What Karl Pearson has to say in these premises, e.g. (The Chances of Death, essays on "Hans in Luck," "Woman as Witch," etc.), may be both interesting and significant, even if the argument is not accepted as conclusive of the somewhat radical deductions which he offers.

[1]Such a conception as a communistic holding of property, whether in land or in chattels, does not come within the legal horizon of these peoples, and such an organisation as the "mark" of scholarly tradition, is as foreign to that scheme of things as the modern stock market.

The conventionally accepted view of early Germanic society has, until lately, been notably different from the one here spoken for. Nor has this earlier view yet been formally abandoned by historians and prehistorians; it appears to be dying by neglect rather than by refutation, although some of the most substantial and ambitious of later studies in Germanic antiquities have been conducted from its point of view and with assumption of its premises. Among the more considerable and valuable of these later works, of which many are of substantial value, may be mentioned as examples: Matthæus Much, Die Heimat der Indogermanen; Herman Hirt, Die Indogermanen (2 vols.); Richard Hildebrand, Recht und Sitte auf den verschiedenen wirtschaftlichen Kulturstufen (vol. i.); and the great work of August Meitzen, Siedelung und Agrarwesen der Westgermanen und Ostgermanen, etc., which affords an extraordinary volume of well-digested material that is equally serviceable whether the author's assumptions are accepted or not. The abandonment, or rather the falling away, of this older view of north-European antiquities appears to be due to the relinquishment of the romantic point of view in historical interpretation and its supersession by an economic and genetic conception. This movement of supersession having taken less effect among German scholars than elsewhere, the older view is still doing service among German historians and ethnologists somewhat more extensively than elsewhere.

heritance very much after the modern fashion in those countries where there is neither entail nor primogeniture; illegitimate children (a category to be counted with in this case) having apparently — at least at the close of the pagan era — no legal claim except in the absence of legitimate issue, though they seem to have had something of an effectual conventional claim.

Marriage arrangements have a similarly modern air, except that polygamy and concubinage appear to have been included in the scheme, — although one gets the impression that the freedom allowed in this respect was not very fully taken advantage of. Separation was easy, on very slight plea, and equally open to either party. The tutelage of children also fell very much into modern lines, much after the fashion that now prevails in those countries where a minimum of restraint is exercised by the parents, and where no restraint is exercised much beyond the age of puberty; girls being held in tutelage rather more closely than boys, and apparently to a higher age. On a separation of the parents, children of tender age apparently went with the mother, quite as frequently as with the father. Such, in a general way, appears to have been the practice; in legal theory there appears to have been a prevalent conception of tutelage of women and children by the male head of the household, but this conception appears not to have made its way successfully in practice. It may be added that, while marriage had its formalities and ceremonial, there is no evidence of its having had a religious or other ritual significance; it is rather to be characterised as a ritualised civil contract only.

The religious faith and life of the late pagan era has had much attention from students of antiquity, and the views current among the adepts on this head, particularly on the side of mythology, have been fortunate enough to achieve an appreciable publicity. And it is to be noted that in this respect Germanic antiquities give a fuller account of themselves than do the antiquities of other, neighboring cultures. That such is the case is due primarily to the work of one man, seconded by the earlier work in the same field of his immediate predecessor among Icelandic scholars. Except for Snorri's *Edda* and the poems of the elder, or "poetic," *Edda* on which he drew, the mythology of the Germanic peoples would scarcely be better known today than that of the Druids; and possibly even less would be known about it if the occasional references to religious practices in the older sagas were also wanting. Any other information, from German, English or classical sources, has no consistency except as it clusters about Snorri's account.

Now, Snorri's *Gylfaginning*, *Bragarœdur* and *Skáldskaparmál* are light literature, the work of an artist gifted with a Shaksperian sense for the ludicrous, and the Asa gods come through his hands in what is perhaps an excessively humanised recension. At any rate, whatever they may have been like in their legendary shapes before they got into his hands, when they leave his hands they are figures of no great stature considered as deities.[1] The mythological passages of the elder *Edda* have a more sedate air than Snorri's anecdotes, and the passing references in the older sagas to occasional rites and observances of a religious or magical nature give more of an impression of sombre superstition than is conveyed by anything Snorri has to say. But when all is said, the fact remains that Snorri is the one chief and indispensable informant, and that his anecdotes will have to be taken, with whatever weighting may seem necessary, as the only consistent body of information extant on this head. Other sources stand to Snorri very much in the relation of marginal notes and glosses.

Barring a certain lightness, approaching flippancy, then, on Snorri's part, and barring the visible influence exercised by the Greek Olympian system on his schematic grading of the Asa

---

[1] Translators and commentators have commonly approached Snorri's work with their minds made up for solemnities, not untouched with filial piety and theological exaltation. The interpretations so arrived at have showed as large an excess of magnitude and divinity in the Asa gods as Snorri's *ipsissima verba* may show too much of horse-play and slack-twisted human nature.

gods and goddesses, his representation of them, their manner of life and their relation to mankind, bears the marks of a veracious account. There is among these northern gods no figure of a divine autocrat, absolute, august, austere and aloof, whose will is the fundamental law and whose good pleasure constitutes good and ill. What vouches for the veracity of this account is the unfailing coincidence of this divine with the human scheme. It is a scheme in which a shrewd and genial elder plays the part of a typical petty king, such as still is met with in the northern folk tales, and in which the several members of the society of gods each pursue their several interests as their several propensities may decide, and within such decent bounds of intrigue and sharp dealing as were currently held permissible, or respectable, among the men of that age, and as still give character to the folk tales. So slight is the theological content of this scheme of divinity that it has required much labor and more bias to satisfy the aspirations of even the more modest seekers for hidden truths in this supernatural underbrush.

And since there is to be had, neither in Snorri's account nor outside of it, anything substantial in the way of a description, or even a characterisation, of the cult of observances, the ritual and the sacred properties that will have given the Asa faith its practical effect, there seems but little to go on in any endeavor to reconstruct a system of worship. Something comes in sight here and there, in references to sacrifice, which appears to have marked both seasonal periods and special occasions — culminating in infrequent but apparently authentic instances of human sacrifice — as also in references to the *hóf* (temple or precincts) and to sacred images. The godhead so propitiated appears most frequently to have been Frey, an agricultural divinity to be conciliated with a view to crops and to material welfare at large. Frey (or Frigg) appears to have been a deity of long standing, being with some confidence traced back to the bronze age.[1]

---

[1] Cf. *e.g.*, Sophus Bugge, "Fricco, Frigg und Priapos," *Christiania Videnskabsselskabs Forhandlinger*, 1904.

The most considerable material survivals of the pagan cult would appear to be the well-known and highly characteristic carved portals that are still to be found in use in the surviving churches dating from the earliest Christian centuries, — valuable also as monuments of the late pagan art work in carved wood. With the exception of slight, late and on the whole inferior specimens, these portals show no Christian symbolism; and their uniform style over large distances argues that they are the outcome of long-continued use and wont, demanding more time than can possibly be allowed within the early Christian period. The leading symbolical motive in this work is the dragon of northern legend, helped out with minor reptilian forms and seconded by a conventionalised tree form. Both by their ubiquitous occurrence and by the excellence and magnificent scale of the work, these material remains would appear to bear witness to a consistent, wide-spread and systematised cult, far beyond what the literary remains independently suggest.

Yet, whatever may have been the reach and systematic consistency of the cult, there is no evidence, literary or otherwise, of a priesthood, — beyond the sufficiently evident discharge of priestly, or at least of ritual, duties by local magnates whose chief duties appear to have been of a civil character. The Icelandic *godi* is the nearest approach to a priest that anywhere comes in sight; and the discrepancy between a priesthood in the accepted sense of the term and these gentlemen-farmers and keepers of the

---

For the latterday conventional view of this pagan cult and creed as they prevailed in late prehistoric times and as seen in the light of current research and scholarship in the Scandinavian countries, see Alex. Bugge, *Norges Historie,* vol. i. part i. sec. v.; where the traits of this paganism will be seen to have greatly unbent from that austere and inflexible state of beatitude that invests it all in Schrader and his contemporaries, particularly among German scholars. The view set forth, or the interpretation rendered, by Dr. Bugge is a conservative and reverent revision of the traditional rendering, but it has the benefit of the later and more matter-of-fact scholarship as well as the authentication of Scandinavian students occupied with these materials today.

sacred properties is sufficiently obvious. A sacerdotal class and an ecclesiastical establishment appear both to be wanting, although some of the functions and equipment requisite for both appear to be at hand. The religious life would seem to have reached a degree of systematisation and, at least for some considerable period toward the close of the pagan era, to have found expression in a cult that embodied passably uniform observances over a relatively wide domain, very far exceeding any national boundaries; but this cult and its observance appear at the same time to have achieved no appreciable hierarchical organisation and no great degree of coercive authority. There are traces of coercion, as in legal penalties for blasphemy (*godgjá*), as also ecclesiastical rights and perquisites, as in a voluntary imposition of tithes for support of the local sanctuary; but taken by and large the impression one gets of this religious life is of much the same character as that given by the civil organisation, — best to be described as a conventionally systematised anarchy regulated by common sense. Such a system of social organisation, whether in the spiritual or in the temporal domain, would be enforceable only within such territorial bounds as would be covered by the habitual range of neighborly contact, — a contact sufficiently close and alert to insure a certain (effective) solidarity of neighborhood sentiment on all matters touching the conditions of life in the group; and the control exercised by such neighborhood surveillance would run within a fairly broad margin of tolerance. Any uniformity of use and wont over a wider tract of country, or over the region at large, whereby an effectually homogeneous culture comes to prevail among these various autonomous parcels of society, could rest in the long run only on a substantial similarity of material surroundings, and of temperament, a similar state of the industrial arts, free intercourse, and a (consequent) homogeneity of language.[1]

---

[1] What has here been said of the Old Order on the Baltic seaboard draws on the evidence from this region and applies to the culture of this region alone. But it is not thereby intended to claim that this culture

The maintenance of this Old Order under stress of changing technological conditions would be helped out by certain peculiar circumstances of the case. As has been noted above, the Baltic peoples habitually borrowed new technological ideas as well as new elements of decorative art, which they handled with such freedom as would argue that these borrowed elements carried over in their transit little or none of the fringe of conventionalities, magical precautions and tabus, that customarily attach to such elements among the people among whom they have arisen or have gone through a protracted development. That they borrowed freely of all those things that could leave a material residue to testify to their presence would argue that they will also have borrowed with some facility of such immaterial elements as would leave a residue only in the texture of the institutional fabric of succeeding generations.[1] Such persistent borrowing has a direct effect in the way of discouraging a growth of rigid conventions or a reduction of institutional details to ultra-rigorous authenticity.

---

differs widely from what has been prevalent in other places and among other peoples on a similar general level of civilisation. It is only that these other instances do not immediately concern the subject under inquiry. In fact, it will be found that the cultures loosely classed as upper-savage or lower-barbarian quite commonly show much the same institutional traits as those here indicated. The like loose, quasi-anarchistic, non-coercive social organisation comes in sight as a matter-of-course, *e.g.*, among the Eskimo, particularly the eastern and central Eskimo, who are by force of circumstances more habitually at peace than their western relatives; so, again, in a degree and with a difference, among the Indians of the Northwest Coast, or among the Pueblo Indians, and there are similar resemblances and reminiscences to be found here and there in Indonesia and Polynesia. All of which argues that this Old Order of the north-European civilisation is neither erratic, exceptional, nor of a precarious kind; and that there is all the more reason to look for recrudescence of its underlying spiritual attitude in cases where the current circumstances favor or admit a reversion to conditions of peace.

[1] Some evidence to this effect is to be seen in the borrowed Gods included in the Asa mythology, as well as in the shifting fashions of sepulture.

On the other hand the borrowing implies continued and passably amicable intercourse with other cultural areas; at the same time that it shows what may be called a receptive attitude toward foreign usage and ideas. The net yield of such intercourse should be more of flexibility than of authenticity in the resulting scheme of life, so that adaptation to new exigencies should be made with relatively slight reluctance, or relatively slight lesion to the accredited principles of right and honest living. Within limits, relatively wide limits, the scheme would bend rather than break. At the same time such changes as make for a longer reach and larger organisation of the industrial forces will commonly also conduce to a wider effectual human contact; so that, as one consequence of the technological advance, the effectual reach of neighborly solidarity will be somewhat increased and the system of anarchistic neighborhood control will be competent to cover a larger population. An increasing density of population, due to the same set of changes, will have the like effect.

It follows that the enhanced scale and reach of the industrial arts, working toward the destruction of the Old Order, in a measure carries its own corrective. But it is none the less evident that the increased viability so given the old order of institutions is due to be overreached by the technological changes which condition it; since technological advance is of the nature of cumulative habituation, while the practicability of anarchistic neighborhood control depends on native traits of human nature that do not change and whose channels of efficiency must always continue to be personal contact through the senses, however this contact may be helped out at one point and another by mechanical expedients. By analogy it might be said that an anarchistic system works by manual labor and its scope can not exceed the manual reach of those engaged, with whatever slight equipment of tools may be conceived to add to the reach of manual contact; whereas the industrial arts are of the nature of a mechanical process which may indefinitely exceed the manual reach of the individual workman. The substantial fact in the one is the personal force and temper of the human individual; in the other it is the impersonal interplay of mechanical processes.

So, the Old Order began to disintegrate and presently broke so soon as the state of the industrial arts pushed the reach of individual initiative beyond the scope of this control exercised by an undifferentiated consensus of neighborly sentiment. The particular point at which the advance of industry finally and decisively disestablished the conditions requisite to the Old Order in the Baltic countries appears to have been in the arts of navigation; although excessive improvement in other means of communication, as, *e.g.*, in roadways and wheeled vehicles, may have contributed materially to its decay and displacement in Denmark and Sweden, as perhaps also in the countries farther to the south. The conditions that made dynastic coercion possible made local autonomy impossible. Not that the resulting coercive system proved itself eminently expedient in any other sense than that nothing else could stand in competition with it when once the technological conditions had overpassed the breaking point of the Old Order. Indeed, the situation that supervened with the triumph of state and church in the Scandinavian countries, *e.g.*, and particularly in Norway, can not well be characterised as anything but imbecile and nasty. But the technological advance had passed the point beyond which the Old Order ceased to be viable; and no retreat could be made to a line of defense so far rearward that the new order, having once taken over the powers of the community, could be dispossessed in favor of the old. It is true of institutional systems as of personal claimants: *Beati possidentes.*

In the course of time, though it appears to have occupied several thousand years of slow but scarcely broken advance, their excessive efficiency in the mechanic arts pushed the north-European peoples out of that state of culture answering to their natural bent. And ever since they so passed the technological limit of tolerance of that archaic scheme of use and wont they have been restlessly casting back for some workable compromise that would permit their ideal of "local self-government" by neighborly common sense to live somehow in the shadow of that large-scale coercive rule that killed it. Now, it happens that insubordination is the vital principle of this defunct system of local self-government, whereas it is the sin against the Holy Ghost of dynastic coercion. So the compromise has not been found, or it has not been found to work; and yet this ideal of insubordination, of Live and let live, has eaten too close to the bone in the north-European hybrid to let him settle down into wholesome content without its realisation.

As has appeared above, and as has been argued more at length in an earlier passage, such a quasi-anarchistic system of neighborhood control — "local self-governing autonomy" — can run on and do well only in case the population which carries on such a cultural scheme is endowed with a type of human nature suited to this manner of life. A short-term success may attend any scheme of institutions, even if it is not eminently suited to the moral genius of the people, particularly if it is seconded by propitious material conditions and a serviceable state of the industrial arts; but where there is a wide discrepancy between the temperamental bent of the people and the system of control and habits of life superinduced by their material surroundings and industrial organisation, no enduring continuity of popular welfare is to be looked for, and the life-history of such a culture or such a community will be marked by catastrophic disturbances and recurrent collapse.

Conversely, where the material surroundings and the current state of the industrial arts are such as to offer mankind a living only on these terms, as would be true through the long prehistoric ages in the Baltic region, the only type of human nature that could make good its survival would be of the fashion suitable to this neighborhood management by common consent. So that the north-European population is adapted to this manner of life by its hereditary bent. Not that this need be conceived as a unique distinction of the north-European hybrid peoples. The conditions of life in prehistoric times — in the days of selective elimination of the unfit types — will in this respect have commonly been of much the same character elsewhere; and the same natural bent is visible, in more or less effectual force, among many of the peoples of the lower cultures, particularly among peaceable, sedentary peoples, such as the Pueblo Indians or the Eskimo. But these others do not immediately concern the present inquiry, and there is no need here to point a contrast in this respect between the peoples of the Baltic culture and any others. For all that concerns the present argument, this anarchistic animus may well mark a generic bent of the human race at large.

So far as bears on the relations between man and man, and between the individual and his social group, this anarchistic morality is formulated in the homely aphorism: Live and let live. It has been the peculiar merit of this archaic anarchism — a merit at least in the eyes of the north-European — that it allows the common man to live as good him seems, within the margin of neighborhood tolerance; at the same time it is involved in this scheme of things, as a condition precedent to its working, that the common man must by natural bent be gifted with a penchant for letting his neighbor live as good him seems, within the same margin of neighborhood tolerance. This is the ideal of "justice" according to the anarchistic conception, — called also, by way of euphemism and compromise, the individualistic or democratic conception.[1] These are the two spiritual foci about which the orbit of right and honest living swings; and so long as this orbit

---

[1] In historic times the moral attitude underlying this principle of justice has reasserted itself with notable resiliency from time to time, in the development of the common law and of, so-called, free institutions. It is nearly the whole of the moral wisdom embodied in the system of Natural Rights, and it is the foundation of the utilitarian school of morals, from Bentham to Spencer.

The ubiquity and persistence of this moral bent is by no means a newly discovered fact, of course. It is precisely this manifest ubiquity and persistence of it that makes this human trait — perhaps human infirmity — an invaluable premise in any inquiry into the practicability

maintains its balance it meets the demands of justice, because such is the moral bias native to man, as selectively determined in the archaic days when the extant types of human nature made good their survival.

That a man should live as good him seems will mean that he is to do his own work in his own way, to the limit of such initiative and capacity as there is in him, — always with the reservation that he will not transgress the margin of tolerance rooted in the moral common sense of his neighbors. The confines of this margin of tolerance appear to be fixed by the current apprehension of what is serviceable for the common good on the one hand and what is disserviceable on the other hand; so that, in so far as it is a question of tolerance, individual idiosyncrasy runs free so long as its bearing on the common good is indifferent. Settled and persistent disserviceability is morally odious, presently becomes obnoxious, and so falls under the corrective intervention of common sense as soon as it swells to such excess as to stir the neighborhood into action. Evidently, what has been called the "instinct of workmanship" comes in for a large share in this moral bias, particularly in respect of the limit of tolerance; economic reprobation has much to do with the intolerance that eventually moves the community to concerted measures for putting down an obnoxious superfluity of naughtiness. Evidently, too, individual grievance suffered by one and another in the community will have much to do in bringing on such a common-sense reprobation of any such superfluity.[1]

Several causes contributed to the decay and eventual collapse of this old order of things, but they may all be run back to the one common ground of an excessive advance in the industrial arts, — excessive, of course, only in the sense that it was inconsistent with

---

or expediency of any given scheme of control or any projected line of collective enterprise.

[1] It is characteristic of this archaic system of justice that no public authority and no legally concerted action ordinarily is called in to redress grievances. The award of the court enforces no penalty; it only gives due legal sanction to reprisal.

the working arrangements that had been sufficient under the Old Order.[1] As has been noted in an earlier passage, the archæological evidence indicates the presence of property and distinctions of wealth as far back as an early period in the stone age, and the evidence of such a difference in wealth grows more pronounced from that time on. A difference of this kind sets up a disparity between the members of the group, so that to Live and let live no longer means an equal, or equitable, chance for all in the use of the group's natural resources or in the utilisation of the state of the industrial arts. Accumulated wealth confers a differential advantage on its owner, so that, with the same free hand as his neighbors and with the added reach given by his "means," he is in a position to benefit beyond the ordinary; which means, conversely, that the common man lies under a corresponding differential disadvantage as against his wealthy neighbor, both in the use of the natural resources and in the usufruct of the community's technological knowledge. So that the accumulation of wealth in private hands works, from its beginnings, at cross purposes with the principle of Live and let live; in so far as the wealthy, in full accord with the principle, is allowed to live as good him seems, and to do as he will with his own, the common man with fewer means has less than an even chance to live as good him seems and do as he will with his own.[2] But the accumulation of wealth and the consequent exercise of power may go some length and still be

---

[1] Cf., Graham Wallas, *The Great Society*, especially ch. i.; also H. C. Adams, "Economics and Jurisprudence"; Presidential Address, Am. Econ. Assoc. 1896, especially sec. ii.

[2] All this, of course, implies no criticism or derogation of the institution of private property at large, either as to its defensibility on moral grounds or as to its expediency on economic grounds. Ownership with full discretion in the use of property appears, both by logical congruity and by the test of use and wont, to be an intrinsic effect of the rule of Live and let live; it is only in its consequences that it comes in conflict with that rule, and these consequences appear to have come seriously into play only gradually and in the course of institutional growth.

amenable to control by neighborhood sentiment, and it may go still farther without effectually escaping all such control or totally defeating the social order.[1]

Under the anarchistic rule of Live and let live the institution of property readily finds lodgment in the fabric of use and wont. If a metaphysical rationale need be sought for it, it is easily found in the shape in which John Locke formulated it at that modern epoch when the right of pecuniary contract again came into the central position in the scheme of civil rights. The psychological ground of it is not difficult to find, whether on the side of the owner who comes in for the property or on that of his neighbors who countenance him in his possession and use of it. And so long as the whole matter runs its course within the range of effective neighborly surveillance, no serious difficulty arises out of such a practice, which commends itself to each as expedient for his own purposes. Meantime it grows into a settled usage, is given definite formulation by use and wont, as to its reach and incidents, and becomes one of the assured points of support in the legal system,

---

[1]The history of the Icelandic republic shows how the accumulation of wealth was itself sufficient to put an end to the Old Order. The republic never had an executive or administrative organ, and grew by deliberate adaptation and improvement out of a system of neighborhood autonomy. It came of an aggregation of settlements made, in the main, by refugees from Norway, who had made their escape from the increasing, and to them intolerable, pressure of a coercive state organised by Harald Fairhair and his immediate successors, and modeled on the pattern of the feudal principalities lying farther to the south, — on the principle of duty as contrasted with that of right. This "anarchistic" republic appears to have served its purpose passably from the outset, but with increasing difficulty, hardship and loss, as wealth and power progressively accumulated in the hands of fewer families, and so came to be managed in appreciable masses under anarchistic rules by competing chieftains — "bosses" they would be called in latterday colloquial speech — who swung the forces of the community for their own ends; until the collapse came as the close of a protracted season of internal raids, lawlessness, civil war and assassination, carried out in the endeavors of these magnates each to live as good him seemed.

— an ancient right, sanctioned by unbroken usage from time immemorial.

IV

(Note to Chapter VI, page 193)

It is no part of this inquiry to pass appraisal on American business enterprise or on the dealings of American business men with the country's resources and opportunities. Yet certain relevant considerations may contribute something to the comparison undertaken between the English and the German case at this point.

In public speech much is made of the unlimited possibilities of this country, and of the utter freedom, boldness and assiduity of its enterprising captains of industry. It is true, these encomiums come most commonly and most volubly from among the members of the craft, but they are after all so integral an article of the popular faith that any question of them becomes an ungrateful if not an odious heresy. It will accordingly be more to the point to recite the circumstances of the case than to add fruitless asseverations.

There need be no deduction allowed on the count of America's unlimited opportunities for profitable business enterprise. Within the circle of industrial countries the material resources of the country may well be admitted to have no counterpart; and its working population is also to be rated as of unexceptionable quality. But accepting these premises, the industrial outcome should logically be something quite unexampled, rather than second best.

In respect of its business community America is the country of the self-made man; such was the state of the case unqualifiedly in that brief past when current business traditions took on what consistency they have, and such is still the state of the case as touches not less than nine-tenths of the volume of traffic or of the personnel. While one does not lightly lay profane hands on this palladium of the republic, it seems unavoidable in this connection to inquire somewhat into the current process of production of this self-made man, and so into his bearing on the state of enterprise in the business community.

The raw material out of which he is made is substantially the same as that which goes to make the American politician, and the arts of production employed and serviceable are also much the same in both cases. As is true of most native Americans, he comes from the farm, in the sense that he has commonly been born outside the limits of any properly urban community; but he will commonly have left the farm for the country town in boyhood. It is in the country towns, and in the smaller cities, so-called, that far and away the greater number of American business men have their beginnings; and the greater number of them, indeed, spend their later life and endeavors in the same surroundings. Success in these surroundings becomes the test of fitness to do business, or to be trusted with discretion in business aside from or beyond these surroundings. For all but a vanishing minority, it is these country-town circumstances that selectively decide whether a given candidate for self-made business enterprise is fit to survive. So that the great proportion of those who have the country's business, and therefore its industry, in hand are those who have proved their fitness for survival under the conditions imposed by the country town, or by the small city, which is an overgrown town.

The American country town, and the small city in its degree, is a peculiar institution, little appreciated by observers from oversea. It is a business community; that is to say it lives for and by business traffic, primarily of a merchandising sort. It is often spoken of as a center or sub-center for the distribution of goods to the country population, and for the receipt and transmission of country produce; but this is definition by enumeration of mechanical facts only. The reason of its being is the gain to be got by doing business in this particular place. The nucleus of its population is the local business men, whose interests constitute its municipal policy and control its municipal administration. These local business men are such as the local bankers, merchants of many kinds and degrees, real-estate promoters, local lawyers, local clergymen. In the typical town all these have something of a hand in municipal politics, which is conducted as in some sort a public or overt extension of that private or covert organisation of local interests that watches over the joint pecuniary benefit of the local business men. It is a means of rewarding serviceable local politicians with salaries and perquisites, especially the latter, and of safeguarding the local business community against interlopers and against any evasive tactics on the part of the country population that serves as host to this businesslike growth. This politico-pecuniary enterprise in municipal policy and perquisites is a case of joint action rather than of collective action, since each and several of the participants, overt and covert, takes part as strategist or diplomatic agent for his own pecuniary interest.

The nature of this country town will be better appreciated if one takes a genetic view of it. Typically it is a product and exponent of the American land system. In its beginning it is located and "developed" as an enterprise of speculation in land values; that is to say it is a businesslike endeavor to get something for nothing by engrossing as much as may be of the increment of land values due to the increase of population and the settlement and cultivation of the adjacent agricultural area. It never (hitherto) loses this character of real-estate speculation. The business men who take up the local traffic in merchandising, litigation, church enterprise, and the like, commonly begin with some share in this real-estate speculation. This affords a common bond and a common ground of pecuniary interest, which commonly masquerades under the name of local patriotism, public spirit, civic pride, and the like. This pretense of public spirit is so consistently maintained that most of these men come presently to believe in their own professions on that head. Pecuniary interest in local land values involves an interest in the continued growth of the town. Hence any creditable misrepresentation of the town's volume of business traffic, population, tributary farming community, or natural resources, is rated as serviceable to the common good.

And any member of this businesslike community will be rated as a meritorious citizen in proportion as he is serviceable to this joint pecuniary interest of these "influential citizens."

The American country town, considered as an institution and an engine of cultural discipline, is chiefly a growth of the nineteenth century, and it has grown to its fullest efficiency in that north-middle region that was effectively brought into the republic during the later three-quarters of the century, more particularly during the period of large immigration from northern Europe. It owes much of its character to this immigration. The immigrants settled over this stretch of country as tillers of the soil, while the American population from the east at the same time scattered over the same region in the towns; with the result that the foreign immigrants did the work necessary to the reclamation of this stretch of fertile land, and the native-born in the towns did the business.

This business was prevailingly of a prehensile character, being carried on by men well at home in the common law of the land and directed to getting something for nothing at the expense of the foreign immigrants who were unfamiliar with the common law. Being, in the view of their masters, aliens in the land, the foreign immigrants were felt to have no claim to consideration beyond what the laws that they did not know would formally secure to them in case matters were brought to the legal test. The presumption in the mind of honest business men at all points was on the side of their own pecuniary advantage, leaving any doubts to be settled by eventual litigation that might be brought by the foreign immigrants, — who could with great uniformity be relied on most meticulously to avoid all litigation under a system of law with which they had no acquaintance, before local magistrates (business men) whom they had no reason to trust, in a language which they did not understand. So, within these premises, the civil law in great measure became a dead letter, except in so far as it served the pecuniary advantage of the business men in the country town; but the formal legality that so inured to the consequent system of astute depredation served to make it morally blameless in the eyes of its beneficiaries and to give it the meritorious appearance of thrift. Whereby the moral frontiers between chicane and thrift have eventually fallen somewhat into abeyance in American business ethics, particularly in the country-town business community that has been specially exposed to this devastation of American morals by the foreign immigrants.

The number of self-made men that have emerged from this traffic, however, has been very considerable. So considerable, indeed, as still to give its distinctive character to the American business community at large, in spite of an increasing contingent, especially of younger men, drawn from other sources and different antecedents. There is consequently enough of a country-town animus pervading this community selectively to bring any recruits from other breeding-grounds into conformity with these country-town ideals of what is the suitable conservative temper that a man should possess in order to be trusted to do business.

The successful man under this state of things succeeds because he is by native gift or by training suited to this situation of petty intrigue and nugatory subtleties. To survive, in the business sense of the word, he must prove himself a serviceable member of this gild of municipal diplomats who patiently wait on the chance of getting something for nothing; and he can enter this gild of waiters on the still-born increase, only through such apprenticeship as will prove his fitness. To be acceptable he must be reliable, conciliatory, conservative, secretive, patient and prehensile. The capacities that make the outcome and that characterise this gild of self-made business men are cupidity, prudence, and chicane, — the greatest of these, and the one that chiefly gives its tone to this business life, is prudence. And indispensable among the qualities that command that confidence of his associates without which no man can make himself as a business man, is a conservative temper.

The ways and means to the making of the self-made man in American business are of this character, and the product is of such a quality as these ways and means may be expected to yield, acting as they do with great uniformity both by training and by selection. It by no means follows that either the business men created by this means, or the business community built out of this select and carefully seasoned material, lacks enterprise of a sort. But it is enterprise in the way of pecuniary strategy, in the getting of something for nothing by shrewd management of pecuniary values. It is enterprise of the kind that eschews innovation. Adventures in new, untried, unstandardised industrial projects and expedients are alien and anathema to the prudent, conservative business community. It is only after such excursions have proved their pecuniary gainfulness in spite of the business community's astute incredulity, that they come to be taken over as a source of gain. But in expeditiously intercepting the gain derivable from such industrial innovations as have proved their gainfulness in spite of the incredulity of the business men, or from the usufruct of such resources as are known to lend themselves to the standard methods of pecuniary manipulation, this business community shows a high degree of efficiency.

America is the land of unlimited possibilities, it is believed, both in respect of material resources and in respect of inventive genius. But it is a notorious commonplace that the mechanical inventions which have in a sense made America what it is in the industrial respect have not only not been made by the business men — they are astute and conservative pecuniary strategists, with neither insight nor aptitude in technological matters — but have also not been made with their support.

It is worth noting that the country-town method of selecting and training the community's business men, in that it makes its selection on grounds of astuteness, caution and cupidity, at the same time and by the same tests rejects such candidates as are endowed with technological insight or an aggressive curiosity in matters of industrial innovation. And connected with this selective bidding up of pecuniary astuteness and quietism is the well-known inefficiency of business management in American industry, — well-known among men competent to speak on these matters, though not well credited among the business men at large, who commonly lack even the degree of technological insight necessary to appreciate the pecuniary loss involved in their own astute mismanagement. The "efficiency engineers" have no hesitation about saying that the business men's management of industry has resulted in a wasteful use of the equipment and labor employed, sometimes rising to figures fairly incredible to the common layman. This waste may be more or less, but it is a systematic result of the management of industrial enterprises by the self-made business man. At the same time the efficiency engineers' criticism takes no account of the waste involved in downright unemployment or stoppage of workmen and plant, due to the pecuniary strategy of the same conservative business men, although this item of waste doubtless exceeds by several fold that caused by incompetent management while the plant is running.

Something is always to be allowed for exceptions and side issues in any generalisation so broad as this, and the broad proposition just set down in characterisation of the American business man is not to be taken as applying without such qualification. But when all desired qualifications have been allowed there remains this unflattering state of the facts, notorious and comprehensive: America has unrivalled material resources and a working population nowise inferior to any other for industry under the machine technology; American business men have had a free hand and a minimum of burdens in the way of taxes or other government exactions (American taxation has, as is well known, fallen chiefly on the farm population and other classes not engaged in business, and has not been extremely high at that); the American achievement in this field within the same period has been notoriously less conspicuous and less substantial, e.g., than that of Germany since the formation of the Empire. Nowhere have the business men had so full and large a discretion, nowhere have they been favored by government regulations to the same extent — for the reason that nowhere have they controlled the making and administration of the laws in anything like the same degree; and nowhere have they fallen short of their opportunities by so wide a margin.

It is true, there is much said of American boldness and resourcefulness in business enterprise; and there is some substance to this boast in so far as "business enterprise" is taken as a synonym for "pecuniary intrigue," also called finance. But if it is to be taken in any more substantial sense it is useful only as evidence that men like to be flattered by imputation of virtues which they do not possess. The country-town self-made man is not the only kind comprised in the American business community, nor is the self-made man's country-town spirit of conservative chicane the whole scope and method of business in this community; but he is far and away the most numerous species of business man in this community; and he has been so by tradition so long and consistently that business usages, relations and ideals in this community have been conventionalised on his lines; so that by force of conventions, in good part embodied in law, and by force of the like spirit in an effective majority of the living generation, it comes about that this country-town conservative chicane is accepted as the type of safe and sane business enterprise.

Even the larger business finance and the larger American business financiers accordingly still show the earmarks of this country-town derivation, — not that these individuals who hold the industrial fortunes of the country in their hands have therefore individually come up through the country town to their later stations of responsibility, but only that the authentic conceptions of business methods and animus, to which all safe and sane business men must conform, are of this derivation, and that therefore the business community at large will do business only on this footing. American business is eminently of a financial character, and the traffic of these financiers runs within the closed circuit of money-market strategy, with any industrial effects of this financial management coming in as incidentals. The controlling incentives are those of the market for securities, not those of the output of goods; and the final discretion vests in the investment banker, not in the engineering staff or the manager of the works. The discretionary direction of affairs has in effect passed into the hands of these financiering houses, whose ostensible relation to the industrial concerns is that of underwriters only. While these financiers exercise the discretion, they have no responsibility for the conduct of the industries dependent on their discretion.

It is well known now, though there is commonly not much said about it, that the "trust movement," so called, of the late nineties and later, began as an enterprise on the part of certain great financiers to secure "bonuses" and similar gains through the recapitalisation and combination of certain industrial and railway corporations, which had, in some cases, been manœuvred into such financial difficulties as to call for a heroic remedy. In great part, indeed for the greater part, these industrial corporations so organised have continued in a state of dependence on these financial houses, instrumental to their financial traffic. There is little surprise and no censure of this arrangement; the reason being that in this community it is altogether typical and commonplace.

It may be noted by way of parenthesis in this connection, and as illustrating how much of a matter of course this large-scale strategy for the interception of the "rake-off" has become, that the head of one of the greatest of these investment-banking houses, which is at the same time probably the greatest discretionary power in control of American industrial corporations, has recently testified that in his opinion the directors of such corporations can not properly be considered responsible for the conditions of work at the establishments of the corporations, since the directors are financial agents only and have no direct connection with the working of the corporations' plant. About the same date and in the same connection another, the spokesman of perhaps the second greatest of these financiering interests, has with grave deliberation put forth the view that the direction of these same establishments must equitably be left in the discretion of these same directors, without surveillance from the side of the public authorities and with full authority.

V

(Note to Chapter VIII, page 274)

It may be in place to indicate in a more articulate way how these large loans and high rates of interest work out in the industrial situation and the redistribution of ownership. The immediate results are twofold: the general rate of discount rises; and a large volume of funds is placed at the disposal of the debtor governments. From the rise in the rate of interest (as, *e.g.*, from 4% to 6%) it follows immediately that the market value of previously outstanding securities declines by a corresponding amount; other vendible property similarly declines, although much of the industrial plant will very shortly recover, owing to secondary effects of the transfer of funds involved in the loans. The immediate (and transient) effect of the loans is to withdraw funds from the general loan market, leaving the business community short in respect of the funds currently employed in industrial financiering and as "working capital" among industrial business concerns; hence a pronounced depression, as the first consequence, which is heightened by the prevalent short-sighted timidity of business men. The war loans, however, have not decreased the volume of funds currently available; on the contrary, this volume has doubtless been increased by the operation, inasmuch as the new inducements offered will have led to an added strain on the part of the possible lenders; the financiering houses will "trade on a thinner equity" under provocation of an advancing rate of discount and an unexceptionable security offered by the governments. The borrowed funds are shortly thrown into the goods market as a demand for articles of use, directly and indirectly, in the prosecution of the war; which increases the demand and advances the price of such goods, and brings on activity in the industries that supply these goods or the raw materials and subsidiary materials required for the purpose. Other lines of industry will apparently not be affected, for the time being, and so will fall into a more lasting depression. Industrial plant (and common stock) in the industries that so come in for an era of prosperity due to the war demand will then probably advance in market price, to answer to these increased gains. Here, again, specially provocative inducements and an assured market for output will lead to "trading on a thinner equity" than is usual in ordinary times. There results, in effect, a voluminous credit extension, such as will in good part supply the place of the funds drawn off from the business community by the war loans; and as these war funds now come back into the business community in payment for the output of goods, the money market (*Kapitalsmarkt*) will recover its buoyancy; but since the traffic in war loans unavoidably goes on throughout the season of hostilities, neither the rate of discount nor the prices current for such goods as are wanted are likely to return to the ante-bellum level so long as these conditions continue.

The resulting state of the case at the close of the war period, therefore, so far as bears on the point immediately in question, may be summarized. Business men engaged with industries subject to the war demand will have gained, while industry in other lines will have lost, though proportionately less; industrial property (plant and securities) will have been recapitalized, on a thinner equity and an enhanced rate of dividends, at an aggregate valuation probably exceeding that of an equivalent equipment before the war; the effectual outstanding capitalisation (largely funded and therefore irrevocable) of the industrial community will presumably be no smaller than it was before the war loans were floated; to this capitalisation are to be added the government securities covering the war loans; which are, in effect though not in form, a further bonded capitalisation of the community's wealth, and the interest on which constitutes a "fixed charge" on the community's income and therefore a deduction from the community's earning capacity. This deduction may conceivably rise to 100% of the net income; it may, indeed, pass that point. It will be seen, then, that, barring unforeseen changes in the industrial situation, such a season of war prosperity should be followed by a liquidation, to bring the aggregate capitalisation into passable correlation with earning capacity, and to determine the resultant ownership of the net earnings.

SELECTED ANN ARBOR PAPERBACKS

works of enduring merit